History of
AMERICAN
INDIANS

History of
AMERICAN
INDIANS
Exploring Diverse Roots

Robert R. McCoy and Steven M. Fountain

An Imprint of ABC-CLIO, LLC

Santa Barbara, California • Denver, Colorado

Copyright © 2017 by ABC-CLIO, LLC

Library of Congress Cataloging-in-Publication Data

Names: McCoy, Robert R. (Robert Ross), 1962– author. | Fountain, Steven M., author.
Title: History of American Indians : exploring diverse roots / Robert R. McCoy and Steven M. Fountain.
Description: Santa Barbara, California : Greenwood, 2017. | Includes bibliographical references and index.
Identifiers: LCCN 2016057556 | ISBN 9780313386824 (pbk. : alk. paper) | ISBN 9780313386831 (ebook)
Subjects: LCSH: Indians of North America—History.
Classification: LCC E77 .M1147 2017 | DDC 970.004/97—dc23
LC record available at https://lccn.loc.gov/2016057556

ISBN: 978-0-313-38682-4
EISBN: 978-0-313-38683-1

21 20 19 18 17   1 2 3 4 5

This book is also available as an eBook.

Greenwood
An Imprint of ABC-CLIO, LLC

ABC-CLIO, LLC
130 Cremona Drive, P.O. Box 1911
Santa Barbara, California 93116-1911
www.abc-clio.com

This book is printed on acid-free paper ∞

Manufactured in the United States of America

Contents

Acknowledgments

We have many people to thank for helping us to write this book. We have both been fortunate to live and teach in places where indigenous people continue to live, work, and go to school. The main campus of Washington State University sits on the homeland of the Palouse and Nez Perce peoples, and WSU Vancouver is located at the overlapping conjunction of Chinookan, Taidnapam, and Cowlitz homelands. In addition, the Portland-Vancouver metropolitan area is home to one of the largest urban populations of Native Americans in the United States. We have both learned a great deal from the native people and communities who make their homes in the Pacific Northwest.

While there have been many people who have assisted us in the writing of this book, we would like to thank a few special friends and family who have made this work possible. Rob's dear friend and mentor Clifford Trafzer taught him how to see the vibrant and distinct histories of native people that have often been hidden by the powerful narratives of the dominant culture. Steve's interactions with Jack Forbes and David Weber continue to shape his thinking even though both men have walked on in recent years. Many others have contributed through brief conversations, shared knowledge, and ongoing scholarship. Friends and colleagues continue to help us both learn more through their scholarship and example. Barbara Aston, Katy Barber, Trevor Bond, Mary Collins, Steve Crum, Andy Fisher, Michael Holloman, Mike Iyall, Ron Pond, Sam Robinson, and Orlan Svingen are only a few of the people we want to acknowledge for their wisdom and tireless work on behalf of indigenous communities.

Thanks also go to Rob's and Steve's families who supported them throughout the process of writing the book. Rob's children, Lilly and Liam, and Steve's son, Huxley, have served as needed distractions and medicine. We have also enjoyed telling them the stories of the native people whose homeland we live in and have been honored to have our children welcomed to events and ceremonies they will remember all of their lives. Rob's wife, Amy, and Steve's wife, Kathi, have been constantly supportive, serving as both encouragement and copy editors. Without their help, we would not have been able to complete this work.

Robert R. McCoy and Steven M. Fountain

Introduction

Writing a history of American Indians has been a daunting task. Perhaps a better title for the book would have been *Histories of American Indians*, since there are 562 federally recognized tribes and a large number of unrecognized tribal communities in the United States. Each of these communities has their own story and history that deserves to be told. While we could only touch on a few strands from this vast tapestry of history, we want to recognize the importance and worth of all these varied stories and the important part that they have played in the creation of our shared history here in the United States.

Yellow Wolf, a Nez Perce warrior and cousin of Chief Joseph, asserted in his collaboration with L. V. McWhorter:

> This is all for me to tell of the war, and of our after hardships. The story will be for people who come after us. For them to see, to know what was done here. Reasons for the war, never told before. Nobody to help us tell our side—whites told only one side. Told it to please themselves. Told much that is not true. Only his own best deeds, only the worst deeds of the Indians, has the white man told. (McWhorter, 291)

Yellow Wolf's succinct appraisal of the burden of history that Native Americans carry is quite remarkable and is a blistering critique of how the dominant culture in the United States has crafted narratives about Indians. These narratives have been disseminated through varied medium, including art, film, historical monographs, photography, and scientific discourse. Many of these narratives continue to hold sway in the popular imagination of various groups within the United States. Some of the iconic representations generated by these discourses include the "vanishing Indian," the

"Savage," the "Spiritual Indian," or the "Drunk Indian." Each of these narratives and many others have served the broader non-Indian culture to understand and justify the often complicated, violent, and coercive nature of the history of interactions with Native Americans in North America. In addition, most of these narratives use the arrival of Europeans as the starting point of history for Native Americans, disregarding millennia of tribal communities' history in the Americas.

In *History of American Indians* we seek to disrupt these narratives and place Native Americans as the central actors in the history of North America. Using the most current research and scholarship, we emphasize the agency and adaptation of Native American communities and cultures while also recognizing the daunting challenges that they faced through their long history of interactions with outsiders in the Western Hemisphere. Those outsiders are also important to the histories here, as those relations have shaped much of Native American history. Over time, outsiders increasingly affected the framework of everyday life for most people.

As we crafted this narrative, we organized our writing around three themes. The first theme centers on the diversity of native communities and cultures. Too often Native Americans are lumped together as "Indians," forcing the incredible diversity of their cultures into a single portrayal or understanding, based on the preferred image of Indians at any given moment. We have attempted to lead readers down a path that emphasizes the different ways that native communities lived, worked, practiced religion, and sought to deal with newcomers to their homelands.

Second, our narrative focuses on the dynamic adaptation and agency of American Indians throughout their interactions with Europeans and Americans in North America. Native people often faced difficult choices when confronted with these newcomers and their culture. Some communities resisted militarily, some converted to Catholicism or some form of Protestant Christianity, while others sought to distance themselves from these massive changes. Sometimes these choices were life and death decisions that ultimately could destroy their way of life and culture. Some of the circumstances that native people faced could not be controlled like the demographic decimation of disease or the environmental consequences of the introduction of new animal and plant species. In the end though, as all human beings do on this planet, native people made choices to protect their families, communities, and cultures.

The third theme highlighted in *History of American Indians* is persistence. Many narratives created by Europeans and Americans have focused on the inevitable disappearance of Native Americans. These portrayals were often couched in discussions of the progressive nature of history and that native people, because of their "primitive " and "backward" ways, were doomed to be assimilated into the larger culture. Our narrative rejects these notions and instead emphasizes the enduring nature of Native American culture and communities. Even in the face of devastating loss and confinement to reservations, native people and their communities continued to fight for sovereignty and control over their own lives and destinies. Far from disappearing from the stage, Native Americans have continued to make their presence known and still influence the course of our history to this day.

Words and names matter, so a brief note about usage is necessary. As you may have noticed, we use a variety of terms to refer collectively to people indigenous to North America. You will find this to be the case in our narrative, in academic life, and in the larger world. "Native Americans" is appropriate and acceptable in most instances. "American Indian" is also widely used (as in the title of this book), even though some individuals have rejected its use. In Canada, the official designation is "First Nations." "Native" has also found wide use but may carry offensive baggage if used without care. "Amerind" has not been generally accepted but enjoyed a brief heyday in academic writing. "Indigenous" is a more apt description in an academic context, but "Indian" is the preferred term that most indigenous people within the United States use for themselves in everyday conversation.

When appropriate, we use a specific tribal designation such as Shoshone, Mohawk, or Seminole rather than more monolithic terms. Here too, be aware that people's names for themselves are preferential to those used by outsiders. In an increasing number of cases, names such as Tohono O'odham have replaced offensive names like Papago. Where these reassertions of tribal identity have entered common use, we use tribes' preferred names.

REFERENCE AND FURTHER READING

McWhorter, Lucullus Virgil. *Yellow Wolf: His Own Story*. Caldwell, ID: Caxton Printers, 1940.

Chronology of Key Dates in American Indian History

ca. 34,000 BCE	Occupation of Beringia by early migrants.
ca. 13,500 BCE	An unknown trader caches spear points and tools near the banks of Buttermilk Creek, Texas.
ca. 12,300 BCE	Ancient hunters live in a shelter overlooking a shallow lake at Paisley Caves, Oregon.
ca. 11,500 BCE	Clovis spear point technology spreads across North America.
ca. 10,000 BCE	Ancient Na-Dene migrate across North America.
ca. 9,500 BCE	Ice sheets retreat, leaving an ice-free corridor along the eastern slope of the Rocky Mountains.
ca. 8,000 BCE	Indigenous peoples domesticate squash, one of the first of several North American food crops.
	Atlatls spread to hunters in the Southwest.
ca. 7,500 BCE	Kennewick Man dies near the banks of the Columbia River.
ca. 5,000 BCE	Indigenous peoples near the Great Lakes use copper to make a variety of tools and ornaments.
ca. 4,000 BCE	Hunters begin nearly four millennia of use of Head-Smashed-In buffalo jump in Alberta.
ca. 2,000 BCE	Earliest mound building complex rises at Poverty Point, Louisiana.
ca. 1,000 BCE	Inuit peoples spread across the Arctic.

ca. 800 BCE	The Adena Complex of mound builders rises in the Ohio River Valley, continuing over 900 years of shared cultural traits.
ca. 200 BCE	The Hopewell Culture spreads across eastern North America.
ca. 600	Ancient Puebloans begin seven centuries of living at Mesa Verde in southwest Colorado.
ca. 800	Mississippian Culture begins to spread across much of eastern North America.
ca. 1000	"Skraelings" (likely Beothuks or Inuits) encounter "Vikings" in first documented contact between Native Americans and Europeans. The Norsemen abandon the settlement after twenty years.
ca. 1000	Cahokia reaches its height.
ca. 1040	Chaco Canyon grows over next century as the center of a network of villages in northwestern New Mexico.
1165	Cahokians build a log palisade separating the elites from commoners in North America's largest city.
ca. 1370	Tuzigoot Pueblo abandoned as Western Apaches and Yavapais attack and burn Montezuma's Castle, Arizona.
ca. 1400	Cahokia abandoned as peoples disperse into smaller villages.
ca. 1450	Pawnees and Arikaras separate as the latter shift north to the Missouri River.
1492	Taínos encounter Spaniards as Columbus lands at several islands in the Caribbean, including Hispañola and Cuba.
1493	Taíno-Spanish warfare follows the return of Columbus to Hispañola as Spaniards move inland to capture the cacique Caonabo.
1494	First shipment of Taíno slaves leaves Hispañola for Spain.
1497	Mikmaqs abducted from Cape Breton Island and enslaved by John Cabot.
1509	Perhaps the first of many Spanish slaving expeditions strikes Florida Indians.
1512	Laws of Burgos outlaw the enslavement of Indians unless found to be in rebellion against Spain.

1607   Powhatan allows English to establish Jamestown in Virginia, welcoming new trade partners.

1610   Membertou, a Mikmaq headman, enters an alliance with French settlers at Port Royal and is baptized with more than one hundred of his people.

1613   Pocahontas, daughter of Powhatan, kidnapped by English and taken to England the following year.

1615   Hurons ally with newcomer Samuel de Champlain and his French colonists.

1616   A four-year smallpox epidemic sweeps across New England, decimating indigenous peoples.

1620   Tisquantum, a Patuxet who had been taken captive and lived in Europe, acts as interpreter and teacher to newly arrived English Pilgrims.

1622   Opechancanough, the new headman of the Powhatans, leads an attack on Virginia English that nearly destroys the colony.

1628   Mohawks defeat the Mahicans, securing a monopoly on Dutch trade in guns and other supplies at Fort Orange.

1633   Smallpox epidemics strike the St. Lawrence-Great Lakes valley repeatedly over the next two decades, spreading from Huronia to New England.

1636   Pequot War pits Narragansetts, Pequots, and other New England Indians against encroaching English colonists and their Mohawk allies.

1638   The Beaver Wars commence with Iroquois conquest of Wenro lands on Lake Erie and warfare continues across much of the Pays d'en Haut through the 1660s.

1639   Taos Pueblos flee to El Cuartajelo among Plains Apaches.

1641   The French reverse a policy and allow guns to be traded with Hurons; Iroquois react by expanding warfare with their Huron rivals and defeat them by 1650.

1655   Lucas Menendez leads Timucuan rebellion in response Spanish demands that they ally against the English.

1655   Peach Wars pit several small tribes against Dutch New York, ultimately removing Indians from their lands adjacent to the colony.

1675   Metacom leads Wampanoags and other New England tribes in King Philip's War against Puritans.

1676	Bacon's Rebellion turns from rebelling against the Virginia government to attack Susquehannocks and tribes of the Powhatan Confederacy
1680	Popay leads the Pueblo Revolt, expelling Spaniards from New Mexico for twelve years.
1692	Spaniards return to New Mexico, rebuilding an uneasy alliance with Pueblos reeling from Apache raiding.
1701	Iroquois and other native nations sign the Great Peace of Montreal with France.
1710	Fox Wars break out as French arm their enemies, eventually leading to the resettlement of Fox-Mesquakies in Iowa.
1711	Tuscaroras fight English traders but are defeated after two years of warfare and many survivors move north to join the Iroquois Confederacy.
1715	The two-year Yamasee War results in the defeat of those people and their allies who flee to join Creeks and Seminoles.
1720	A combined Pawnee-Oto force defeated the Spanish Villasur Expedition, turning New Spain back from the Great Plains
1737	The Delaware Walking Purchase results in Pennsylvania colonists deceiving Lenapes out of much of their land.
1743	Russian fur companies began exploiting Aleut labor, eventually working as far south as Baja California.
1748	Choctaw Civil War breaks out, dividing the nation between pro-French and pro-English factions.
ca. 1750	The Makah village of Ozette is buried by a mudslide, remaining undisturbed until excavations began in 1970.
1754	Iroquois Six Nations and British colonies engage in failed Albany Plan of Union negotiations.
1754	Virginia Militia led by Col. George Washington launch an attack against French near Fort Duquesne, followed by Seneca-French counter-attack that forced his surrender and sparked the Seven Years' War.
1761	Neolin, the Delaware Prophet, experiences his first vision and leads a spiritual revival of Great Lakes peoples.
1763	The Paxton Boys murder twenty-two Conestoga Susquehannocks in Pennsylvania, including those placed in protective custody.

1763	Britain established the Proclamation Line of 1763 in an attempt to separate colonists from a designated Indian Country west of the Appalachians, but British colonists continued to move westward.
1763	Ottawa headman Pontiac leads a successful confederacy against the British, but ultimately signed a peace treaty in 1766 after his French allies failed to return to North America.
1768	Iroquois cede traditional Shawnee homeland to the British in the Treaty of Fort Stanwix.
1769	Spanish Colonization of California extends the mission system.
1774	Spaniards enter Nootka Sound and trade with Nuu-chah-nulth. Two years later British James Cook would visit, triggering a rush of Europeans to the North Pacific sea otter trade.
1774	Virginia Governor Lord Dunmore declared war on tribes south of the Ohio River, forcing cessions of land.
1775	Ipai and Tipai revolt against Spanish missions on southern California.
1780	The American Revolution strikes Iroquois and Cherokee villages as the Rebels attack British allies; Joseph Brant and Cornplanter retaliate but retreat northward to Canada.
1781	Quechan Revolt at Yuma cuts Spaniards off from overland contact with California.
1782	Col. David Williamson carries out the Gnadenhutten Massacre in Ohio, executing ninety Christian Lenapes.
1785	Ecueracapa negotiated a treaty between Comanches and Spanish New Mexico in which they joined forces against Lipan Apaches.
1790	U.S. Congress passes the first of several Trade and Intercourse Acts to regulate the Indian trade and restrict Indian land sales to be between a tribe and the federal government.
1790	Miami Little Turtle and Shawnee Blue Jacket defeat U.S. forces under Gen. Josiah Harmar, followed by an even larger victory over Gen. Arthur St. Clair the following year.

1795	Blue Jacket and other leaders of the Western Confederacy forced to sign the Treaty of Greenville ceding northern Ohio.
1799	Seneca leader Handsome Lake experiences a vision that establishes a revived Longhouse religion after dying and coming back to life.
1803	The Louisiana Purchase brings multiple native nations within the United States and the Lewis and Clark Expedition is charged with forging peace and swaying trade away from European rivals.
1805	Lewis and Clark spend the winter at Fort Clatsop in Chinook lands.
1811	Tenskwatawa defeated in Battle of Tippecanoe and William Henry Harrison burns Prophetstown in the aftermath.
1813	A dispute between anti-U.S. Creeks influenced by Tecumseh and pro-U.S. factions becomes the Red Stick War. The Fort Mims Massacre brings retaliation the following year in the Battle of Horseshoe Bend.
1815	Tecumseh killed in the Battle of the Thames, ending organized Indian resistance in the Midwest.
1817	Andrew Jackson invades Florida in the First Seminole War.
1817	The "Old Settler" Cherokees begin their migration westward to the Arkansas River Valley to escape conflict with white settlers. They are the first of a lengthy exodus.
1821	Sequoyah introduces his Cherokee Syllabary.
1822	The U.S. Factory System limiting the Indian trade to a small number of government traders ended.
1823	*Johnson v. M'Intosh* decision states that Indian tribes have a right to their land and can only transfer that right to the federal government.
1824	The Hudson's Bay Company embarked on its fur desert policy, using Metís, Iroquois, and other indigenous and European labor to destroy the fur resources south of the Columbia River.
1828	Cherokees form a Constitution and declare the Cherokee Republic under Chief John Ross.

1830   The Indian Removal Act makes practice the official policy of the United States: all Indians east of the Mississippi are subject to removal west of the river.

1831   *Cherokee Nation v. Georgia* establishes tribes as "domestic dependent nations."

1832   Black Hawk leads Sauk and Fox in resistance to removal from Illinois.

1832   Kennekuk, the Kickapoo Prophet, separates from Black Hawk and preaches a message of nonviolent accommodation with white settlers.

1832   President Jackson and the State of Georgia ignore *John Marshall's Worcester v. Georgia* decision that states have no right to extend laws over sovereign Indian tribes.

1833   Secularization of the California Missions planned to divide the land among the Indian neophytes but most of the land was instead sold off.

1835   The fraudulent Treaty of New Echota ceded all Cherokee lands east of the Mississippi River even though many leaders, including John Ross, did not sign.

1835   Osceola, Coacoochee and others struck at the United States in the wake of the Treaty of Payne's Landing to begin the Second Seminole War.

1835   William Apess publishes *Indian Nullification of the Unconstitutional Laws of Massachusetts* to bring attention to the struggles of the Mashpee people.

1836   The first in a series of mid-nineteenth century smallpox epidemics sweeps over Plains Tribes.

1838   Gen. Winfield Scott led a forced removal of Cherokees to Oklahoma on the ten months long Trail of Tears.

1847   Cayuse Indians kill Marcus and Narcissa Whitman and eleven other Americans; five Cayuses were executed after an 1850 trial.

1847   Tomás Romero leads Taos Pueblos in a revolt against U.S. rule, killing appointed Governor Charles Bent. U.S. troops retaliate against Taos killing 150.

1848   The discovery of gold led to over 300,000 people pouring into the homelands of dozens of California Indian tribes, especially with the arrival of the 49ers.

1848   The Treaty of Guadalupe Hidalgo stripped Indians of
            their citizenship and promised that the United States
            would aid in stopping Comanche and Apache raids into
            Mexico.

1850   California statehood brings a bounty against Indians and
            the failure of the eighteen treaties negotiated with Cali-
            fornia tribes.

1851   The Treaty of Fort Laramie gathers over 10,000 Indians
            from several Plains tribes to sign an agreement for tribal
            lands and a cessation of hostilities along the overland trails.

1852   First "modern" reservation established at Fort Tejon by
            California Superintendent of Indian Affairs Edmund
            Burke.

1855   Resistance to treaties negotiated by Isaac Stevens triggers
            the Yakima and Puget Sound Wars in Washington.

1860   Led by Manuelito, Navajo warriors attack Fort Defiance
            in Arizona, the first action in the long war between the
            United States and the Navajo in the Southwest.

1860   Conflict between miners and Northern Paiutes, Shoshone
            and Bannock begins in Oregon Territory.

1861   Jefferson Davis sends Albert Pike to negotiate new trea-
            ties for the Confederacy with tribal communities in
            Indian Territory.

1862   For over two months, many Santee Sioux rise up against
            the United States in Minnesota.

1862   Apache tribes begin their long resistance against the
            United States. At the Battle of Apache Pass the Army
            wounded Mangas Coloradas forcing the withdrawal of
            the Apache to Mexico.

1863   The U.S. Army fights against the Navajo using scorched
            earth tactics. By 1864, nearly 10,000 Navajo make the
            Long Walk to the Bosque Redondo Reservation where
            they face hunger, despair, and poor conditions.

1863   The "Thief" Treaty of 1863 is signed by the U.S.
            government and Lawyer's people, ceding the majority of
            the 1855 Nez Perce Reservation to the government.

1864   On November 29, the villages of Black Kettle and Left
            Hand are attacked by the U.S. Army and militia forces

	at Sand Creek, Colorado. As many as 400 Cheyenne and Arapaho are killed.
1867	Senator James R. Doolittle issues the "Doolittle Report," an investigation of the conditions of Indians in the United States.
1867	Congress creates the Peace Commission as a way to deal with the "Indian Problem."
1867	Kiowa, Cheyenne, Comanche, Arapaho, and Kiowa-Apache sign the Medicine Lodge Treaty.
1867	The United States purchases Alaska from Russia.
1868	Sioux leaders sign the Fort Laramie Treaty of 1868. In it, the United States promised to withdraw troops from the region, close the Bozeman Trail, and guarantee hunting rights outside the reservation.
1868	General George Custer attacks Black Kettle's village on the Washita River, killing Black Kettle and many others.
1868	President Grant institutes the "Peace Policy" designed to deal with corruption and appoint Christian missionaries as Indian Agents.
1869	Congress creates the Board of Indian Commissioners to regulate reservations and Indian Agents across the United States.
1870	The Supreme Court issues the Cherokee Tobacco decision, stating that federal law supersedes treaties.
1870	Senator Benjamin Rice introduces bill to organize the Oklahoma Territory.
1870	Wholesale slaughter of buffalo begins across the Great Plains.
1871	Congress declares that no future treaties will be negotiated with Indians in the United States.
1872	The forced removal of the Modocs fails, and the Modoc War starts. Fighting continues into June 1873. The Modocs surrender and many of their leaders are executed including Captain Jack and Schonchin Jim.
1873	The Apache continue their resistance against the U.S. government. Fighting ends in 1886.
1874	The Red River War ends with the defeat of the Cheyenne, Arapaho, Kiowa, etc. and confinement to the reservation.

1874	Gold is discovered in Paha Sapa (the Black Hills).
1876	The Sioux are ordered to the reservation after the Grant Administration abrogates the Fort Laramie Treaty by allowing a gold rush to the Black Hills.
1876	A U.S. force under General Crook begins a military campaign against Lakota, Cheyenne, and Arapaho people. As part of this force General Custer led the Seventh Cavalry against Indian encampments on the Little Big Horn River. He and his whole command are killed in the ensuring battle.
1877	Crazy Horse is killed during an attempted arrest.
1877	The Nez Perce War begins after the U.S. government orders nontreaty Nez Perce onto the reservation in Idaho. Fleeing toward Canada, Nez Perce survivors surrender on October 1 at the Bear Paw Mountains.
1877	The Bannock War begins in southern Idaho and northern Nevada. The U.S. Army fought the Paiutes and Bannocks until the fall of 1878.
1879	Richard Henry Pratt establishes first Indian Boarding School at Carlisle Barracks in Pennsylvania.
1879	*Standing Bear v. Crook* is decided by the Supreme Court. In this decision, the Court declared that Indians were persons and are subject to all the rights and privileges of persons under the Constitution.
1881	Sitting Bull returns from Canada and surrenders to the U.S. military.
1883	William Cody, also known as Buffalo Bill, organizes the Wild West Show. The show ran until 1913 and employed many Native Americans.
1884	The Supreme Court rules in *Elk v. Wilkins* that Indians are not citizens of the United States but are part of distinct political communities.
1886	In *United States v. Kagama* the Supreme Court decides that Congress can pass laws and exercise jurisdiction over Indian-on-Indian crime in federal courts.
1887	General Allotment Act passes Congress. Better known as the Dawes Act, it required Indians to take an allotment of land on the reservation. "Surplus" land was purchased by the U.S. government from the tribes and sold.

1889	First Oklahoma land rush occurs as Congress opens land in Indian Territory not assigned to tribes during their settlement.
1889	Wovoka has a near-death experience and returns to preach. He begins the Ghost Dance Movement.
1890	Sitting Bull killed by reservation policemen during an attempted arrest.
1890	The U.S. Army detains Spotted Elk's band of Lakota and then opens fire on them, killing over 150 men, women and children.
1896	Gold is discovered in Alaska and Yukon Territories. A gold rush begins with thousands of miners traveling to the region.
1898	Congress passes the Curtis Act, which extends allotment to the Five Civilized Tribes in Indian Territory.
1902	The Territory of Oklahoma is created by Congress.
1903	The Supreme Court rules in *Lone Wolf v. Hitchcock* that Congress's plenary powers give it the right to revoke treaties and treaty rights.
1904	The allotment of the Sioux Reservation begins.
1906	Edmund Curtis begins photographic documentation of American Indians.
1906	Congress passes the Alaska Native Allotment Act. The Act extends allotment to Alaska Natives but no reservations are set up in the territory.
1910	Incorporation of Indian Shaker Church. The Church was founded by John and Mary Slocum in Washington State in 1881.
1911	Society of American Indians established.
1912	The Alaska Native Brotherhood and Sisterhood established.
1913	Northwest Federation of American Indians founded by tribes in the Puget Sound area.
1913	In *United States v. Sandoval*, the Supreme Court rules that Congress has jurisdiction over the Pueblo Indian community and by extension all Indians.
1917	The United States enters World War I. Nearly 12,000 Indian men serve in the military.

1918	The Native American Church incorporates in Oklahoma. The use of peyote in its ceremonies causes protest and prosecutions throughout the United States.
1919	Congress passes a law granting citizenship to Indian veterans.
1924	Congress passes the Indian Citizenship Act, which granted citizenship to all Native Americans born in the United States.
1924	Pressure from Indian rights groups and the Pueblos force Congress to pass the Pueblo Lands Act, which recognized Pueblo title to their land.
1928	The Meriam Report is issued, detailing the conditions on reservations and Indian boarding schools. The Report will serve as a major impetus for the Indian New Deal during the Great Depression.
1929	Start of the Great Depression. The U.S. Army and the Red Cross feed Indian people during the winter of 1931.
1932	Franklin Delano Roosevelt elected.
1931	John Collier is appointed Commissioner of Indian Affairs.
1934	Congress passes the Indian Reorganization Act and is the centerpiece of the Indian New Deal. The Act reversed the government policy of assimilation and started many tribes on the road of self-government.
1934	Congress passes the Johnson-O'Malley Act, which required the Bureau of Indian Affairs to contract with state and local officials to provide education, social services, and medical care to tribes.
1935	Indian Arts and Crafts Act is passed by Congress.
1936	The Indian Reorganization Act is extended to Native Alaskan communities.
1941	The Japanese Empire attacks the U.S. Naval base at Pearl Harbor.
1941	The United States declares war on Japan, Germany, and Italy. 22,000 Indians serve in the U.S. military during the war.
1942	Training of Navajo Codetalkers begins.
1942	Japanese Internment camps are located on Indian reservations by the U.S. government.

1942	The Supreme Court rules in *Seminole Nation v. United States* that the U.S. government must pay trust monies to Native Americans.
1944	National Congress of American Indians is founded in response to termination policies in the United States.
1945	Ira Hayes and his fellow Marines raise the American flag on Mount Suribachi during the battle for Iwo Jima.
1945	John Collier resigns as Commissioner of Indian Affairs.
1946	Indian Claims Commission established by Congress.
1949	Hoover Commission and beginning of termination policy. By 1953, termination was the official policy of the U.S. government.
1953	Congress ends the ban on the sale of alcohol on reservations. They delegate this power to tribal governments. Shortly thereafter Congress also ends the ban on the sale of firearms and ammunition.
1954	Klamath Termination Act is the first termination act passed by Congress.
1955	The U.S. Public Health Service takes over health care for Native Americans.
1956	Congress passes the Indian Relocation Act also known as Public Law 959. The Act is intended to encourage Native Americans to leave the reservation and assimilate into the broader population.
1958	California Rancheria Termination Act is passed by Congress.
1961	Menominee Termination Act is passed by Congress.
1961	At a conference of the National Congress of American Indians, Native Americans dissatisfied with the leadership of NCAI form the National Indian Youth Council. This marks the beginning of an era of greater activism and militancy.
1961	The first fish-in occurs in the Pacific Northwest. Fish-ins were protests for treaty rights.
1962	The Washington State Supreme Court rules against the right of Indians to fish with nets.
1964	The Office of Economic Opportunity is created. The OEO formed an Indian desk to facilitate distribution of federal money to tribes.

1965	Alaska Natives form Alaska Federated Natives to promote land claims and advocate for native communities in Alaska.
1968	M. Scott Momaday receives the Pulitzer Prize for *House Made of Dawn*.
1968	The American Indian Movement is founded in Minneapolis.
1969	Indians of All Tribes occupy Alcatraz Island. The occupation continued until 1971 when the federal government removed the small group of occupiers that remained.
1970	AIM leaders lead a protest on Thanksgiving Day in Plymouth, Massachusetts. During the protest they occupied the *Mayflower II*.
1970	The Native American Rights Fund is founded, which provided legal assistance to tribes and individual Native Americans.
1971	AIM organizes a protest at Mount Rushmore that garners national press coverage and attention.
1971	Congress passes the Alaska Native Claims Settlement Act, which gave nearly a billion dollars and 44 million acres to Alaska Natives to extinguish land claims. Regional corporations were set up to bolster economic development for Alaska Native communities.
1972	Raymond Yellow Thunder, an Oglala Sioux, is tortured and murdered in Gordon, Nebraska. AIM leaders and a thousand followers forced local authorities to prosecute two white men for the murder.
1972	AIM leaders and leaders from the Alcatraz Occupation organize a cross-country trip called "The Trail of Broken Treaties" that ends in Washington, D.C. The protesters, after being rebuffed by government officials, occupy the Bureau of Indian Affairs building and issue the Twenty Points List.
1972	Congress passes the Indian Education Act, which provided funding for Indian children to attend public schools.
1973	AIM activists and local residents of the Pine Ridge Reservation occupy the town of Wounded Knee. They are surrounded by federal and local law enforcement. The siege ends on May 8 after the federal government agrees to

	investigate conditions and corruption on the reservation. After the occupation, the federal government seeks to prosecute AIM leaders and bankrupt the organization.
1973	Congress passes the Menominee Restoration Act, which reversed termination on the Menominee Reservation and restored their status as a federally recognized tribe.
1974	Native American women activists start Women of All Red Nations.
1974	Revelation that the Indian Health Service had systematically sterilized Indian women.
1974	Congress passes the Hopi Land Settlement Act, which caused the removal of 12,000 Navajo people from the Navajo-Hopi Joint Use Area. It was the largest removal since the nineteenth century.
1976	The Indian Healthcare Act is passed by Congress, allowing tribes to manage Indian Health Service programs.
1978	Congress passes Indian Child Welfare Act, mandating that courts must use native values and tribes should be informed when placing Indian children for adoption.
1978	The American Indian Religious Freedom Act is passed by Congress. The law stated Congress's desire to protect Indian religious freedom but did not contain enforcement provisions.
1978	The Supreme Court decides in *Santa Clara Pueblo v. Martinez* that tribes had the right to determine their own membership.
1979	Seminole Nation is the first tribe to introduce gaming on their reservation.
1980	U.S. census reports that 1.5 million Native Americans live in the United States.
1985	Wilma Mankiller elected as principal chief of the Cherokee Nation of Oklahoma. She is the first woman to lead a major tribe in modern times.
1988	Congress passes the Indian Gaming Regulatory Act that provides a regulatory framework to govern Indian gaming in the United States.
1991	The Pequot tribe opens Foxwood Casino, which would eventually become the largest casino outside of Las

	Vegas. By 2016, there would be 493 Indian gaming operations in the United States, generating nearly 30 billion dollars in annual revenue.
1990	Congress passes the Native American Graves Protection and Repatriation Act (NAGPRA). NAGPRA required that any institution receiving federal funding must inventory their collections, inform tribes of relevant materials for repatriation, and then comply with the tribe's request to return items or human remains.
1996	Kennewick Man is found on the banks of the Columbia River. After twenty years of legal battles, DNA testing reveals that Kennewick Man is related to the native people of the Columbia Plateau.
1996	Elouise Cobell files suit in federal court over discrepancies regarding trust assets of Native Americans held by the U.S. government. The case was settled in 2009 for 3.4 billion dollars, some going to the plaintiffs and some to a fund to purchase lands for tribes across the United States.
1999	Ground breaking for the U.S. National Museum of the American Indian occurs.
2000	The Bureau of Indian Affairs turns 175, and the head of the agency, Kevin Grover, offers a formal apology to Native Americans for the transgressions of the agency.
2000	The Seminole Nation votes to remove freedmen descendants as members of the tribe. The U.S. government responds by cutting off most federal programs and will not authorize gaming. The freedmen descendants are reinstated.
2004	California tribes sign a compact with the state to authorize gaming.
2008	Federal legislation designates the day after Thanksgiving as Native American Heritage Day.
2011	The Cherokee Nation of Oklahoma formally removed descendants of black slaves from tribal membership. The federal government orders the tribe to restore membership but the tribe refuses. The case is still being litigated in court.
2013	Hopi and Apache tribes fail to stop an auction of sacred masks in Paris, France. The masks are sold to a foundation

            that vows to return the items to the Hopi Nation and the San Carlos Apache Nation.

2016   The Lummi tribe successfully blocks the construction of the largest coal port in North America based on their treaty rights from the 1855 Point Elliott Treaty.

2016   The Standing Rock Sioux protest the building of the Dakota Access oil pipeline near their reservation, threatening their water and sacred sites. Joined by other native people and supporters, the Standing Rock Sioux confronted local, state, and federal law enforcement over the pipeline construction.

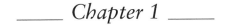

Chapter 1

A Native America

Ice had formed ahead of them and it reached all the way up to the sky. The people could not cross it. Raven flew up and struck the ice and cracked it. Coyote said, "These small people cannot cross the ice." Raven flew up again and cracked the ice again. Coyote said "Try again, try again." Raven flew up again and broke the ice. The people ran across.

This account from Paiutes in the desert sagebrush country of Nevada tells a story of long ago when Coyote led people from the north to the Paiute homeland in the Great Basin. That ice was the central obstacle to overcome (with the help of Raven and Coyote) fits one of several anthropological theories of the peopling of the Americas. Almost all evidence indicates that Native Americans' ancestors were from Northern Asia and for many decades, the explanation for this has hinged upon the Bering Strait theory.

There are three major contenders for the route of entry into the Americas from Asia. Beringia, the thousand-mile wide grassland steppe that finally resubmerged about 8,000 years ago was the only route for any overland approach to North America. Two are overland variations. The Ice-Free Corridor hypothesis posits that people made their way via an unglaciated region of North America that would have opened roughly 13,000 years ago. A second, less supported route would have proceeded through the mountains of what is now British Columbia, mostly through areas that would have been scoured by subsequent glaciers. Archaeological evidence is thus impossible to gather and this route remains speculative.

A more recently theorized route is along the now-submerged coast of Alaska and British Columbia, extending south to California. Kelp, seaweed, marine mammals, and fish would have provided abundant food to the earliest Americans along this marine route. Whether by land or by sea, or in combination, such sites are also difficult to access. Any migration during an ice age would have been along a coast later submerged by melting ice. However, supporters of this hypothesis point to the peoples of the North Pacific using boats at least 30,000 years ago. Archaeological findings from the Catalina Islands off southern California testify to the use of watercraft there some 13,000 years ago. Academics have increasingly accepted that earliest settlement of North America likely involved a maritime component and several peoples well inland of the sea also reference the sea in their origin stories. One of several Hopi origin stories references water everywhere in the beginning.

Peoples may have lived in those Beringian lands now submerged by the sea for some 10,000 years before moving on to North America as the ancestors of Na-Dene/Athapskan speakers and to Asia as Yeniseian-speaking peoples. Linguists believe that the origins of those related languages may be in a population that originally shifted out of Asia some 25,000 years ago. Whether they exited through the Ice-Free Corridor or gradually fled the rising water by another route remains a mystery. Some recent evidence indicates that Northern Asia itself may have been the meeting place of migrations out of western Eurasia and an older East Asian population and this too complicates any simple story of a small band of hunters stumbling into a new continent. Taken together, what has become clear in recent years is that the Bering Strait theory can no longer be accepted as a simple, one-way stage in the peopling of the Americas.

Two more controversial theories should also be mentioned. One suggests the movement of peoples from Europe across the northern Atlantic ice margins in something of a mirror image of the Pacific migrations. This theory has relied primarily on similarities of lithic technologies between European Solutrean spear points and the Clovis points of North America but has not been widely accepted. Even more marginalized in academic discussions are suggestions of approaches to the Americas from the South Pacific. Connections between Polynesians and mainland South America rest on scanty and controversial evidence.

ANCIENT AMERICANS

In recent years, archaeologists have verified human occupation far older than the 11,500-year-old "Clovis first" horizon. Since the 1960s, most anthropology has proceeded on the assumption that ancient peoples in the Americas could not have arrived earlier than 12,000 years ago and the technology represented by Clovis spear points marked the arrival of the earliest humans. A succession of sites has moved that date back thousands of years. The Manis Site in Washington revealed a spear point embedded in a mastodon rib dating to 13,800 years ago. At the Paisley Caves site in Central Oregon, coprolites (human fecal remains) are among the oldest direct evidence of human settlement and date to 14,300 years ago. At Buttermilk Creek in Texas, a cache of thousands of spear points and tools dates to 15,500 years ago. On the Aucilla River in Florida, a mastodon kill site dates to 14,500 years ago. More controversial material and sites in the Americas have offered even older dates.

As academics continue to debate the validity of the oldest indications of human presence, the timelines extend even deeper into the past. It is difficult to grasp the time depth of dates tens of thousands of years old, but a few more comparisons might help: Britain was not an island until about 8,500 years ago when melting ice flooded lowlands that now form the English Channel. If we take the Paisley Caves date as a baseline, over 700 generations have lived in North America. In contrast, we live only ten generations removed from the American Revolution, a hundred from Julius Caesar's Rome, and a little more than 200 from the building of the Great Pyramid at Giza. People looked across an ancient lake from Paisley Caves and lived in many other places across North America thousands of years before anyone lived in what is now Britain. It makes a pretty compelling argument for "forever" being an accurate assessment of Native American presence.

Of course, many indigenous people believe that they have been in the Americas forever and that they came into being when their ancestors emerged from the earth (Navajos and Mandans), transformed from trees into people (Algonquians), emerged from a hollow log (Kiowas), or fell from the sky (Iroquois). Many origin accounts explain the connections between people and animals and those intertwined relationships stand at the center of spiritual understandings of the world. Yokuts' origin story centers on Eagle and Coyote shaping people from clay. Nez Perces and Miwoks also credit Coyote with making or helping the first people. The Nimipoo (Nez Perce) account of Coyote tricking a monster and distributing parts of his body explains the origins of not only the Nimipoo but also all of the peoples scattered across the Columbia Plateau and northern Plains. Tribes as scattered as the Blackfeet, Potawotomis, and Nipmucs also tell stories of a creator making peoples from clay. What nearly all origin stories have in common is a deep connection to place and a continuing role in tribal culture.

Some indigenous accounts and anthropology indicate that there were at least three major waves of ancient migration to the Americas, though this is also likely an oversimplified view. The first wave appears to be the ancestors of most Native American groups. A second wave of Na-Dene ancestors arrived some 12,000 years ago, followed by another wave of Inuit ancestors 3,000 years ago. Diffusion of these populations was complicated and overlapping but these were the ancestors of later indigenous peoples.

Early Americans coexisted with a long-vanished array of large animals dubbed megafauna. Older theories asserted that the arrival of hunters across the Bering Land Bridge brought the end of animals such as mammoths and mastodons; ancient horses, camels, and bison; wooly rhinoceros; and giant sloths, beavers, and more. According to this blitzkrieg hypothesis, the pursuit of more game drew people wielding Clovis-pointed spears deeper into the continent until they had both covered the Americas and eliminated the largest animals of the Pleistocene era. Little evidence supports that scenario and it has become increasingly apparent that in many locations, people and megafauna overlapped for centuries. As the earliest dates for archaeological findings recede deeper into the past, those centuries have become millennia. Humans may have reduced herd numbers, but end-of-ice-age climate change may have been a more significant factor. Human arrival coincided with the transition of much of the Great Plains from forest to grasslands, for example. More complicated interactions between fire, changing habitats, competition between predators, and even disease may also be at the root of the disappearance of megafauna roughly 11,000 years before present.

What is more apparent is that peoples filled nearly every available ecological niche across the Americas and rapidly came to a deep understanding of these places. Overexploitation of game or vegetation would have resulted in disaster. While experimentation and learning were undoubtedly part of understanding the ancient world, the taboos, stories, and means of conveying indigenous knowledge allowed some peoples to remain in place for thousands of years. Practices shifted with ecological changes, making adaptation a central feature of many native cultures.

SHAPING THE LAND

One early marker of indigenous peoples in the North American landscape was fire. Making and maintaining forest openings, encouraging new plant growth, and drawing animals to open meadows for grazing made fire a primary tool. Burning maintained open meadows and drew game such as deer into convenient hunting zones. Small fires also increased the extent of edge habitats where many animals concentrate. Removal of brush and competing grasses allowed easier access to berries and seeds while it also promoted growth of straight new shoots for a variety of uses. Regular use of fire also created places in which all of the food plants were roughly of the same age. Where berries and seeds matured at once, cooperative harvesting could yield hundreds of pounds of food in a single day's harvest.

In part due to a different relationship with the natural world, Native Americans domesticated few animals. The primary companion animal and beast of burden was the dog. There were likely more varieties than we now know, but the "Indian dog" was widespread across North America. Peoples developed other breeds, including the Chihuahua in Mexico and a large wooly-coated dog whose coat filled a fiber niche parallel to sheep.

The invention of agriculture is not an accidental process. Lengthy experimentation with plants and horticulture are necessary to reach a reliable and stable resource and this happened in the Americas at about the same time as in the ancient Middle East and Asia; squash from southern Mexico dates to 10,000 years ago, with other crops such as maize, quinoa, and peanuts arriving not long after. Distribution of food and technology through trade routes made for a gradual expansion of these foods. By about 4,000 years ago, farmers raised squash, sunflowers, gourds, and barley in the rich soils along rivers in the Ohio Valley in eastern North America.

Elsewhere in North America, peoples cultivated other plants by diverting water, thinning, and selective harvesting. The abundance of the Pacific Coast allowed peoples in California and the Pacific Northwest to manage their landscapes in ways that Europeans did not recognize as agriculture. By increasing the productivity of valuable plant species, indigenous peoples supplied food, basketry materials, fibers for clothing and rope, medicines, arrow shafts, and more. Acorns, nuts, berries, and seeds all provided sustenance and dried or made into flour these could also be stored.

By about 250 BCE, some Native American communities had shifted their economic base to raising crops. By 800 CE, many communities specialized in maize growing and, by 1200, the familiar "three sisters" of corn, squash, and beans characterized many eastern farming communities. All three of these crops had originated in Mexico as fields spread and game diminished. Agricultural villages grew and in many cases were larger than those in Europe. With surplus food, trade increased, but so too did economic stratification. Although agriculture is closely linked with the development of artisanship and even the origins of civilization, it was also a strategy that held dangers. Droughts, disease, or insects could destroy crops and plunge entire regions into difficulty. Concentration of people into towns also increased the transmission of diseases such as tuberculosis and made sedentary peoples targets for raiding.

In drier regions, such as the Southwest, irrigation systems extended from streams and springs to water fields.

Where wild or cultivated foods continued to be abundant there was little pressure to fully invest in an entirely agricultural way of living. However, for much of North America, agricultural crops supplemented other food sources. Storable grains were especially important in hedging against poor growing years and animal population crashes. The reverse was also true since agriculture also had its disaster. Hunting, fishing, and gathering helped to even out seasons in which disaster struck agricultural crops.

On the Great Plains, people relied on a different strategy of abundance. Using buffalo jumps or *pishkuns*, Plains peoples were able to make use of the largest animals on the Plains. Sites like Head-Smashed-In in Alberta date to over 6,000 years before present and were still being used as recently as the early 1800s. The longevity of this strategy speaks to its efficiency and utility. Archaeologist Jack Brink makes the case that when a hundred or more bison plunged over the *pishkuns*, Plains peoples generated more food in a shorter amount of time than anywhere else on earth. Hide, bone, and sinews produced from massive kill sites not only supplemented the needs of mobile villages but also provided trade goods to networks radiating out from *pishkuns*, buffalo pounds (corrals where herds could find no easy exit), and other communal hunting sites. An event generating such a windfall would have brought people together in much the same way trade fairs did for thousands of years.

Such successful strategies as communal hunting on the Great Plains helps also to explain interactions between mobile hunters and more sedentary riverine villages. Surpluses of meat could be exchanged for harvested items, allowing both strategies to flourish. Pemmican, a blend of dried meat, berries, and rendered fat, also came from the buffalo hunts and could be stored or carried over long distances.

Bow and arrow technology eventually replaced spear-atlatls across North America, but did so at widely different times. It is difficult to separate small atlatl dart points from arrowheads, but if archaeologists are correct, bows and arrows may have appeared at least 8,000 years ago but did not immediately replace older atlatl technology for hundreds of years. Bow and arrow technology provided greater accuracy and could be fired from more positions, but it may not have been as efficient as buffalo jumps and pounds.

Archaeological evidence and oral accounts indicate that North America was not a consistently harmonious place. Warfare, drought, starvation, and disease existed in the ancient world as well. In the Aleutian Islands, for example, there were no large land animals to hunt and bows and arrows seem to have been reserved exclusively for warfare. When resources failed or population increased too rapidly, competition led to violence. Many later cultural practices may have originated in tragedy, leading to stories that caution about excessive selfishness or departure from practices that maintain a steadier supply of materials and foods for people. It also appears that violence played a role in the demise of many of North America's ancient societies.

MOUND BUILDING SOCIETIES

In part due to the inability to access detailed records of the past, many anthropologists have characterized ancient peoples by the artifacts they have left behind. Point complexes may reflect a shared technology, but tell us little about the political and social relationships of people who happened to employ similar tools. Similarly, mound building signified a series of cultures that rose in the eastern half of North America, but it would be a mistake to assume that sharing mortuary or ceremonial practices unified people across such vast distances.

The oldest mounds in the United States date to at least 5,400 years ago. Mounds along the Ouachita River in northern Louisiana were not used for burials, and no clear ceremonial role has been discovered. Yet later societies would continue to build mounds. The Adena complex centered in present-day Ohio rose about 2,800 years ago. Unlike the Mound Builders of thousands of years before them, Adena era people made pottery and used mounds as part of burial rituals.

Conical Adena mounds and burials sprinkled with ochre continued until about 100 CE when mound buildingappears to have become more complex and entered a larger scale phase. From about 200 BCE to 500 CE, the Hopewell Culture flourished across the eastern half of North America. Once thought to be a unified entity, more examination of the Hopewell tradition has revealed a broad set of shared cultural traits that signaled lengthy, ongoing interaction between peoples in the Mississippi, Missouri, and Ohio River valleys.

A later Mississippian Mound Builder culture reached from the Gulf Coast to the Great Lakes, but a city just east of present-day St. Louis was at its center. Cahokia became the largest city in North America in the decades after the year 1000, with a central complex of rammed-earth pyramidal

Painting of Cahokia Mounds, ca. 1150-1200 CE. In this artist's conception of downtown Cahokia, Monks Mound and the main plaza sit within the palisade at the center of a community of some 20,000 people. A combination of flooding and fire may have contributed to poor maize harvests and by the late 1300s, the people of Cahokia had dispersed into smaller communities, abandoning the largest city in North America. (Cahokia Mounds State Historic Site, painting by William R. Iseminger)

mounds surrounded by smaller mounds and homes. Fields of maize supplied food for perhaps as many as 20,000 residents. Artifacts and remains in and near the nearly 200 mound structures built at Cahokia give a glimpse of the complex society there. The largest, Monks Mound, is billed as the third tallest pyramid in the Americas and stood at the center of the city. To the west a circular calendar-dubbed Woodhenge was one of several features aligned with movement of stars, sun, and moon.

Another mound contained the remains of more than 270 sacrifice victims, though interpretations of how human sacrifice fit into Cahokian belief systems and rituals remain a matter of debate. Six presumed elites were also buried in this mound, surrounded by beads, ceramics, copper goods, and other trade goods indicating their great wealth. Recent studies have found that the victims and elites alike were a mix of male and female local residents. The mixed genders and that those sacrificed were not captive strangers has forced a rethinking of an older theory of young women being sacrificed in honor of a society dominated by male warriors. The evidence indicates something quite different.

In about 1165, Cahokia erected a massive log palisade around the town, either to protect the central city from attackers or to separate elites from the rest of the population. Whether this labor-intensive structure was the result of political competition with nearby villages or a signal of increasing separation between classes still puzzles archaeologists. The preceding century had been one of rapid expansion of Cahokian mound building and culture across a vast region. Anthropologist Timothy Pauketat has called the sudden emergence of large-scale building at Cahokia a "big bang" for Native American culture. Monks Mound may have risen in less than twenty years and Cahokian building and artifacts can be found from Wisconsin to Ohio to Louisiana. City making was apparently a sudden, good, and compelling idea in the eleventh century.

However, it seems that not too long before the wall went up around the city that Cahokia suffered a fire that destroyed a substantial portion of the city. Cahokians did not rebuild the hundred burned buildings and ongoing droughts deepened. By the 1200s, the droughts had abated, but another series of ecological disasters arrived. An earthquake and several Mississippi River floods may have signaled the slipping power of Cahokia's leaders and triggered the demise of the city. Many of Cahokia's former residents left, likely dispersing to become the ancestors of peoples such as Choctaws, Osages, Pawnees, and others. By 1400, the site was abandoned.

Mound building continued in eastern North America as part of the Fort Ancient tradition, again centered on Ohio. Perhaps the most famous of the effigy mounds, the Great Serpent Mound in Ohio, has long been connected with this later tradition. Estimates for the Great Serpent Mound's construction range widely, but recent core sampling has confirmed dates of 2,300 years ago. Though Great Serpent is still presumed to be ceremonial, little evidence exists to indicate in what way the animal effigies functioned. The ancient secrets of mounds built thousands of years ago may not be clear, but their complexity should force a reassessment of ancient societies.

THE ANCIENT SOUTHWEST

Far to the west of the Mound Builders lived Ancient Puebloans. (Many people know this society as "Anasazi," a Navajo term meaning "enemy ancestors" that some Hopi and Pueblo descendents find offensive.) Known best for their black-on-white pottery and impressive buildings, they gradually shifted from pit houses near agricultural fields to the defensive cliff dwellings of Mesa Verde, Chaco Canyon, Canyon de Chelly, and other locations.

Chaco Canyon in present-day northwestern New Mexico was the center of a culture rivaling the eastern Mound Builders. Long-distance trade goods from Mesoamerica including macaw parrots appear to date from as early as the ninth century. Chocolate, caffeine, and copper bells appeared later and indicate an ongoing connection to peoples well to the south. Chaco experienced a period of rapid growth during a period of increased rainfall from 1040 to 1140 (roughly coinciding with Cahokia's peak) even though wood used in the mostly stone structures had to be carried from forests more than fifty miles away. Chacoan building designs spread across much of the Four Corners region and many of the pueblos with "great houses" were connected by linear road network radiating from Chaco.

A decades-long drought that struck in the 1130 may have triggered the collapse of Chaco and the dispersal of peoples to the Rio Grande River valley and other sites across the Southwest. By 1250, Chaco and many of its associated pueblos were abandoned. A controversial theory advanced by Stephen Lekson asserts that Chaco was the center of an empire whose seat of power shifted to nearby Aztec Ruins in the 1100s–1200s, and then much farther south to Paquimé in northern Mexico from about 1250 to 1450.

A different strategy can be seen at Mesa Verde, just over the Colorado border to the north of Chaco. There, mesa-top housing structures dating to the seventh century were abandoned in the 1190s. An influx of new residents from Chaco may have been the impetus to move into more defensive positions on or against cliff faces. These cliff dwellings collectively housed more than 20,000 people at their height. The late 1200s brought both increased drought and warfare. Archaeological evidence and oral accounts hint strongly at outsiders competing with the Mesa Verdeans for scanty resources, but by the 1300s, most of the region had been abandoned. Not all ancient sites in the Southwest were abandoned. Acoma Pueblo and the Hopi village of Oraibi are both contenders for the oldest continually inhabited sites in North America, each founded in the early 1100s.

To the south of these Ancient Puebloan sites, an older complex of canal-building agricultural peoples known as the Hohokam appear to have coalesced over several centuries. Characterized by their red ceramics, Hohokam was one of the most persistent cultures in North America. Snaketown, outside present-day Phoenix, was occupied nearly 2,300 years ago. By the year 800, Hohokam cultivated a variety of crops as diverse as cotton, agave, and tobacco. At around 1200, Snaketown was abandoned and the center of Hohokam culture shifted to Casa Grande. By the 1400s, Hohokams appear to have shifted cultural strategies and became the O'odham whose descendants still live in Southern Arizona today.

THE AMERICAS BEFORE 1492

Population estimates range widely but about one-fifth of the earth's population, between forty-five and sixty-five million people, lived in the Americas prior to European colonization. About eighteen to twenty million Native Americans lived north of what is now Mexico. They spoke more than 300 different languages across over fifty language families. A variety of strategies allowed indigenous people to fill nearly every ecological niche across the continent, and their ability to adapt allowed for some peoples to settle in place for hundreds of years. Others shifted to new strategies and new territories. Taken together, North Americans were dynamic and resilient enough to survive and thrive for millennia.

On the eve of European colonization, several of the more powerful societies of North America were in flux. From Cahokia to Casa Grande, peoples were in the midst of forming new villages and adapting their cultures to new circumstances. The continuing movement of peoples into the Great Plains following a lengthy period of drought brought a new era of relying primarily on bison and other game. The new Plains peoples extended agriculture west and north up the Missouri River as hunters and farmers formed a symbiotic relationship. Numic-speaking Shoshoneans continued their expansion out of the Great Basin into the Rocky Mountains and High Plains.

In the east, the Haudenosaunee (Iroquois) formed their Great Law of Peace, likely in 1451. A solar eclipse marked the date in oral histories, but it remains a matter of controversy as to which solar eclipse this may have been. Some scholars have posited that the date may instead be in the mid-1100s while Haudenosaunee tradition asserts an even older origin. Recorded in and conveyed by wampum, with the Great Law of Peace, Deganawidah and other ancient leaders urged Senecas, Cayugas, Onondagas, Oneidas, and Mohawks to strive together for unity. This oral constitution, symbolized by the Tree of Peace and five arrows bundled together, was the organizing principle of the Haudenosaunee Confederacy. Each tribe took a specific role, with Mohawks assuming diplomatic leadership while

Onondagas, as the fire keepers, were changed with calling and maintaining the council. Maintenance of the Great Peace alliance may well have been the key factor that allowed Haudenosaunees to withstand European colonization and maintain their power in the times ahead.

PROFILE: DEGANAWIDAH, JIGONSASEH, AND HIAWATHA

The Great Peacemaker, Deganawidah, according to Haudenosaunee tradition was the originator of the Haudenosaunee Great Law of Peace or *Gayanshagowa*. Several versions of his story state that he was born to a Huron mother in a virgin birth. His mother had a vision in which her son would plant the Tree of Peace at Onondaga. Deganawidah performed several feats along the way, including reforming a notorious cannibal, which brought several followers to his prophet's vision. His urging of tribes to cease warring earned him the advocacy of a Seneca woman named Jigonsaseh, "She Who Lives On The Road To War." She was tired of housing, feeding, and treating warriors on their way to and from raids. Warriors often met in her home to argue or resolve disputes and in that role, Jigonsaseh became a trusted voice of reason among the tribes and when she advocated for Deganawidah's plan, people listened.

Hiawatha was a renowned Onondaga with a critical role in convincing skeptical leaders of the value of a lasting confederacy of nations. Haudenosaunee accounts of Hiawatha should be separated from the image invented and popularized in the nineteenth century by poems and plays. Most critically, he demonstrated the utility of wampum to carry messages and used belts of wampum as part of his ceremonies to convey the message of the Great Peace to other villages. Senecas became the final tribe to join in the Great Peace when the sudden darkening of the sun that swayed doubters to join the alliance. Generations of scholars have attempted to pinpoint the date based on this solar eclipse, but no matter how old the alliance is, tales of the Great Peacemaker and his allies have shaped Iroquoian governance to this day.

PROFILE: KENNEWICK MAN

When two young men stumbled across bones jutting from the bank of the Columbia River just upstream from Kennewick, Washington in 1996, they touched off a controversy that took two decades to resolve. The bones were on U.S. Army Corps of Engineers property but several tribes immediately contested ownership of the remains. When anthropologists studying the remains initially announced that the bones were of a man in his late forties who lacked Native American characteristics, the issue of whether the 9,000-year-old bones belonged to regional tribes became much more complicated. A group of anthropologists sued for access to the bones initially turned over to tribes.

Umatillas, Colvilles, Yakamas, and Nez Perces brought a countersuit under the Native American Graves Protection and Repatriation Act (NAGPRA) to protect the Ancient One and return him to the soil. In 2004, the Ninth Circuit Court of Appeals ruled in favor of the anthropologists, largely due to the lack of a clear connection to any modern tribe required under NAGPRA.

Kennewick Man lay in a museum at the University of Washington for eleven more years before a 2015 DNA test demonstrated that Native Americans were the closest modern match. During that time, studies revealed that he had been wounded in the hip by a spear. He had, at some point, broken ribs and suffered other injuries to his shoulder and leg. Kennewick Man led a difficult life. Only through a rider on a federal Congressional bill did Kennewick Man begin his road home. He was reburied by a group of Columbia Plateau tribes in early 2017.

REFERENCES AND FURTHER READING

Brink, Jack W. *Imagining Head-Smashed-In: Aboriginal Buffalo Hunting on the Northern Plains*. Athabasca, AB: AU Press, 2008.

Delcourt, Paul A., and Hazel R. Delcourt. *Prehistoric Native Americans and Ecological Change: Human Ecosystems in Eastern North America since the Pleistocene*. New York: Cambridge University Press, 2008.

Deloria Jr., Vine. *Evolution, Creationism, and Other Modern Myths: A Critical Inquiry*. Golden, CO: Fulcrum, 2002.

Fagan, Brian M. *The First North Americans: An Archaeological Journey*. New York: Thames & Hudson, 2011.

Hurt, R. Douglas. *Indian Agriculture in America: Prehistory to the Present*. Lawrence: University Press of Kansas, 1996.

Mann, Charles C. *1491: New Revelations of the Americas before Columbus*. New York: Knopf, 2005.

Meltzer, David J. *First Peoples in a New World: Colonizing Ice Age America*. Berkeley: University of California Press, 2009.

Pauketat, Timothy R., and Susan M. Alt, eds. *Medieval Mississippians: The Cahokian World*. Santa Fe: School for Advanced Research Press, 2014.

Peck, Trevor R. *Light from Ancient Campfires: Archaeological Evidence of Native Lifeways on the Northern Plains*. Vancouver: UBC Press, 2011.

Powell, Joseph F. *The First Americans: Race, Evolution, and the Origin of Native Americans*. New York: Cambridge University Press, 2005.

Riley, Carroll L. *Rio Del Norte: People of Upper Rio Grande from Earliest Times to Pueblo Revolt*. Salt Lake City: University of Utah Press, 2007.

Steward, Julian H. "Some Western Shoshoni Myths." *Bureau of American Ethnology Bulletin* 136 (1943): 249–299.

Stuart, David E. *Anasazi America: Seventeen Centuries on the Road from Center Place*. 2nd ed. Albuquerque: University of New Mexico Press, 2014.

Wallace, Paul, and John Mohawk. *The White Roots of Peace: The Iroquois Book of Life*. Santa Fe, NM: Clear Light, 1994.

_____ *Chapter 2* _____

New Peoples and Shatter Zones

In December 1492, the Taíno *cacique* Guacanagarí met the newcomers who would establish the first European settlement in the Americas in almost 500 years. Off the shores of his chiefdom, Christopher Columbus's *Santa Maria* ran aground on a reef. One-third of the European sailors would be left behind in a temporary settlement of *La Navidad* on the island they called Hispañola. Taínos were used to the arrival of newcomers from across the Caribbean. However, these Spaniards were stranger than usual, and brought with them cultural beliefs that were outside of Taíno experience.

Both Taíno and European culture shaped the initial confusion and misinterpretations, but for Guacanagarí, the real task was determining how to receive the newcomers. The novelty of Spanish materials was one of the draws of an uneasy partnership, but events would soon reveal insurmountable divisions between Taínos and Spaniards. The marooned Europeans sought to extract food, gold, and sex from the Taínos, abusing their hosts to the point that Taínos turned on the Europeans. By the time Columbus and his fleet of seventeen ships returned in November 1493 to colonize the island, Taínos had killed all of the Spanish refugees.

Guacanagarí told Columbus that Caonabó, a headman from the interior, was responsible for the Spanish deaths. Further, Guacanagarí said that he and his people had fought off Caonabó at great cost. Guacanagarí said that he had been wounded in the leg, but when Columbus demanded proof, the wound had miraculously healed. Despite the dubious story, Guacanagarí and Columbus came to a mutual agreement. Both parties needed the other as an ally, and Columbus especially needed amicable relations with the people who surrounded his settlement site. After a brief uprising among the colonizers that resulted in Columbus sending half of the Spaniards home, he turned his attention to the interior and potential gold strikes. After building a new fort as a base of operations, Columbus gave orders to both pacify and terrorize the interior.

Under Caonabó's leadership, Taínos withdrew from their lowland villages and fields to the mountainous center of the island. In doing so they gave up access to most of their food sources, but also denied Spaniards effective use of their horses. Spaniards captured Caonabó in part with the offer of a horse and metal goods, which turned out to be handcuffs. By 1495, the culmination of this campaign of conquest came with the Battle of Vega Real. Using war dogs, harquebuses, and horses in a dawn raid, the Spaniards decimated refugees gathered into a village.

Spaniards, extending their earlier colonizing experience in the Canary Islands, remade Hispañola into a version of Spain. As the familiar foods and ecology of the island gave way to European plants and animals, Taínos found themselves and their homeland beleaguered by human and nonhuman strangers. Resistance continued on the island for years, including a significant movement led by Anacaona, a female *cacica* in the island's western district, but eventual Spanish domination of Hispañola set the pattern for other Caribbean islands. Cuba was largely under Spanish control by the late 1510s with Spaniards taking advantage of divisions between more than two dozen *caciques*.

CONFRONTING THE SPANISH PROJECT

Spanish ideologies shaped their invasion of the Americas. The culture of the Iberian Peninsula was especially attuned to religious doctrine and warfare due to the centuries-long conflict with Islamic expansion. The centuries of warfare against Islam dubbed the *reconquista* (reconquest) shaped generations of Spanish thinking. Spain declared victory in forcing Moors from southernmost Spain in 1492 and they carried their binary framework to the Americas. Military forces and zealous *padres* worked together to carry out the aims of a Catholic kingdom emboldened by their certitude as claimants of absolute truth. When Spanish expeditions arrived in the Americas, they understood the peoples they encountered as potential new subjects and souls, but also as possible enemies of Christendom.

To claim lands for their empires, Europeans enacted their own culturally specific schemes. Spain employed the *requerimiento*, a practice carried over from the war against the Moors. By reading a document—in Spanish—to indigenous peoples, many Spaniards believed that miraculous, instantaneous conversions could result. The crux of the *requerimiento* was the demand that new subjects become Christian Spaniards under an overseas crown. Any people who did not accept this effectively declared that they were enemies of Catholicism and Spain. Spaniards could then either force conversions or extend their religious warfare against peoples presumed to be in league with the Devil. Enemies captured in such just warfare were subject to enslavement.

Aside from the new ideologies that confronted Native Americans, fundamental changes to American environments also began with European contact. The sudden arrival of plants, animals, germs, and viruses from Eurasia and Africa remade the world. In what historians have called the Columbian Exchange, these changes ranged from the arrival of new foods and domestic animals to new forms of vermin, weeds, and disease. Indigenous peoples across the Americas took advantage of useful items and rejected others. However, invasive species such as dandelions, wood rats, and even horses and pigs escaped human control and moved inland far faster than Europeans.

Native Americans also had no immunity to crowd diseases, many of which developed over millennia of Eurasian animal domestication. Smallpox, measles, chicken pox, swine and avian influenzas, bubonic plague, and dozens of others killed millions in Eurasia and Africa, but destroyed entire communities in the Americas. The speed with which some diseases killed makes it difficult to determine the exact diseases at play in some sixteenth-century epidemics. The rapid spread and overlapping of multiple diseases further muddies the picture. However, it is clear that disease traveled much further than Europeans themselves. Trade and communication with neighboring peoples allowed diseases to strike villages well beyond contact zones.

Perhaps most devastating of all of these diseases was smallpox. A pandemic spread from the Caribbean and Mexico in the 1520s south into the Incan Empire. It remains unclear how far smallpox and other diseases traveled out of central Mexico, but some authors have suggested a hemispheric pandemic may have devastated peoples throughout the Americas. The cumulative impact of such virgin soil epidemics go a long way toward explaining how Europeans could enter the Americas and gradually force their culture into decimated indigenous worlds.

European death rates from smallpox stood at about 30 percent, but Native Americans saw 90 percent mortality. People had few ways to combat unfamiliar diseases and traditional cures often did little to help. Once death rates became high enough, the social network for villages and chiefdoms were quickly overwhelmed. When struck by such an emergency, it is easy to imagine communities so overwhelmed that other key functions such as food preparation, harvesting, sowing, and hunting became increasingly difficult.

In contrast, Europeans generally benefitted from the Columbian Exchange. Indigenous foods, especially, flowed back across the Atlantic to increase the number of calories available for consumption. On any given

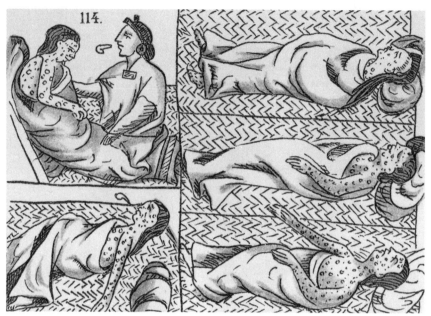

A Nahua image from the 16th-century Florentine Codex depicts the devastating course of smallpox in Mexico. Native Americans suffered disproportionately from European diseases such as smallpox, measles, typhus, and others. Sickness spread quickly among the cities, towns, and villages of North America, killing as many as nine out of ten. (Courtesy of the Peabody Museum of Archaeology and Ethnology, Harvard University, PM# 2004.24.29636)

piece of land, maize, potatoes, and manioc produced more sustenance than traditional European crops such as wheat or barley. Since these American plants also grew better in poorer soils, the amount of arable land increased, leading to exponential growth in food production and population. Europeans were suspicious of some new foods such as tomatoes and maize, but by feeding them to livestock, they increased the availability of milk and meat. The influx of goods and rapidly multiplying population sparked the European economy, but the resulting inflation increased inequality for Europeans. Those conditions led directly to the large numbers of European indentured servants and African slaves who would continue to shape American colonization.

The appearance of Europeans coincided with what Ethnohistorian Robbie Ethridge has called "the Mississippian shatter zone." Throughout the Southeast, the 1500s saw a gradual reorganization of older regional cultures. This era of instability gave rise to chiefdoms such as Apalachee, Coosa, and Natchez. Across the Southeast, palisaded towns were the norm near territorial borders and chiefdoms were separated by large buffer zones.

Archaeologists have taken this as evidence of ongoing warfare amongst rival peoples throughout the shatter zone.

Europeans quickly learned to exploit these rivalries as they entered new territories. Aiding one chiefdom against another and enslaving enemies was a pattern Spaniards extended from their earlier conquests of the Canary Islands. Slave raiders struck Florida as early as 1510, and Spaniards invaded Cuba the following year. In 1519, Hernando Cortés launched an invasion of Mexico, where Tlaxcalans allied themselves with the newcomer Spaniards to strike back against the Mexíca or Aztec Empire.

Native Americans were critical to the joint success of Indian-Spanish campaigns, and indigenous aims often reshaped European intentions. Whether through shared languages or geographic knowledge, *indios amigos* often provided critical information and acted as mediators and translators between natives and newcomers. Tribes seeking advantage over rivals allied themselves with the newcomers and often continued to direct the activities of conquest. The 1524 invasion of Mayan territory served the aims of Tlaxcalan allies from central Mexico at least as much as Hernando Cortés. So too were Spaniards drawn into defending their *indio* allies in northern Mexico. Central Mexican *indios* became the workforce for Mexican mines and ranches and by the mid-1500s and were the primary settlers of northern frontier towns. Spaniards hoped that urban Indians from central Mexico would serve as models to entice more mobile peoples to become sedentary agriculturalists. Where Spaniards found no allies, they often failed to make any inroads. Long supply trains, little familiarity with strange landscapes, and raiding by Indians they collectively called Chichimecas imposed limits on early expansion.

Conquistadors were motivated to continue campaigns by a system in which commanders received an *adelanto* (a fifth of any plunder and jurisdiction over lands conquered) and *encomienda* rights (a share in the labor and annual production of their Indian subjects). In part driven by the example of Cortés, conquistadors struck out into Native America in hopes of easily conquering indigenous cities and enriching themselves and their families. However, even with disease decimating the Indian populations, the Cortés example remained an exception. Over and over, indigenous peoples defeated invading conquistadors or expeditions found no precious metals.

Unlike the Caribbean, the vast scale of the mainland combined with continued indigenous resistance made for a particularly effective defense. For two centuries, peoples of the Southwest and Southeast managed to confine colonization to a handful of outposts surrounded by Indian Country. A 1528 expedition to Florida was representative in its floundering. After spending months traveling from Sarasota Bay to the chiefdom of Apalachee in northern Florida, the 250 survivors killed their remaining horses and took to the Gulf of Mexico in rafts. As survivors came ashore in Texas, they seem to have been treated well, but after some of the Spaniards resorted to cannibalism, nearby Coahuiltecans enslaved the would-be conquistadors.

Alvar Núñez Cabeza de Vaca eventually led two other Spaniards and an African overland to La Junta on the Rio Grande and Casas Grandes before encountering a Spanish slaving expedition in Sinaloa. Eight years after landing in Florida, Cabeza de Vaca and the African Estebanico de Dorantes had developed reputations as healers and a large entourage of Indians escorted them to the Spanish frontier. There, despite Cabeza de Vaca's protests, the slaving party captured 500 of those Indian followers. Having encountered dozens of indigenous societies in his journeys, Cabeza de Vaca had also come to the conclusion that conquest of Native Americans was counterproductive and unnecessary. However, he argued in vain against continued campaigns of violent conquest against the indigenous peoples of New Spain.

During this critical contact period, the region between central Mexico and the Pueblo villages on the Rio Grande paralleled the Mississippian shatter zone in its rapid changes. Indigenous populations shifting away from Spanish slaving gave rise to new dynamic multiethnic communities on the lower Rio Grande. Further north, Jumanos controlled trade across the southern Great Plains. Between 1450 and 1550, they supplied even greater amounts of bison meat, hides, and other goods to their trading partners on the lower Rio Grande and in Pueblo villages on the upper river. It was a time of relative abundance as the Little Ice Age brought greater moisture to the southern Great Plains. More grass grew and Jumano hunters encountered more bison. From the Plains came bison hides and flint from quarries just north of present-day Amarillo, Texas. At the same time, Pueblo fields may also have been more productive and agricultural villages traded the "three sisters" (corn, squash, and beans) and more in a network extending to central Mexico and eastward across the Mississippi.

During the mid-1500s, perhaps drawn by the increased resources of the southern Plains, Athapaskan-speaking peoples shifted southward. These Apaches eventually drove a wedge between Jumanos and their Pueblo allies, becoming the new critical link between the Pueblo agricultural settlements and the bison of the plains. Almost simultaneously, Spaniards began to arrive in the region. Cabeza de Vaca's return sparked even greater interest in the lands to the north and a series of three major expeditions and several smaller ones began in 1539 with Father Marcos de Niza, led by Estebanico, toward the Seven Cities of Cibola.

The Pueblo villages of the upper Rio Grande were close enough to Spanish legends that the promise of another population center full of riches drew Spaniards northward. The expedition ended suddenly with Estebanico's death. There is reason to doubt that he reached the Zuni village of Hawikuh, but Zuni accounts that they had killed a man for insulting their women correspond with some of the expedition details. In any case, de Niza immediately returned to Mexico where his failed expedition made clear that there was indeed a population of settled people in cities north of the Chichimeca. Francisco Vásquez de Coronado led a larger, better-equipped expedition to the north in 1540. Nearly three-quarters of the 1,100-person expedition were *indios amigos* from central Mexico, some of whom remained in New Mexico when the failed expedition returned to New Spain in 1542. The 1,500 horses and mules that made up the other substantial portion of the expedition brought large numbers of these animals into the interior of North America for the first time. Collectively, these expeditions served to expose Pueblos, Apaches, and other natives of the greater Southwest to Spanish goods and ideologies that would shape colonization efforts.

THE MISSISSIPPIAN SHATTER ZONE

The same year as the de Niza-Estebanico expedition, Hernando de Soto led an expedition that passed through most major villages of the Southeast. From Tampa Bay, the Spaniards traveled north through Apalachee, then northeast to modern North Carolina before turning west and following the Tennessee River valley through Coosa. At Mabila in central Alabama, Tascalusa nearly defeated the Spaniards in a surprise attack. Tascalusa's men killed several Spaniards, horses, and many of the pigs herded as provisions for Soto's force. Soto struck back by burning several nearby towns and word spread quickly through trade networks.

Soto settled into the food-rich province of Chicaza for the winter of 1540 where the Chicazans opposed the Spaniards but avoided an all-out battle. The following spring, as the Spaniards prepared to return to exploring, he demanded 200 Indian bearers to serve as beasts of burden for his troops. Instead, Chicaza warriors attacked with flaming arrows. The Chicazans may have destroyed the Spaniards had there not been such confusion from the remaining horses running wild through the fiery battle. Again, Spaniards lost dozens of horses and pigs to the flames. On top of their losses at Mabila, this was a turning point for the expedition. Traveling northwest to Arkansas, then southwest through Caddo territory in Texas, Soto repeatedly took Indian leaders hostage as a means of extorting food and safety along his route. When Soto died in 1542, the remaining Spaniards began a desperate march to the Mississippi to escape. Four years of death and destruction had yielded nothing for the Spanish Empire.

In part due to the continued failures of Spanish expeditions, it was not until 1565 that Pedro Menéndez was able to establish a permanent European outpost in the Southeast. The Saturiba village of Seloy on the coast of Florida became the site of St. Augustine, Spain's fortress to guard treasure fleets riding the Gulf Stream out of the Caribbean into the Atlantic. A French settlement in Saturiba territory at the mouth of the St. Johns River triggered the Spanish effort. Less than two weeks after landing at Seloy, the Spaniards marched against their European rivals, guided by Saturibas. Destroying both the French settlement and the survivors who had come ashore south of St. Augustine, Menéndez established Spain as the primary European power in the region. However, while he was absolutely dependent upon Saturibas and other Timucuan allies, he also maintained a low opinion of non-Catholics. He explicitly compared Indians and French Protestants as both having Satanic beliefs. By 1572, desperate to assert control of the region, Menéndez urged a war of fire and blood be waged, with survivors sold into slavery offshore so that there was no possibility of return. In this, the Spanish of Florida mirrored their brothers in northern Mexico. Unconverted Indians resisting Spain were to be met with total war and potential extermination.

Events in northern Mexico and Florida intensified a Spanish conversation about the place of *indios* within New Spain. Instead of direct enslavement, a system of *repartimiento* put Indians to work legally building new towns, repairing roads and bridges, and accompanying caravans. They also tended fields, tilled land, herded animals, cut firewood, and acted as house servants. In Florida, Indians cut stone and built fortifications such as San Marcos and unloaded ships. In part due to a shortage of horses, Florida's mission Indians also served as bearers, packing goods by foot between Spanish towns and missions. To defend such practices from accusations of enslavement, Spaniards applied legal limits on the length of service and issued token payments to Indians so as not to be accused of slavery.

The Orders for New Discoveries in 1573 were meant to both relieve Indians from excessive colonial demands and to reduce the costs of seemingly wasteful efforts to extend conquest further into North America. The Orders officially ended conquest and encouraged peaceful and charitable relations with Indians. Specifically, the Orders limited encomienda demands to a single blanket or hide and a single *fanega* of maize. The practice of governors often purchasing their offices and indebting themselves effectively cancelled such protections. Extorting money from the preceding governor, often to cover up abuse of Indians, became regular practice. Governors and other colonizers turned to illegal but locally accepted practices.

A NEW MEXICO

In the Spring of 1598, Don Juan de Oñate led 500 colonists (a number that included more than one hundred soldiers and seven friars) to found a new colony in the midst of the Pueblos. Promising better treatment than they had received from Coronado, Pueblos put up little initial resistance. Pueblos' motives may have been borne of expediency. It was easier to integrate newcomers than to fight, and the goods and military assistance offered by Spaniards were likely factors in their reception.

The promised cooperation in New Mexico did not last long. Spaniards seized a Tewa pueblo and evicted its occupants rather than building their own housing. Soldiers demanded goods from the Pueblos and took maize, deerskins, cotton blankets, buffalo robes, firewood, and Pueblo women. Spanish cattle invaded fields, damaging the crops necessary to both feed villages and trade. In an observation at once astute and ignorant, a Spanish soldier noted that the Pueblos remonstrated, wept, and acted almost as if they were being killed. When a Pueblo leader attempted to shame Oñate for stealing food from his people, the governor had him killed by throwing him off the roof of his pueblo.

Another incident stands out as representative of the violence inflicted by Spaniards. The episode was so traumatic and cruel that inhabitants of the mesa-top Pueblo of Acoma still recount the grisly story. In December 1598, Oñate's nephew Juan de Zaldivar led a patrol to the Pueblo far to the west of

In this imagined version of the January 1599 siege of Acoma, Pueblos (here wearing Plains headdresses) fight a pitched battle with conquistadors. In retaliation for Acoma's resistance to seizures of their food stores, Spaniards killed over 800 men, women, and children. To demonstrate Spanish intolerance for rebellion, each captured man had one of his feet cut off in a public ceremony. (Universal History Archive/UIG via Getty Images)

the Rio Grande to extort provisions. When Zaldivar arrived at the well-defended village, Acoman warriors killed Zaldivar and ten of his soldiers. Oñate, isolated from Mexico by weeks of travel, determined to make an example of such resistance. In January, he brought the full force of the Spanish soldiers against Acoma. After three days of intense fighting, the Spaniards managed to storm the village. When the battle was over, 800 men, women, and children lay dead. Soldiers herded 500 survivors on foot east to the Rio Grande where they held a trial for treason and murder. As punishment, all over the age of twelve were enslaved for twenty years, with all men over twenty-five having the additional punishment inflicted of one of their feet being cut off to prevent their running away. Under Spanish law, all children under the age of twelve were declared innocent, but they were removed from the influence of their families. The children were sent to the mining frontier of central Mexico to be raised as servants in good Christian households.

Friars in the Southwest looked toward the Pueblo towns as the next population ripe for conversion to Christianity. They preferred a colony with few other Spaniards so they could keep Pueblos away from the corrupting influences of civilians and military alike and limit competition for Indian labor. They demanded that Pueblo converts abandon all of their ceremonies, dress, food, and language. In conflict with Pueblo culture, they demanded monogamy and chastity before marriage. Fertility ceremonies in particular clashed with the Padres' sensibilities as an event that combined indigenous religion, language, and a reenactment of the earth being impregnated.

Backed up by soldiers with horses, dogs, and guns, the missionaries reinforced their conversion with the threat of violence. Most Pueblos appeared to cooperate with Spanish efforts by accepting as much of the Spanish conversion as they had to in order to continue friendly relations in the face of Apache and Navajo raiding. Metal tools; new crops, including watermelons, wheat, apples, and grapes; and new domesticated animals such as sheep, goats, cattle, and pigs appealed to Pueblos. The apparent acceptance of European crops and Catholicism afforded some protection against enslavement and outside raiders.

By 1607, the Viceroy removed Oñate from his governorship at the behest of missionaries. Spain nearly deserted its unprofitable colony, but the same missionaries convinced the Viceroy that they had 7,000 provisional converts and that Spain could not desert these new subject souls. In an effort to retain these Pueblo converts, the Viceroy issued a series of additional reforms in 1609. The first was to end Spanish occupation of Indian villages and the result was the founding of a new town site: Santa Fe. In an explicit effort to reduce rapes, only a small garrison of fifty married men were to serve as soldiers in New Mexico. Further exploration and use of Indian labor to raise crops was prohibited.

The *rescate* provided an alternative source of labor for Spanish colonies. This practice ransomed captives in the name of Christian charity. In 1694, Navajos beheaded children when Spaniards refused to pay ransom and after that, Spaniards seem to have eagerly rescued captives in trading fairs and elsewhere. Paid for out of the royal treasury, the reality was that individuals gained servants by spending thirty to forty pesos of the King's money. For roughly the price of a mule, children could be placed with good families where they learned to do chores for their keep. Others ended up sold southward into Mexico. The *rescate* operated under a pretense of distinguishing between the rescue of captives and outright slavery, though even this sometimes fell away. For example, authorizing a strange combination of conversion and enslavement, Governor Juan Ignacio Flores Mogollon simply ordered that Apaches be baptized before sold.

Even relatively poor households had at least one *indio de depósito* servant by the mid-1700s. Though they had little legal standing, these servants could be freed and could not pass their condition of servitude on to their children. They may not have been chattel slaves, but it is clear that many were demeaned, marginalized, and brutalized. Open slavery was illegal, but it remained profitable if owners could deliver slaves to the labor hungry Mexican mines. Only thirty-five families retained their encomienda rights in New Mexico and with no silver mines or obvious source of revenue, human labor was the only obvious means for profit for colonizers.

In spite of the harm inflicted upon Pueblo people, Spaniards and Pueblos remained linked together in an alliance against raiding Navajos, Utes, Apaches, and Comanches. Perhaps due to the reduction in goods available for trade as a result of Spanish policies, surrounding tribes raided New Mexico villages to obtain the food and trade items they needed. Ironically, the system imposed by Spaniards made Pueblos more reliant upon them for joint defense even as their numbers plummeted. In the century following Spanish colonization, the Pueblo population dropped to less than 17,000. Spaniards reacted by consolidating pueblos whose population no longer appeared viable for food production or defense. From over a hundred at contact, only twenty-one Pueblo towns remained.

At the same time, the power struggle between the missions and the governors provided some room for Pueblos to navigate among restricted options. Governors often refused to enforce the discipline sought by missions, allowing dances and ceremonies to continue. In large part, this amity allowed governors and their friends to tap into the Indian slave world. Non-Christians could be employed as servants and as illegal slaves for sale to the labor hungry mines to the south. Friars attempted to protect their charges from seizure but also tolerated little backsliding away from the path of conversion. The Franciscan priests used punishments such as whipping followed by smearing slashed backs with turpentine. To give Indians a taste of the fires of hell that Christianity was meant to save them from, they sometimes then lit the turpentine on fire. In the minds of many priests, it was far better to experience the pain of such tortures, or even death, if it meant saving souls in perpetuity. At least one scholar has argued that the fathers in New Mexico were especially prone to seeking martyrdom in this most violent of frontiers. In any case, Pueblos seem to have been caught in an untenable position. They were at once besieged by outside raiders and navigating carefully within a Spanish system that could result in punishment, hunger, and further death by disease. While there were many small victories in using Spaniards for their own ends, a gradual erosion of Pueblo power and repeated crises made seventeenth-century New Mexico a particularly difficult and complicated place for indigenous peoples.

PROFILE: EL TURCO

The semimysterious figure of man Coronado called "The Turk" reveals much about the complex interactions of Pueblo peoples of New Mexico with a continental network. As El Turco led the Coronado expedition away from the heart of Pueblo territory in 1541, Spaniards' willingness to believe appears to have driven them to put their faith in tales of golden cities. Along with another non-Pueblo Indian, Ysopete, El Turco represented the promise of riches among other Indians farther afield. Even when Pueblos denied that El Turco had knowledge of any city of gold, Coronado elected to follow him toward Quivira.

El Turco led Coronado eastward across northern Texas and at each meeting spoke with the Indians he encountered. His knowledge of languages ranging from Nahuatl to the sign language employed by traders across the Great Plains enabled him to interact with Coronado's *indios amigos* and the Pueblos, Querechos, and Teyas they met. These people confirmed at least a version of his story and indicated that there were dense settlements farther to the east. However, Ysopete contradicted El Turco and indicated that Quivira was to the north, not the east. Further, the Wichita villages were not filled with gold. Coronado seems to have trusted neither of his guides completely and the lure of possible riches led him on with a smaller party to a point near the Kansas-Nebraska border. There, with Ysopete's account proven true and months of travel resulting in nothing, Coronado and his men became convinced that El Turco must have had supernatural assistance in leading them to such a disappointing end. Coronado had El Turco garroted to death.

The Spaniards managed, with the assistance of a compass, to make their way back to the Pueblo villages on the Rio Grande, but the journey was something of a precursor for the Spanish inability to expand beyond occupying sedentary agricultural villages. Coronado returned to Spain in chains for abuses against the Indians (in part because his expedition revealed no riches and only served to alienate potential subjects). In many ways, El Turco's deception was the turning point for Spanish expansion in North America; New Spain would never effectively extend into the Great Plains.

PROFILE: THE LADY OF COFITACHEQUI

The Lady of Cofitachequi encountered the other major European incursion into North America in 1540. Soto had tortured Indians he met by burning them alive until they indicated the way to Cofitachequi and they may have stumbled upon her location by accident. She had only been visiting a village on the banks of the Wateree River in South Carolina admonishing some of the local headmen to pay their tribute. In a show of her power, her subjects bore her on a litter draped in fine white cloth, and the Spaniards were impressed with her bearing and status. The Lady of Cofitachequi appeared to embody the rumors they had gleaned from Apalachees weeks earlier of a rich kingdom in the north ruled by a woman. After she crossed the river in a canoe similarly covered, she gave gifts of hides and food to the strangers, and a string of pearls to Soto. Greeting Soto as she might a visiting *cacique*, the Lady of Cofitachequi attempted a diplomatic solution to the arrival of a foreign army to her lands. When Spaniards expressed awe at the number of pearls in one of the mound temples, she attempted to impress her power upon them further by expressing disdain for the local treasure. She had far more at her seat of power a few miles away.

The situation turned when after days of constant demands from the Spaniards, the Lady absented herself. She may have thought that withdrawal of her authority would make it more difficult for the Spaniards to acquire food and goods, or she may have realized the failure of her strategy. A few days later, Soto entered the town of Talimeco and made the *Lady of Cofitachequi* his hostage. Bringing several female attendants with her, the Lady continued her sovereign role and was an instrument for the invaders' continued demands for food and supplies. She escaped her captors near the boundaries of her lands, with at least three of her entourage bringing her baggage with her. By that point, it was clear that no silver or gold was forthcoming from Cofitachequi and Soto continued carrying his violent invasion farther into North America. Presumably, the Lady of Cofitachequi returned to Talimeco and resumed her rule over one of the richest of the Mississippian chiefdoms.

REFERENCES AND FURTHER READING

Anderson, Gary Clayton. *The Indian Southwest, 1580–1830: Ethnogenesis and Reinvention.* Norman: University of Oklahoma Press, 1999.

DuVal, Kathleen. *The Native Ground: Indians and Colonists in the Heart of the Continent.* Philadelphia: University of Pennsylvania Press, 2007.

Ethridge, Robbie. *From Chicaza to Chickasaw: The European Invasion and the Transformation of the Mississippian World, 1540–1715.* Chapel Hill: University of North Carolina Press, 2010.

Forbes, Jack D. *Apache, Navajo, and Spaniard.* 2nd ed. Norman: University of Oklahoma Press, 1994.

Gallay, Alan. *Indian Slavery in Colonial America.* Lincoln: University of Nebraska Press, 2009.

Galloway, Patricia. *Choctaw Genesis, 1500–1700.* Lincoln: University of Nebraska Press, 1995.

John, Elizabeth A. H. *Storms Brewed in Other Men's Worlds: The Confrontation of Indians, Spanish, and French in the Southwest, 1540–1795.* 2nd ed. Norman: University of Oklahoma Press, 1996.

Kelton, Paul. *Epidemics and Enslavement: Biological Catastrophe in the Native Southeast, 1492–1715.* Lincoln: University of Nebraska Press, 2007.

Milanich, Jerald T. *Florida Indians and the Invasion from Europe.* Tallahassee: University Press of Florida, 1995.

Reséndez, Andrés. *A Land So Strange: The Epic Journey of Cabeza de Vaca.* New York: Basic Books, 2007.

Snyder, Christina. "The Lady of Cofitachequi: Gender and Political Power among Native Southerners." In *South Carolina Women: Their Lives and Times,* edited by Marjorie Julian Spruill, Joan Marie Johnson, and Valinda W. Littlefield, 11–25. Athens: University of Georgia Press, 2009.

Weber, David J. *The Spanish Frontier in North America.* New Haven, CT: Yale University Press, 1992.

Chapter 3

Increasing Colonial Contacts

All along the shores of the continent in the seventeenth century, indigenous peoples encountered newcomers at an increasing rate. The resource-rich meeting of land and sea supported dense native populations and the sea itself was a primary transportation route. It was often far easier for Indians to paddle along the shore than to cross multiple rivers and headlands. Thus, maritime Native Americans often had their first encounters with Europeans in the bays and river mouths. Stymied by unfamiliar shores and currents, those Europeans often relied on local knowledge to navigate coastal waters. Numerous rivers extended transportation routes deep inland through rich farmlands, hunting zones, and towns.

Between what would later be called New England and the Chesapeake Bay, Europeans kidnapped hundreds of Native Americans before they made their initial settlements in the region. The critical information they gleaned slowly allowed Europeans to come ashore and navigate the coastal zone. However, Native Americans also manipulated Europeans with little knowledge of local geography or culture. Epenow, a Wampanoag from Martha's Vineyard, used a common tactic with his English captors. After living in London for three years, his tales of gold lured an English ship back across the Atlantic. When a ship carrying Epenow and two other captives returned to his home island in 1614, he quickly escaped overboard covered by a flurry of Wampanoag arrows fired at the crew.

Of course, Native Americans had encountered Vikings five centuries earlier. The Norse established a colony at L'Anse Aux Meadows, Newfoundland, but abandoned that settlement in the face of *Skraeling* attacks by the year 1000. Whether these *Skraelings* were Beothuks or Inuits remains contested, but it seems that at least one Native American woman may have sailed to Iceland. DNA indicates a small number of Icelanders have a Native

American ancestor, giving credence to claims of contact with non-Inuit North Americans. Europeans only returned occasionally to harvest timber in the years after the Viking abandonment.

Other early contacts between Europeans and Native Americans included fishermen who came ashore in the late fifteenth century to salt and dry their catch. Gaspar Corte-Real abducted more than fifty Beothuks or Micmaqs in 1501. When Portuguese fishermen tried to establish a colony on Cape Breton Island twenty years later, Micmaqs besieged them until the Europeans gave up and went away. When French explorer Jacques Cartier first encountered Micmaqs near the mouth of the Saint Lawrence River in 1534, they surprisingly found a common language in Portuguese. It is difficult to say what impact these relatively fleeting visits ashore had, or even to what extent Portuguese, Basque, or English fishermen interacted with the indigenous peoples of the North Atlantic coast. In at least some cases, Europeans visited trauma upon Native American communities and they responded with resistance to further encroachment. By the late sixteenth century, most indigenous peoples on the Atlantic seaboard certainly had knowledge of Europeans, their goods, and their tactics.

ALGONQUIANS AND ENGLISH COLONISTS

Dozens of separate Algonquian and Iroquoian-speaking peoples lived in the lands extending inland from the Atlantic. Algonquian speakers of several dialects stretched from the Carolina Outer Banks to Labrador and from the Saint Lawrence River to lands well west of the Great Lakes. Iroquoian speakers included Cherokees and Tuscaroras in the south, but the center of Iroquois territory sat between the Saint Lawrence River in the north, the Great Lakes in the west, the Hudson River valley on the east, and the upper reaches of the Delaware and Susquehanna Rivers on the south. Some shared cultural traits between most eastern peoples, such as longhouses, made it easy for outsiders to assume some commonalities across a wide swath of the continent, but the separate interests and politics of dozens of indigenous nations bewildered Europeans as well.

Nearly a century after their earliest official voyages to North America, English and French efforts to colonize North America began with a series of poorly planned and ill-fated attempts. One of the more famous failed colonies has led to an enduring mystery. In 1585, English colonists settled on an Outer Banks island in Roanoke territory and they disappeared with few clues as to their fate. The word "Croatan" carved into a tree near the abandoned site may have referred to a nearby village in the homeland of people with that name. An English attack just before the colonists arrived and a counterattack on the English fort at Roanoke characterized an uneasy relationship with the many different Algonquian-speaking peoples of the region. Poor coordination of relief and resupply efforts gave English sailors little knowledge of local people or of their own colonists' fates. One longstanding theory that some of the English Roanoke colonists either joined or were abducted by indigenous communities may be possible, but without further evidence, remains speculation.

Intermittent contact made coastal peoples familiar with both violence and the value of new metal goods. It also allowed for some individuals to bridge indigenous and European worlds. In one case, Spaniards abducted Paquiquineo and another Native American in 1561 from the peninsula between the James and York Rivers. They traveled across the Atlantic to Spain by ship and when Paquiquineo returned a decade later—renamed Luís de Velasco—he warned his people to attack any Europeans and deny them a foothold in their lands. He eventually reclaimed his indigenous identity, led an ambush against Spanish

Robert Vaughan's engraving of Powhatan presiding over his village of Werowocomoco appeared in John Smith's 1624 account of the Virginia Colony. Powhatan consolidated power as the primary headman over some 15,000 Algonquian-speaking people under thirty sub-chiefs or *werowances*. Though his people at first tolerated the Jamestown colony, the continued English reliance on Indians for food and supplies turned the relationship to one of intermittent raiding and warfare that intensified after Powhatan's death in early 1618. (Library of Congress)

priests, and then disappeared from the European record. Unable to distinguish among the Chesapeake's Algonquian peoples, Spaniards retaliated against nearby Chickahominys, further alienating the region's peoples.

By the time English colonists arrived at Jamestown in 1607, one *sachem* or chief, Powhatan, dominated thirty tribes across the region he called Tsenacomo. Called by the English "King Powhatan," he likely saw the European newcomers as valuable means of acquiring goods and increasing the power of his confederacy of regional towns. When John Smith rose to leadership of the Jamestown colony, Powhatan dealt with him much as he would with any reluctant subchief. In a ritual that has been misunderstood and romanticized for centuries, Powhatan sent a clear message to the Europeans. He abducted Smith, and then conducted a ceremony in which his life was subject to Powhatan's whim. At the moment of mock execution, he had one of his several daughters, Pocahontas, "save" Smith by intervening with his would-be executioners. Though Smith propagated a tale of an Indian princess falling in love with him and saving him from her father, the message and meaning of the ceremony would have been very clear to anyone living in Tsenacomo: Powhatan held absolute power over his subchiefs and tributary villages, including Smith and Jamestown.

After Smith returned to England two years later, relations between the Powhatans and their English neighbors deteriorated. Intermittent war broke out between 1609 and 1614, followed by another, more intense episode in 1622. Powhatan's younger brother, Opechancanough had succeeded him by then and reacted against the spreading English tobacco fields. A surprise attack on Jamestown and the nearby tobacco planters in March killed one-third of the English colonists in North America, but the Powhatans held back from complete slaughter. The Powhatans had reasserted their superiority in the colonial arrangements and they allowed the colony to continue as a weakened vassal community.

The following fall, the English struck back, burning Powhatan cornfields. This became the regular strategy of English troops. By attacking the sustenance of nearby tribes they weakened their rivals and were often able to steal the reserves of corn as part of the booty of war. Rather than press for a peace, English colonists continued these tactics for another decade. As more colonists arrived and more survived in the English outpost, they began to outnumber their Powhatan neighbors and see real profits in shipping tobacco to European markets. In a reversal of the earlier relationship, the English had managed to turn their Indian neighbors into vassals.

To the north, the Pilgrims arriving at Massachusetts Bay in 1620 also met with Indians who were far more familiar with Europeans than the Europeans were with Native Americans. When Pilgrims came ashore, the first man they met (likely a Wampanoag) gave them a simple greeting in English: "Welcome."

Indian communities were still reeling from a series of epidemics in New England that began in 1616. Measles, typhus, plague, and the common cold combined to empty villages and open the way for English settlers to make inroads into areas already cultivated and, until recently, thickly settled. For their part, English colonists explicitly understood epidemics as the will of God, simultaneously punishing the failures of non-Christian Indians and making way for His chosen people. Indians were thus caught between perceptions that they must convert to escape punishment and the lackluster attempts of English to aid Indians in that conversion. Once Puritans began arriving in 1630, their numbers rapidly overwhelmed both the earlier Pilgrims and their Indian neighbors in Massachusetts.

In what came to be called the Pequot War, Dutch-supported Pequots lost to the united alliance of the New England colonies, Narragansetts and Mohegans. Pequots had been spared the ravages of the 1610s epidemics that decimated much of New England, but a 1633 smallpox epidemic killed four fifths of their people; perhaps 3,000 remained. Pequots had gained control over the lower Connecticut River valley in part through their dominance of the *wampum* trade. Pequots had exchanged strings of *wampum* shell beads for furs from people farther inland, but Europeans quickly transformed the trade good into a currency. Puritans and Dutch alike demanded large quantities of *wampum* and displaced Pequots and their tributary tribes from their position in the regional trade network.

The divided peoples of the region between the Dutch Hudson River valley colony and the English on Massachusetts Bay jockeyed for position in the new, more complicated arrangement. In part to remove his people from their status as tributaries to the Pequots, Mohegan *sachem* Uncas joined with the English to make war on the Pequots. After a series of counter-attacks in 1637, Narragansetts and Mohegans led Puritan forces undetected to the primary Pequot village of Mystic. Setting fire to the town, the Puritan forces under John Underhill watched as Pequots either died from smoke and flames or fled into their musket fire. Though some resistance continued into the following spring, Puritans had broken the most powerful Indian confederacy in New England. In the aftermath, shocked by English conduct in the war, the Narragansett *sachem* Miantonomi proposed that the Indians of the region join together so as to stave off the Puritans. This, too, failed as rival tribes continued to position themselves as allies or partners with the Europeans who threatened their very existence.

Puritans were mostly ambivalent about conversion, in part because they focused on the perfection of their own community. The Pequot War solved the English problem of a potential indigenous threat to Puritan towns. However, Indians did not disappear from New England and the solution for indigenous peoples seeking Christianity as a possible answer to catastrophe were praying towns. John Eliot was the Puritan most interested in conversion of New England Indians and he relied on Cockenoe, a captive, in translating English into the Massachusett language. Together, Eliot and Cockenoe eventually produced a Massachusett bible that was the first bible printed in the Americas. Beginning in the 1640s, Eliot and Samson Occom, a Mohegan, founded fourteen praying towns. However, Occom and other so-called Praying Indians stood halfway between worlds. As cultural intermediaries, they were neither fully accepted by their Puritan neighbors or by their tribes. Many of the residents joined simply because there was no other place for Indians in a rapidly growing New England. However, Praying Indians did enjoy some autonomy and a brief reprieve from displacement by colonists.

IROQUOIANS AND FRENCH COLONISTS

French colonization focused on the Saint Lawrence River, which they hoped would be a passageway across the continent to China. The river fell short of reaching the Pacific, but it was and is the major waterway in eastern North America. Along its shores, Iroquoian-speaking people lived in long-house villages. To the south lay the confederacy of the Iroquois Five Nations: Mohawks, Oneidas, Onondagas, Cayugas, and Senecas. To the west was the land of the Hurons and other Algonquians. The French shared the Catholic impulse to send missionaries to convert Indians to Christianity, but after initial attempts to follow the Spanish model, the Jesuits adjusted their tactics. They learned native languages and went to live in Indian villages. In part because French fur traders also sought out relationships with First Nations, they, too, pushed far into the interior. Without the military investment of Spain, French colonists, fathers, and traders had to adopt different relationships with their indigenous neighbors.

From bases at Quebec and Montreal, the French engaged in trade with Hurons and Montagnais and joined raids against their Iroquois enemies as early as 1609. Jesuits and *voyageurs* alike moved ever farther into the Algonquian Great Lakes, and peoples quickly became dependent on European trade goods, especially steel. By the 1630s, beaver were nearly extirpated east of the Great Lakes in peoples' efforts to continue trading. At the same time, disease swept the region, hitting French allies especially hard.

By the 1640s, this trading dependency and the effects of disease drove Five Nations Iroquois expansion into the Ohio River Valley. Across New England and the Saint Lawrence, mourning wars had become a regular feature, as tribes raided enemies to replace their own population. As Five Nations Iroquois collectively had the largest population in the region, their raiding of Ohio River valley peoples was on a far larger scale. They also needed to expand their beaver hunting territory to maintain their fur trade. In this intense warfare across what historian Richard White called the Middle Ground, tribes began shifting westward, away from Iroquois raiders and European disease. Some villages and even tribes disappeared entirely, absorbed into other villages and cultures, while others essentially became Iroquois. French traders and missionaries traveling in the midst of this chaos became, in many instances, the neutral parties whom villages appealed to in order to negotiate peace. Warfare was bad for business and French voyageurs were eager to see Indians return to hunting instead. However, the violence spurred retaliations. Raids sparked counter-raids.

In the confusing violence of these "Beaver Wars," Indians were often able to benefit from French weakness. France could not dictate terms from a position of military power and the fur trade was reliant upon Indian labor and knowledge. However, in a five-year span, an estimated half of the Huron population died from European diseases. The new warfare for territory changed from small-scale captive raiding to large-scale destruction of Huron villages. Senecas, especially, sought to displace Hurons from their territory to gain new hunting grounds and eliminate their rivals. In 1649, a grand council made the decision to abandon the Huron homeland and seek protection elsewhere. Hurons joined smaller tribes in the diaspora of the Middle Ground or relocated to the French colony on the Saint Lawrence.

INCREASING CONFLICT

From the 1614 founding of a trading post at the junction of the Mohawk and Hudson Rivers to that point, the Dutch West India Company had formed trading relationships with many of the region's peoples. Trade with Mohawks was specially favored as guns and powder could be used against their French rivals and their allies. When Holland decided in 1640 to end the Dutch West India monopoly on trade in their New Netherland colony, it brought a surge of immigrants and increased tensions with nearby peoples.

The arrival of William Kieft signaled a change in policies. Kieft attempted to force local Indians to pay tribute to the Dutch colony and attacked Raritans under the pretense of retaliating for a stolen pig. Using wampum bounties, he enticed other Indians to carry out violence on Dutch enemies. Wappinger Lenapes on Manhattan Island had fled from attacks by Mahicans and Mohawks, but following the murder of a Dutch man, they came under attack by Kieft and his followers. On October 1, 1643, Dutch soldiers murdered 120 men, women, and children in the Pavonia Massacre on the site of what is now Jersey City, New Jersey. Outraged by this indiscriminate killing, Lenapes and other Algonquian-speaking people of the region united against the Dutch. Mohawks and their Dutch allies repeatedly attacked Wappingers living near New Amsterdam, perhaps killing half of their people over the following two years. The Pound Ridge Massacre was a notable low point in which Wappingers who had retreated to a Long Island village were again killed indiscriminately by surrounding Dutch troops, this time led by the English mercenary John Underhill. As many as 700 Wappingers and Siwanoys gathered in a ceremony died in a single moonlit evening with only one Dutch soldier killed. Only eight Indians survived.

A decade later Wappingers and Munsees allied with Susquehannocks in a large-scale attack on Dutch settlements throughout the region. The Susquehannocks had become the primary trading partners of the New Sweden colony and in part were caught up in the Dutch-Swedish rivalry. Dutch forces conquered the Swedes in September 1655, prompting Susquehannocks to strike back against their Dutch enemies. Paddling to the Hudson River, they joined with Wappingers in driving Dutch colonists into a retreat to New Amsterdam. They selected Pavonia as the initial point of attack and killed 100 Dutch colonists there, taking another 150 as captives. The Dutch explained this sudden resumption of Indian warfare as retaliation for the murder of a Wappinger woman, Tachiniki, for the theft of a peach. Susquehannocks and Lenapes clearly acted in their own interests, and coincidentally in the interest of their European allies. Across the region, Native Americans could no longer escape the entanglements of military alliances and economic partnerships.

In Virginia, English colonists forced a series of land cessions across the former Powhatan Confederacy. In 1651, reacting to rumors of a conspiracy to poison colonist wells, an English force marched against the Indians of the Delmarva Peninsula. The Nanticokes suffered the worst of the sudden attack and when fearful colonists turned the leader of the vigilantes over to colonial authorities in Jamestown, all charges were dropped. Other Indian complaints of encroaching colonists and trespassing animals grazing in Indian fields met with little response. Across Virginia, colonists slowly pushed Indians from their land. Some retreated as a practical matter when hunting failed and animals could not be kept from food crops. Others faced continued manipulation in colonial courts and documents. In one instance in 1660, colonial leaders demanded as part of treaty negotiations that the Potomac headman, Wahanganoche, hand over four of his subjects who were suspected of murder. When the four Potomacs arrived, the county commissioners immediately released them from jail and then imprisoned Wahanganoche for his failure to deliver. In the end, they extorted a land cession from the Potomacs to resolve the case.

The general practice of Virginians in their dealings with Indians set the stage for a critical turning point in American history. By the 1670s, English plantations extended from almost every waterway flowing into Chesapeake Bay. The dozens of villages encountered only a couple of generations earlier were gone. Tobacco had caught on as a valuable export in the 1630s and plantation owners had used thousands of indentured servants to clear the land and develop their fields. The promise of release upon the end of an indenture appealed to Europeans in desperate straits. Only in America could individuals from lower economic standing claim (Indian) land and get a fresh start. However, former indentured servants found fewer and fewer opportunities. The tidewater lands had been taken and the appointed colonial Governor, William Berkeley, held a monopoly on licenses for the Indian trade. When Berkeley refused to retaliate against Indians for a series of small-scale incidents in 1675, Nathaniel Bacon, an opportunistic member of the Virginia Council, led former indentured servants against the Governor at Jamestown.

Only two years earlier, Maryland had invited Susquehannocks to live in their colony, partly to serve as a buffer against potential Iroquois raids. However, they were soon enmeshed in antagonisms similar to their Indian neighbors. Conflicts over trade and payment, destruction of Indian crops, colonists' domestic animals, a rising trade in Indian slaves, and more made this an era of almost continual clashes among colonists and Doegs, Piscataways, and others. Berkeley's attempts to protect friendly Indians such as the Susquehannocks, or at least to prevent open warfare pitted the Governor against many Virginians.

When English colonists attacked the friendly Susquehannocks (instead of Doegs who had recently raided a farm), they triggered counter-attacks. Bacon seized upon Virginians' fear and promptly marched against nearby Pamunkeys, Occaneechees, and Mataponis. As her people fled into hiding, the "queen" of the Pamunkeys, Cockacoeske, appealed directly to Berkeley to stop the unprovoked attacks. Berkeley led an army and put down the rebellion in early 1677, but the damage had been done to Virginia's Indians. Cockacoeske was the first of a dozen leaders to sign the Treaty of Middle Plantation, which surrendered indigenous land claims in exchange for mutual protection from attacks. The treaty reserved a small parcel of land for the Indians and swore their allegiance to the English king.

To the north, New England Indians also faced war against English colonists in 1675. The Wampanoag *sachem* Metacom (called by the English "King Philip") reacted to the execution of three of his subjects for murdering a Praying Indian named John Sassamon. Ironically, Metacom was the son of Massasoit, the *sachem* who greeted the Pilgrims and helped them through their first winters on Massachusetts Bay. Puritans reacted to the initial Wampanoag attacks by assaulting whatever Indians they could find. In so doing, they managed to turn much of the region's indigenous population against the English. Narragansetts, Nipmucks, and Abenakis joined Wampanoags in destroying twenty-five towns, forcing English settlers to flee for Boston. However, the English enlisted Praying Indians against their cousins, requiring each to bring in scalps to prove their loyalty. One, John Alderman, would kill Metacom the following year. Mohawks also remained on the side of the English, fighting against their old Algonquian enemies.

Engraving of Nipmuc Indians attacking Brookfield, Massachusetts, in August 1675. Demands for more power over Indians and their lands led to widespread violence. The combined Native American forces destroyed one-third of New England towns including Brookfield, but by the summer of 1676 Mohawk raiding against rival tribes and a united strategy by the English colonists combined to end the war. (Peter Newark American Pictures/Bridgeman Images)

Though English colonists feared an uprising of united Indians across the frontier from Bacon's Rebellion in Virginia to King Philip's War in Massachusetts, they and their allies managed to wear down the New England Algonquians. In the December 1675 Great Swamp Fight, Pequots joined the English in the siege of a Narragansett town. Navigating through a frozen swamp, the English-Pequot force overwhelmed a brief defense and set fire to the town. In a brutal attack reminiscent of the Mystic Massacre during the Pequot War, the English and Pequots killed perhaps 1,000 men, women and children, losing only seventy of their own. Other Narragansetts died later, wounded or without food in the depths of winter. By the following spring, Narragansett *sachems* Canonchet and Quaiapen would both be dead.

Both sides suffered enormous casualties, with over 1,000 English killed. But, caught between English colonists to the east and Mohawks to the west, the combined forces probably killed as many as one-third of the remaining Algonquian people. Those taken captive by English colonists were sold into slavery and shipped to Barbados and the Caribbean. The last effective native resistance to English colonists in New England was broken. Only four praying towns remained after the war and Mohawks shortly resumed their raids on these last strongholds of their enemies.

THE GREAT PEACE OF 1701

By the late 1600s, tribes in the west increasingly looked to the French as allies against the continuing Iroquois juggernaut. Guns made warfare more deadly and disease continued to spread, affecting Iroquois and rivals alike. However, using their Dutch and English guns against French allies, Iroquois quickly gained an advantage. In the 1630s, Hurons, Neutrals, Petuns, Ottawas, and others to the north came under attack and by the 1650s many of these peoples had either left their villages for the west or consolidated near the French colony.

For at least thirty years, Shawnees, Miamis, Illinois, Peorias, Sacs, Foxes, Potawatomis, and other peoples living between the Ohio River and the Great Lakes faced attacks, captivity, or relocation. One Jesuit described the wars as an Iroquois hammer crushing people against a Sioux anvil in the west. Many survivors reformed their communities west of the Great Lakes or south of the Ohio River. The bounty of the lands closer to the Mississippi included bison and provided some temporary relief while much of what is now Ohio and Indiana became a vast depopulated Iroquois hunting zone.

French traders continued their journeys into Indian Country in order to trade more directly with tribes such as the Potawatomis and Foxes. French traders, of course, preferred to receive valuable beaver furs and sometimes demanded that their gifts take only that form. Such demands in hunting territories pushed to their limits alienated many Algonquian tribes and even triggered occasional violence. However, over time, Indians and their French counterparts came to an accommodation in which French traders acceded to Algonquian demands for better gifts and Algonquians responded with a continued alliance against their Iroquois rivals. Reciprocal gift giving was central to overcoming the Iroquois. By the 1690s, French and their indigenous allies invaded Iroquoia itself. Iroquois attempted to ally with French enemies, the English, but the alliance was ineffective and Iroquois pressed for peace in 1701.

Combined French-Indian attacks and English colonists' steady encroachment into Pennsylvania drove Iroquois to agree to the Great Peace of Montreal in 1701. Some 1,300 representatives of thirty-eight different native nations met and negotiated a treaty obligating Iroquois to be neutral in the imperial contest between France and England and allowed many peoples to return to their old homelands. Shawnees and Miamis shifted back eastward into old territories that remained rich farmlands, but were no longer suitable for the fur trade. The Beaver Wars had taken their toll on the animals and the richest trapping areas were now west and north of the Great Lakes. The prices for furs also dropped and once again strained the Algonquian-French alliance. Michipichy, a Huron-Petun chief, encouraged to relocate near the new French post at Detroit, felt betrayed when the result of peace with the Iroquois appeared to be directly connected to lesser gifts. He secretly carried on his own negotiations with Iroquois while coordinating attacks on rival Ottawas who were still aligned with French interests.

French efforts to maintain the Great Peace included their encouraging Ottawas to return Iroquois captives to their people in 1705. When they could not do that, Ottawas agreed that they would get slaves from western Sioux as compensation for Iroquois losses. Indian slaves provided a particularly high value gift to bestow upon Frenchmen and were thus a strong means of sustaining a reciprocal obligation. Fox Indians in particular carried on a trade in Plains Indians captives. In a conflation of identities of Pawnee slaves from the central Plains, the name *panis* or Pawnee became a catchall term for Indian slaves from the west. Peoples as far west as the Pawnees themselves supplied slaves from other peoples captured in warfare. Plains Apaches, Arikaras, and Wichitas were almost certainly among the enslaved individuals French called *panis*. Once in the French world, these slaves became part of the delicate balance between various Algonquians and Iroquois. Some also entered the wider world of European slavery, sold off to the Caribbean, traded as Mediterranean galley slaves, or acquired by seafaring owners who took them even farther from home.

Caught in this loop, French colonists not only benefitted from an increased trade in Indian slaves but also faced the ongoing requirement to give gifts in return or risk insulting their western allies. When gifts ceased, so too did the relationship between Indians and their French counterparts. When the French invited over 1,000 Foxes to return to their former homelands near Detroit, in 1710, they reached out to their largest supplier of Indian slaves. The French strategy to concentrate their allies near their western outpost at Detroit made mutual sense for Foxes returning home and for a weakened New France. However, in a demonstration of how difficult diplomacy had become, the Huron-Petun chief Michipichy and others who had already relocated to Detroit protested. Soon, the so-called Fox Wars would again pit the peoples of the Middle Ground against each other.

PROFILE: KATERI TEKAKWITHA

In 2012, Kateri Tekakwitha became the first Native American saint in the Catholic Church. She lost her Mohawk father and Algonquian mother at a young age and suffered from some of the aftereffects of a smallpox epidemic that swept Iroquois Country in the 1660s. The French priest who authored the first account of her possible saintliness attributed Tekakwitha's purity to her damaged eyesight and sensitivity to light. It may well be that Tekakwitha was predisposed to accept Christianity due to her mother's being brought up by priests before her capture by Mohawks. There is little to indicate that Tekakwitha's mother did not fully integrate into Iroquoian life, but she—and other villagers at Ganadauuagué—surely retained some of her Christian teachings. Isolated from her community and after rejecting two marriage arrangements, she and other Christians were at odds with their community when a priest arrived in her village and attempted to convert Iroquois. However, the priest arrived at harvest time and most of the villagers were in the fields. Tekakwitha had injured her foot and remained behind where she received the individual attention of the Jesuit. After a long winter in which he told her about his faith and worked toward conversion, he baptized her as Catherine on Easter Sunday 1676.

Her new faith clashed with Iroquois traditions, and when she snuck away to one of the Jesuit missions near Montreal, she was part of a movement of a substantial number of Iroquois and Algonquians who sought relief from disease and declining fortunes in the Catholic Church. Tekakwitha's guardian, a chief of the village, faced a crisis in which the older traditions seemed ineffective against the new problems of the seventeenth century. Converts were traitors to Iroquoia, but Tekakwitha and others were determined to capture the power of the newcomers. Once at Kahnawake, her celibacy and deliberate suffering included flagellation, enduring long periods of cold, mortification by placing thorns on her sleeping mat, and even use of fire to burn herself. She lived only four years as a Catholic, but her demonstrated devotion and stories of her smallpox scars disappearing upon her death led to her becoming a Canadian symbol of the power of conversion.

PROFILE: JOHN SASSAMON

As the cultural mediator at the center of King Philip's War, John Sassamon remains a symbol of the complicated changes sweeping across North America in the late seventeenth century. A Massachusett, his parents converted to Christianity but died when Sassamon was still young. He learned to read and write English and acted as an interpreter during the Pequot War. By 1651, he became the teacher at the praying town of Natick and briefly attended Harvard. He would later preach in another praying town, Namasket. For many years, he remained close to his Wampanoag relatives and when Metacom became *sachem* in 1662, Sassamon was one of his primary aides. There is some evidence that Puritans were displeased with his return to allegiance among Wampanoags, but it is clear that Sassamon's literacy and linguistic skills were valuable to Metacom.

Another turning point may have come in 1671 when colonial officials demanded Metacom surrender all of his arms and to cease planning for hostilities. Relations between Wampanoags and Puritans had hit a low point, and Sassamon was caught in-between. His allegiance may have shifted again, or he may have simply wanted to prevent warfare when, in January 1675, Sassamon told Plymouth's Governor that Metacom was again preparing for a surprise attack on the English colonies. Sassamon had the credibility to deliver such a warning, but the English appeared to have given his report little credence. Telling the officials that their inaction would likely result in his death, he disappeared shortly after. In February, his body was found in a frozen pond. Another Praying Indian, Patuckson, claimed that three Wampanoags had murdered Sassamon and tried to disguise that act as a drowning. Following a trial before a mixed Indian-English jury, Tobias, Mattashunannamo, and Wampapaquan were hanged. Wampapaquan's rope broke and he then confessed, but was later executed by firing squad. Scholars continue to debate whether those men were guilty, or even whether there was any clear evidence for Sassamon's murder.

REFERENCES AND FURTHER READING

Greer, Alan. *Mohawk Saint: Catherine Tekakwitha and the Jesuits*. New York: Oxford University Press, 2004.

Gutiérrez, Ramón. *When Jesus Came, the Corn Mothers West Away: Marriage, Sexuality, and Power in New Mexico*. Stanford, CA: Stanford University Press, 1991.

Knaut, Andrew L. *The Pueblo Revolt of 1680: Conquest and Resistance in Seventeenth-Century New Mexico*. Norman: University of Oklahoma Press, 1995.

Lepore, Jill. *The Name of War: King Philip's War and the Origins of American Identity*. New York: Alfred A. Knopf, 1998.

Lipman, Andrew. *The Saltwater Frontier: Indians and the Contest for the American Coast*. New Haven, CT: Yale University Press, 2015.

Otto, Paul. *The Dutch-Munsee Encounter in America: The Struggle for Sovereignty in the Hudson Valley*. New York: Berghahn Books, 2006.

Rice, James D. *Tales from a Revolution: Bacon's Rebellion and the Transformation of Early America*. New York City: Oxford University Press, 2012.

Rushforth, Brett. *Bonds of Alliance: Indigenous and Atlantic Slaveries in New France*. Chapel Hill: University of North Carolina Press, 2012.

Salisbury, Neal. *Manitou and Providence: Indians, Europeans, and the Making of New England, 1500–1643*. New York: Oxford University Press, 1984.

Sando, Joe S., and Herman Agoyo, eds. *Po'pay: Leader of the First American Revolution*. Santa Fe, NM: Clear Light, 2005.

Townsend, Camilla. *Pocahontas and the Powhatan Dilemma*. New York: Hill and Wang, 2004.

White, Richard. *The Middle Ground: Indians, Empires, and Republics in the Great Lakes Region, 1650–1815*. New York: Cambridge University Press, 1991.

Chapter 4

Colonial Alliances and the New Nation

Native Americans' changing relationship with European colonization and neighboring tribes made the seventeenth century particularly dynamic. In the wake of the Beaver Wars and the Mississippian shatter zone, many villages and towns coalesced into confederations or previously separate people formed new communities. This dynamic process of creating new people, or ethnogenesis, reordered old relationships. It also produced new tensions within and between tribes as new people worked to find a new political and economic balance.

Many tribes' histories testify to the disruption and increasing violence of the era. For example, the Eries were one of the casualties of the Beaver Wars when the Five Nations Iroquois overwhelmed them. Fleeing their homeland on the southern shore of Lake Erie in 1656, they relocated among their Susquehannock trading partners near Chesapeake Bay. There they encountered the turmoil of the weakening Powhatan Confederacy as dozens of displaced tribes struggled to survive between expanding English colonies and other refugee people shifting away from Iroquoia. Only three years later, the former Eries moved again to the Georgia-Carolina frontier. Identified by Europeans as Westos, they maintained their trading connections with Virginians. With the aid of English guns they forced their way into the southeastern Indian slave trade. Eager Virginian buyers sold captives on to the Caribbean to prevent runaways from returning to their homelands.

Westos' power rose and fell quickly. In 1673, warfare broke out between Westos and Carolina colonists. Throughout the war, Westos maintained a flow of guns, lead, and powder until they brokered a deal shifting their slave-trading partnership to the Carolinians. Losing the Westos as their suppliers, Virginians turned to Cherokees and the rival group outpaced the Westos. In part because Carolina could not deliver the quantities or quality of trade goods as the Virginians could, Westos once again felt the squeeze of a better-armed, more powerful people. By 1679, Savannah Indians began replacing Westos as the primary Carolina allies and when Westos sent peace emissaries to negotiate their way out of their reversed position, the Savannahs took them captive and sold them into slavery for more guns.

MUSKOGEES AND THE YAMASEE WAR

The Muskogees, or Creeks, formed a confederacy of several towns and people emerging out of the Mississippian shatter zone. By the late seventeenth century, they had absorbed Shawnee refugees fleeing Iroquoian expansion, Apalachees fleeing Spanish missionization, and coastal people escaping English colonization. Creeks also found themselves nearly surrounded by English and their allies on the east, Choctaws and French on the east, and Spanish and missionized Apalachees and Timucuans to the south. In the 1680s, trade in deerskins created initial ties to the fledgling colony of South Carolina, but they remained central to the imperial rivalries between Spain, England, and France.

Initially, South Carolina had attempted to prohibit colonists from purchasing land from Indians, exploring to the west, or even settling within two and a half miles of an Indian village. The colony's directors, the Lords Proprietor, hoped to control Indian relations and avoid costly conflict. At the same time, however, they allowed for the continued enslavement of any individuals captured by others. The robust trade in Indian slaves that developed from the interior shaped the coastal colony. Frontier violence convinced the Lords Proprietor to begin issuing licenses for the Indian slave trade in 1683. A panel of chiefs and the elected colonial assembly had to jointly verify that captives had been taken in just war.

Yamasees and Creeks rose to prominence in this slave trade. For a few years, Yamasees dominated a trade in "justly captured" Timucuan Indians captured in raids on the Spanish missions of northern Florida. This sparked counter raids and dragged Spaniards into direct conflict with the English. However, Creeks controlled access to the interior and Europeans sought to sway them to their side and shift the balance of power. A Spanish effort to force Creeks to submit to their control in 1685–1686 only pushed Creeks into a closer relationship with English South Carolina. When Spaniards sought to arrest English traders, Creeks hid them, even at the cost of Spanish retaliation. Spaniards burned four Creek towns, but English guns continued to arrive. Colonists also ignored paper restrictions and by the 1690s English, Spanish, Yamasees, Savannahs, Creeks, and Choctaws all intertwined in a complicated and violent cycle of raiding. A 1696 smallpox epidemic extended into the interior and may have been a final blow to the older Mississippian order.

In April 1715, Creeks and Yamasees gathered at a meeting with South Carolinian Indian agents. In an attempt to break their dependency on trade with Europeans, they opened fire on the Carolinians and began what would be called the Yamasee War. During the war, Indians captured many African slaves and escorted them to Florida, out of reach of their British owners. Two years later, the war sputtered to an end with each Indian nation pursuing its own course. Yamasees caught between powerful Creeks and Carolinian colonists fled to the same northern Florida missions that they had raided in the past.

In the wake of the Yamasee War, South Carolina deliberately shifted from Indian to African slavery to reduce their dependence on Indian relations. It was also clear to all involved that the rising Creek Confederacy of between 15,000 and 20,000 people held more power and could mobilize more "gun men" than any of their neighbors, including the struggling European colonies. Skillfully playing British against Spaniards, Creeks could and did make demands of Europeans. When Georgia Governor James Oglethorpe agreed to a joint expedition against Spanish Florida in 1743, Creeks designed the plan of attack and, once aboard ship, took the cabins for themselves. The British forces, including Oglethorpe, had to resign themselves to sleeping on the open deck exposed to the weather. Over the 1700s, Creeks also intermittently raided frontier settlements to force their European counterparts into negotiations. More often than not, Creeks compelled colonists to agree to favorable terms while avoiding all-out war.

THE GREAT SOUTHWESTERN REVOLT

The mid-seventeenth century brought increased conflict to the Southwest as well. In 1639, Jemez, Picuris, and Taos all revolted, killing Spaniards and destroying churches. Afterwards, many Pueblos fled to refuge among Plains Apaches at El Cuartejelo and Spanish officials became suspicious of any interactions with Apaches. They saw the Apache newcomers to the Plains as rivals for control of Pueblo commerce and allegiance. Throughout this period, Apaches continued their expansion into modern Mexico where they threatened the northernmost Spanish-Indian settlements. New Mexicans raided the Plains for Apache slaves and regularly disrupted trade between eastern Pueblos and their Plains partners. Redirecting surplus goods into the colonial economy, Pueblos often had little remaining to exchange with their neighbors. In response to this reduced supply, Apaches stepped up their raiding of agricultural towns.

Drought struck in the late 1660s, forcing abandonment of several pueblos. More Pueblos joined the El Cuartejelo Apaches and others retreated to villages closer to the Rio Grande. In a sign of increasing discontent and intolerance, the arrest and public whipping of forty-seven Pueblo spiritual leaders and execution of four more may have marked a turning point in Pueblo-Spanish relations. Pueblo warriors gathered to threaten the Governor and demanded the release of the remaining shamen.

Continued punishment of Pueblos practicing their traditions struck at the heart of their culture. By 1680, Pueblos had faced drought, intermittent epidemics, increased raiding, occasional famine, and a declining population. One religious leader, Po'pay, led the planning to overthrow the oppressive Spaniards, and leaders from several Pueblo communities soon joined him. Using Catholic saints day gatherings as cover, a series of secret meetings led to messengers contacting most of the pueblos in New Mexico. However, when three villages refused to join the conspiracy, they alerted the Governor. Pushed into action four days early, the rebellion broke out on August 9 in the pueblo of Tesuque. The violence spread rapidly as Pueblos and Apaches joined to destroy the Spaniards, killing nearly 400 of the settlers, soldiers, and priests. A nine-day siege of Santa Fe broke the Spanish resistance and the remaining 2,000 colonists fled in a long retreat south to El Paso. Governor Antonio de Otermín retook Isleta Pueblo the following year, but after holding a brief trial revealing the depth of anti-Spanish sentiment, he returned to exile.

In part because of continued Apache raiding and French encroachment into Texas, Spaniards were initially unenthusiastic about the difficult task of retaking New Mexico. Meanwhile, revolts spread across much of the Southwest. Janos, Mansos, Conchos, Pimas, and Hasinais all threw off their would-be colonial masters and cut off relations with New Spain. Once successful, Pueblos quickly returned to their separate agendas in the face of continued Apache raids, drought, and disease. When Diego de Vargas led a diplomatic mission north to the Rio Grande pueblos in 1692, he was able to secure promises from more than twenty Pueblo leaders that they would return to Catholicism and Spanish rule. In December, he fought his way into Santa Fe and executed seventy of the perceived leaders of Pueblo opposition. Over the next two years, Vargas continued his campaign to quash the revolt, and when Pueblos attempted to renew the uprising in 1696, they failed. Some Pueblos relied upon Spanish protection from raiders and others continued to clash with Spaniards taking land, food, and other resources. The Great Southwestern Revolt had defeated and expelled Europeans from the region, but the mix of issues confronting Pueblos and other Native Americans could not be entirely solved by simple removal of colonists.

Only a generation later, Spaniards made one last effort to exert their authority beyond New Mexico's Pueblos. Fearing that westward moving French traders would align even more tribes against them and supply them with guns, Pedro de Villasur set out to expel France from the Great Plains. In an August 1720 battle recorded in the Segesser Hide Paintings, Pawnees and Otoes used French guns to destroy the Spanish-Pueblo force at the junction of the Loup and Platte Rivers in Nebraska. Spaniards would never again attempt to force their way into the Great Plains, acknowledging that they could not overcome Plains Indians.

IROQUOIA AND THE SEVEN YEARS' WAR

William Penn's colony of Pennsylvania managed to strike an unusually amiable relationship with Indians in part because the Quaker had no interest in military conflict. Lenape chief Tammany insisted on Europeans' outright purchase of lands, and he and others signed a series of deals beginning in 1682. Penn's successors were less scrupulous. In 1737, they instigated the "Delaware Walking Purchase," using an agreement with nearby Iroquois and fraudulent documents to insist that they had already purchased more Lenape land. Using hired runners and a deceptive map, the Pennsylvania agents nearly doubled the distances the Lenapes had understood in negotiations. Though popular accounts of this event pitch Lenapes as victims of a simple trick, the "walk" only sealed a deceptive deal already created on paper. Similar instances and the tide of expanding colonial farms slowly displaced Lenapes from their homeland.

For their part, Iroquois played one imperial power off of the other. By maintaining neutrality, the Iroquois Confederacy (which after 1722 included Tuscaroras who had moved north from the Carolinas) became a fulcrum in the English-French rivalry. Iroquois were able to gain concessions from Europeans simply by leaning toward one side of the other. As part of this strategy, Iroquois ceded their claims to the Ohio River Valley in the 1752 Treaty of Logstown. That served British aims but the region was the homeland of Mingos, Wyandots, and Shawnees.

As part of a scheme to survey and sell the ceded land, Virginia Governor Robert Dinwiddie sent George Washington and the Virginia Militia to the headwaters of the Ohio River in spring 1754. Their aim was to oust a small French detachment and seize control of the Ohio River Valley. Mingo warriors Tanacharisson and Scarrooyady led the force of 130 Virginians through the Appalachians to the French post at Fort Duquesne. What Washington found was not a small garrison, but a sizeable force of Oneidas and Senecas in alliance with France. Washington's force, after ambushing a French scouting party, was quickly routed by the much larger and more experienced Iroquois-French force. The French commander, hoping to avoid all out war, risked alienating his Indian allies and allowed Washington and his men to return to Virginia unmolested.

The 1755 Battle of the Monongahela, also Known as "Braddock's Defeat," from a 1903 painting by Edwin Willard Deming. The overwhelming victory over the regular British army drove home the centrality of indigenous allies in the conflict between France and Britain. British victory finally came in 1760, reordering indigenous-colonial relations in eastern North America. (DeAgostini/Getty Images)

Overlapping with these events, a delegation of Six Nations Iroquois met with the British Board of Trade in Albany in the summer of 1754. The British aim was to avoid warfare while increasing their land claims. The Iroquois sat for a few days, understood that the Albany Conference was not in their interest, and walked out. Only a few remained behind, leaving none with authority to continue negotiations, but some ended up signing over Lenape lands in the Susquehanna and Wyoming Valleys. In response to the otherwise failed talks, one of the British delegates, Benjamin Franklin, proposed a Plan of Union, under which an elected council led by an appointed president would be responsible for negotiating Indian affairs (and by extension, western land exchanges) with a unified voice. The colonial assemblies roundly rejected this Indian affairs council as infringing on their authority.

Meanwhile, Great Britain used the Fort Duquesne incident as the pretext for an all-out effort to remove their French rivals and the supply chain to enemy Indians from North America. They increased taxes to pay for an invasion by thousands of professional troops. General James Braddock, considered Britain's finest military leader, made an early mistake in denigrating the fighting ability of untrained Indians. Only eight Mingo scouts aided in a renewed attempt to take Fort Duquesne. Braddock himself met his end in July 1755 as a combined force of 700 Ottawas, Potawatomis, and French killed, captured, or wounded two-thirds of his 1300-man army.

Over the course of the mid-1700s, decisions to ally with the French, the British, or to stay neutral shattered the old Iroquois League of the Longhouse. A Virginia militia attack on an unrelated Seneca party (themselves en route to raid Catawbas on the Carolina frontier) and the continuing pattern of bad land deals pushed Senecas, Cayugas, and Onondagas to solidify their alignment with the French. Some Mohawks and Oneidas, the two tribes in closest proximity to British colonies, remained on the British side. William Johnson, whom Mohawks called *Warraghiyagey* or "Big Business," swayed many Mohawks to the British side. Johnson had learned the Mohawk language and married a Mohawk woman, Molly Brant, before first recruiting Mohawks in 1746 to fight in King William's War. When war between France and Britain broke out again in 1755, 200 Mohawks joined him against a force of French, Canadians, Abenakis, and Canadian Mohawks. Johnson's victory in the Battle of Lake George was one of the few British wins over the next three years. Elsewhere, the French and their far larger contingent of Indian allies won almost every engagement but they did not have enough French troops to hold the strategic positions and resorted to capturing and burning British forts and settlements. However, the increased expenditures and reinforcements from Britain combined with an adaptation to Iroquois tactics led to key victories. Using their naval strength to cut off the inland French and their allies, the British-Mohawk-Oneida force slowly ground down their opposition. The French ran out of supplies, gifts, and trade goods and their Lenape, Shawnee, Mingo, and Seneca allies slowly abandoned a losing cause.

The fall of Montreal in 1760 marked the end of the French-British war in North America, though it continued elsewhere across the globe. As one of his first decisions, the British commander in North America, Jeffrey Amherst, ended annual gifts to treaty chiefs. He also restricted the supply of trade goods, resulting in increased prices for most trade goods and a shortage of lead, powder, and firearms for Indian hunters. Without a French competitor to drive prices down, the pattern showed no indications of abating.

By early 1761, Senecas called upon their allies to rise up against the British, but only Lenapes and Shawnees responded. Neolin, the Delaware Prophet, provided leadership for a unified response. He taught a rejection of European goods (especially whiskey) and a return to traditional ways as the way forward for Indian people. Pontiac, an Ottawa-Anishinaabe chief, built on Neolin's message and began to organize a revolt against British rule. In 1763, he led a successful offensive against the British occupiers of several formerly French posts. Within a single month, two-thirds of the British forts west of the Appalachians fell to Pontiac's warriors. Only Forts Pitt, Niagara, and Detroit remained as outposts of the British Empire south of the Great Lakes. The siege of Fort Pitt by a combined Lenape, Shawnee, and Mingo force dragged on and Amherst broke it by introducing smallpox with gifts of infected blankets and handkerchiefs to the besiegers. Powder and ammunition ran short in the second year of the campaign and Indians' French allies failed to return.

By 1764, Pontiac was forced to make peace and attempted to ensure more fair trading practices for Indians in British North America. The British agreed to try to halt settlers and simultaneously came to the conclusion that these noble fighters and fair negotiators were far better individuals than the colonial American rabble. Familiarity had bred contempt for colonists, but appreciation of indigenous people. The strange result, a grudging respect for North American Indians and disdain for troublemaking expansive colonists, helped to shape the coming revolution in less than a generation. When it came, most Indians sensibly stood by British allies in opposition to land-hungry American farmers.

In the immediate wake of the 1763 Treaty of Paris, British Parliament strove to eliminate the causes of their enormous wartime debts. The subsequent Proclamation of 1763 drew a boundary along the crest of the Appalachians dividing colonial territory from Indian Country to eliminate further conflict. Many British colonists who had fought the French expressly understanding it as a war of conquest felt betrayed by the requirement to remain to the east of the mountains. As they had so often before, they simply ignored the directive from London.

Other events shaped the Native American reaction to the British victory. Many Cherokees had allied with the British and participated in campaigns against the French in Alabama and in the Ohio Country. When Virginians murdered Cherokees returning to their homeland and Carolinians invaded, Cherokees turned against their former allies. Like their counterparts in the Ohio Country, by 1760, Cherokees found their French supply lines had dried up. British troops destroyed villages and pressed Cherokees for land cessions as conditions for a peace treaty. Little Carpenter (Attakullakulla), who had led the pro-British Cherokees against the French and their allies early in the war agreed to British terms in 1761.

In December 1763, a group of Scots-Irish settlers murdered six Christian Indians at Conestoga, Pennsylvania. The town had been founded by Susquehannocks and chartered by William Penn more than a century before, but the vigilante Paxton Boys reflected the change from Penn's time. When the remaining Conestoga Indians were placed in protective custody, the Paxton Boys broke into the jail and murdered the fourteen survivors. Following this incident, more than 250 colonists marched on the colonial capitol of Philadelphia to demand they be able to take Indian land by right of conquest. Benjamin Franklin was able to turn the mob away from the city, but Pennsylvania's peaceful relations with Indians had ended.

DUNMORE'S WAR AND THE AMERICAN REVOLUTION

In the 1768 Treaty of Fort Stanwix, Iroquois representatives ceded all of their claims to lands south of the Ohio River. This was the result of complicated deal in which Iroquois had earlier agreed to end raids against Cherokees and draw a boundary line between their lands. Iroquois insisted that they were the only Indians with standing to negotiate on behalf of the many peoples of the Ohio Country. However, Lenapes and Shawnees rejected the authority of Iroquois to negotiate away their homelands. British negotiators effectively shifted the Proclamation Line to the Ohio River and settlers began moving into the area almost immediately.

Indians and colonists clashed regularly and the 1774 murder of a party of Mingos tilted one of their chiefs, Logan, into a war of vengeance. Lord Dunmore, Governor of Virginia, took advantage of the situation and mobilized an army of 1,100 men to quash the Indians of the Ohio Country, at least partly to assert Virginia's claims to the newly opened lands in Kentucky and Ohio. Shawnee chief Cornstalk mustered 1,000 Shawnee and Mingo warriors to face Dunmore's army and met them in the October 10, 1774 Battle of Point Pleasant. After hours of fierce fighting, the superior firepower of the Virginians won the day, with 250 Indians and more than 50 Virginia militiamen dead. Dunmore then invited Shawnees to discuss peace even as his army continued to burn Shawnee villages. Compelled to sign, many Shawnees agreed to the land cessions of the earlier Fort Stanwix Treaty.

The American Revolution forced Native Americans to once again make a choice. Most Indians feared that once independent of Britain that the American colonists would accelerate their expansion into Indian Country. Dunmore's War provided a clear example of colonist encroachment followed by military force. Given British attempts to control their colonists, most Iroquois and Shawnees aligned themselves against the American rebels.

The Continental Congress established three departments of Indian affairs in 1775 to attempt to negotiate neutrality for the duration of the war. Three years later they authorized Indians to join the Continental Army, subject to approval by General George Washington. The same year, the United States conducted its first successful treaty negotiations. The United States sought an alliance with Lenapes to prosecute the war in the west and the Delaware Treaty of 1778 recognized their sovereignty, even offering consideration of a future fourteenth Lenape-led Indian state. Chief White Eyes, the principal

Lenape leader who had negotiated an end to Dunmore's War and signed the treaty, died in mysterious circumstances later that year. American initially reported that he was a smallpox victim, but in reality, an American militia officer had killed him. Officers covered up the murder so as not to turn Lenapes against them. This, too, failed when Americans were unable to provide assistance to their allies in the Ohio Country.

In the years after White Eyes' death, American militia would again betray their Lenape allies. In 1782, Pennsylvania militia seized the Christian Lenapes at the Moravian settlement of Gnadenhutten. The militia voted to kill the Indians and imprisoned them for the night. The next day, on March 8, they systematically killed and scalped nearly 100 men, women, and children.

The war split other tribes apart, too. The Six Nations Iroquois divided, with the majority siding with the British, but most Tuscaroras and Oneida sided with the American rebels. Molly Brant's brother Joseph, also known as Thayendanegea, became a commissioned British officer and traveled to England to make the case for Mohawks regaining sole title to their lands and to make Iroquois full participants in the war against the American rebels. Red Jacket, a Seneca chief, urged Iroquois to broker a deal with the Americans, but Brant thwarted his efforts. Brant's raids in New York spread fear among Americans and sparked a retaliatory campaign in 1779. General John Sullivan led an army of 3500 men through Iroquoia, burning villages and crops to punish the Iroquois Confederacy. Following the war, in 1783, Brant and his followers received a land grant on the Grand River in Ontario. These 1,800 Grand River Iroquois included people of many tribes, but they were only one part of the exodus of British allies from the new United States to Canada.

Seneca chief Cornplanter signed a second Treaty of Fort Stanwix in 1784, guaranteeing peace between the Americans and the Iroquois. An Iroquois grand council, however, refused the treaty and Americans embarked on a series of follow-up negotiations. A decade later, the Treaty of Canandaiuga finally established an official peace between Six Nations Iroquois and the United States. The Seneca leaders Cornplanter, Red Jacket, and Handsome Lake were among the fifty signatories of what was nicknamed the Calico Treaty or Pickering Treaty. Under the terms of the treaty, Iroquois retained western New York and the United States was obligated to distribute calico cloth each year, and it does so to this day.

TECUMSEH'S CONFEDERACY AND THE RED STICK WAR

The new nation promulgated a series of laws that shaped the American relationship with tribes. With the 1790 Trade and Intercourse Act, the United States made its first attempt to regulate the Indian trade. At its core,

Portrait of the Seneca chief Cornplanter (Kaiiontwako), by 19th-century American painter Charles Bird King. Though he fought against the Americans in the Revolutionary War, Cornplanter negotiated "the Last Purchase" with the new nation as part of the peace treaty of Fort Stanwix in 1784. The U.S. later granted him and his followers the "Cornplanter Tract" in northwestern Pennsylvania that would be flooded by the Kinzua Dam in 1965. (McKenney, Thomas L. and James Hall. *The Indian Tribes of North America*, 1836–1844)

the Act prohibited transfer of Indian lands to any party except by treaty with the Federal Government. Congress renewed or revised the Act five times and the 1795 version established a government factory system, whereby all trade had to be conducted through licensed trading posts or "factories." These operated with very little profit in an effort to draw Indians into a relationship with government traders. Indebted Indians would then be pressured to cede land in order to clear debts. However, private traders offered higher quality, if higher priced, goods and outside of a few cases, the factory system struggled to compete.

In the South, Cherokees and Creeks had also divided over the Revolutionary War. Alexander McGillivray, the paramount chief of the Upper Creeks, supported the British and opposed Lower Creeks who allied with the American rebels. When those American allies ceded lands in 1783, McGillivray rejected the negotiated a treaty. Instead he made a treaty with Spain that tied Creeks to a British trading company based in Florida. He became a full partner in Panton, Leslie, and Company and coordinated the Creek deerskin trade to continue trading for British weaponry. McGillivray and the Creeks were able to continue resistance against encroaching Americans until the controversial 1790 Treaty of New York in which he agreed to a boundary between Creek lands and the United States. In return for signing the treaty, which included a provision to return fugitive slaves from Creek Country, McGillivray drew a salary from the U.S. government and he quickly became a prominent slave-holder. However, the United States did not hold up their promise to remove illegal settlers and McGillivray and the Creeks renounced the agreement.

The European powers that negotiated the Treaty of Paris ending the Revolutionary War recognized U.S. territory extending to the Mississippi and had made no specific provisions for Native Americans. Settlers continued their predicted expansion into Indian Country, disregarding the arrangements of the Treaty of Fort Stanwix. A confederation of Indians led by Blue Jacket (Shawnee), Buckongahelas (Lenape), and Little Turtle (Miami) attempted to halt the settler advance. When General Josiah Harmar led 1,400 men into Miami territory in late 1790, he suffered a string of defeats. Buoyed by the Miami-Shawnee-Lenape success, Mingos, Ottawas, Potawotomis, and Wyandots joined the effort.

General Arthur St. Clair replaced Harnar when the campaign resumed the following year. Nearly half of his force had deserted by the time Little Turtle attacked in November 1791. In what became known as St. Clair's Defeat, the Indians inflicted a 98 percent casualty rate; only two-dozen men out of over 1,000 escaped unharmed. The U.S. Congress launched an investigation into the death or capture of more than 650 Americans and increased taxes to pay to train and deploy a better army. The August 1794 Battle of Fallen Timbers was the turning point in the U.S. campaign against Indians in the Northwest Territory. Revolutionary War hero Mad Anthony Wayne employed Chickasaw and Choctaw scouts in a defeat of Blue Jacket, Little Turtle, and a small contingent of Canadians. When Indians retreated to the safety of nearby British Fort Miami, the British commander refused to let them in, sealing their defeat.

The American victory affected two treaty negotiations. Unwilling to start another war with the United States, Great Britain abandoned its Indian allies in the Ohio Country. The 1794 Jay's Treaty resulted in the withdrawal of British troops from American territory. The following year, the Treaty of Greenville compelled Little Turtle, Blue Jacket, and others to cede their claims to much of the future state of Ohio.

In 1805, Tenskatawa, the Shawnee Prophet, began having visions in which he interpreted Americans to be the evil offspring of the Great Serpent. He participated in rooting out Lenape witches suspected of causing the death of Buckongahelas and accused those inclined to cooperate with the United States of being witches as well. Tenskatawa developed a doctrine that forbid use of European goods, especially alcohol. His prediction of an 1806 solar eclipse solidified his following and he soon established a new community at the junction of the Wabash and Tippecanoe Rivers in Indiana. Nearly 3,000 Indians joined the community Americans called Prophetstown.

A new pan-Indian confederacy arose, led by Tenskwatawa's older brother, Tecumseh. Both men traveled from tribe to tribe to win further support while arguing against Little Turtle's advice that the time had come to negotiate with and accommodate the United States. Tecumseh believed that treaties should be negotiated with all Indians in solidarity instead of with individual tribes pitted against one another. He was particularly outraged by Little Turtle's signing the 1809 Treaty of Fort Wayne, which had not included Shawnees. In a meeting with Indiana Territory Governor William Henry Harrison, Tecumseh demanded that the Governor nullify the treaty and threatened to join the British. Harrison refused and Tecumseh embarked on a path toward war.

Harrison himself led troops to Prophetstown in late 1811 when he knew Tecumseh was away. Tenskatawa preemptively attacked, but the Americans "won" the battle when the Indians began to run low on ammunition and withdrew. Americans lost three times the number of men as the Prophetstown Indians, but Harrison declared victory. He ordered the town burned, perhaps destroying the one of the largest indigenous settlements east of the Mississippi.

When the War of 1812 broke out, Tecumseh's confederacy stood with the British. Unfortunately, they joined forces with one of the more inept British commanders. When Americans gained control of Lake Erie, the British retreated from Detroit to the Lenape village of Moraviantown. Once there, the British made no effort to fortify the town or reinforce their position. American troops, again led by Harrison, attacked on October 5, 1813, outnumbering the combined British-Indian force by three to one. British troops quickly surrendered or fled, leaving Tecumseh and 500 warriors facing an American Army of more than 4,000. Tecumseh died as American troops surrounded his position and his followers soon surrendered. With this defeat in Canada, the region's last serious resistance to Americans ended.

Tecumseh and Tenskatawa had traveled to Creek Territory and one group, the Red Sticks, responded to his anti-American efforts. Perhaps inspired by Tenskwatawa's prediction of a comet and the 1811 New Madrid earthquake, this faction began to assassinate pro-American Creeks, especially among the more assimilated Lower Creeks. By mid-1813, an American militia force had ambushed Red Sticks returning from a Florida arms deal and in retaliation, the Red Sticks struck back at Fort Mims,

Alabama. After Creeks had overwhelmed the defenders, they killed or captured over 500 American and Lower Creek soldiers, settlers, and slaves. The massacre became a rallying cry and in response, on March 27, 1814, Colonel Andrew Jackson led U.S., Creek, and Cherokee forces to victory over the Red Stick Creeks in the Battle of Horseshoe Bend. The Red Sticks refused to surrender and as many as 800 were killed. Red Stick chief Menewa led 200 survivors to join the Seminoles outside the United States in Spanish Florida.

PROFILE: PO'PAY (OR POPÉ)

A Tewa religious leader from the pueblo of San Juan, Po'pay was the primary organizer of the Pueblo Revolt of 1680. From his base in a *kiva* at Taos Pueblo, he spread word that three *kachina* deities had visited him. The god *Poheyemo* ordered Pueblos to destroy the Spaniards and anyone who supported them.

Many historians point to a 1675 incident in which then-governor Juan Francisco Treviño arrested and ordered forty-seven Pueblo shamen publicly whipped as the trigger for the Pueblo uprising. However, the Revolt was not simply an act of retaliation. Po'pay and other leaders waged a war to reclaim their religion and reject Christianity. At Po'pay's urging, many Pueblos ritually cleansed themselves to reverse their baptisms. However, more than eighty years of Spanish presence had changed Pueblo culture and Pueblos rejected Po'pay's further directive to completely rid themselves of European culture. Spanish crops, tools, and trade goods had become part of the Pueblo world.

Within a year of the successful ejection of Spaniards from the upper Rio Grande, Po'pay's absolutism cost him his authority. Luis Tupatú, a Picurís Pueblo, overthrew Po'pay as leader of the new confederation but he was unable to solve the problems that beset Pueblos. In 1683 Tupatú desperately asked the Spaniards gathered in exile at El Paso to return to the colony. Po'pay briefly resumed leadership in 1688 but died shortly after. Some accounts indicate that Pueblos resentful of his continued dictatorial style may have killed him, but little is known of the splintering Pueblo alliance before Spaniards returned in 1692.

PROFILE: NEOLIN, THE DELAWARE PROPHET

The Delaware Prophet, Neolin, was the most well-known of several Native American prophets of the eighteenth century. He advocated for the rejection of European culture as a means to revive the strength of Native America. In the face of the expanding colonies of New York, Pennsylvania, and Delaware, many Lenapes had relocated west to the Ohio Country. There, they joined together in communities whose common experience was betrayal in their dealings with Europeans. Lenapes who sided with the French in the Seven Year's War made peace with the British when they promised to preserve Indian lands in Ohio. However, once the British claimed victory, they immediately ended the giving of gifts that had sealed Indian-European alliances for generations and began issuing new land grants.

Neolin credited a spiritual journey in which he visited the Master of Life as the basis for a new religion including some Christian elements. In his vision, the easiest path led to a land of fire and only the difficult way led to a restoration of the good life of former times. This required prayer to the Master of Life instead of appealing to shamen and other indigenous spiritual leaders through dances and ceremonies. According to Neolin, the cause of Indians' reduced state was their betrayal of the true way. A rejection of polygamy, promiscuity, and witchcraft were necessary, but Europeans and their foods, guns, and alcohol were the primary sources of evil. Sexual abstinence and purging with an emetic drink were part of a new ritual designed to restore game and success against their enemies. Lenapes began to teach young boys to once again use bow and arrow in hunting

Neolin's mission to unite Indians to drive Europeans out was the philosophy that drove Pontiac's 1763–1764 uprising. Pontiac did not preach Neolin's pure message, in part because he hoped to ally with the French and use their guns to overthrow the more threatening British. Yet, it was Neolin's vision that lent Pontiac authority in a partial rejection of European colonization that returned with Tenskwatawa's movement in the early nineteenth century.

REFERENCES AND FURTHER READING

Bragdon, Kathleen J. *Native People of Southern New England, 1650–1775.* Norman: University of Oklahoma Press, 2009.

Bross, Kristina. *Dry Bones and Indian Sermons: Praying Indians in Colonial America.* Ithaca, NY: Cornell University Press, 2004.

Calloway, Colin G. *The Victory with No Name: The Native American Defeat of the First American Army.* New York: Oxford University Press, 2014.

Cave, Alfred A. *Prophets of the Great Spirit: Native American Revitalization Movements in Eastern North America.* Lincoln: University of Nebraska Press, 2006.

Dowd, Gregory Evans. *War under Heaven: Pontiac, the Indian Nations, and the British Empire.* Baltimore: Johns Hopkins University Press, 2002.

Ethridge, Robbie. *Creek Country: The Creek Indians and Their World, 1796–1816.* Chapel Hill: University of North Carolina Press, 2003.

Fenn, Elizabeth A. "Biological Warfare in Eighteenth-Century North America: Beyond Jeffery Amherst." *Journal of American History* 86, no. 4 (2000): 1552–1580.

Gallay, Alan. *The Indian Slave Trade: The Rise of the English Empire in the American South, 1670–1717*. New Haven, CT: Yale University Press, 2002.

Hall, Joseph M., Jr. *Zamumo's Gifts: Indian-European Exchange in the Colonial Southeast*. Philadelphia: University of Pennsylvania Press, 2009.

Kenny, Kevin. *Peaceable Kingdom Lost: The Paxton Boys and the Destruction of William Penn's Holy Experiment*. New York: Oxford University Press, 2009.

Knaut, Andrew L. *The Pueblo Revolt of 1680: Conquest and Resistance in Seventeenth-Century New Mexico*. Norman: University of Oklahoma Press, 1995.

McDonnell, Michael. *Masters of Empire: Great Lakes Indians and the Making of America*. New York: Hill and Wang, 2015.

Merrell, James H. *Into the American Woods: Negotiators on the Pennsylvania Frontier*. New York: W. W. Norton, 1999.

Sando, Joe S., and Herman Agoyo, eds. *Po'pay: Leader of the First American Revolution*. Santa Fe, NM: Clear Light, 2005.

Schmidt, Ethan A. *Native Americans in the American Revolution: How the War Divided, Devastated, and Transformed the Early American Indian World*. Santa Barbara, CA: Praeger, 2014.

Chapter 5

The Equestrian Plains, 1600s to 1851

Horses and the potential for change that they offered were among the most significant elements of the Columbian Exchange. Native Americans' incorporation of the new animals was also an uneven process. People by people and village by village, word of horses, contact with the animals, and in many cases, acquisition of a set of skills resulted in a new tool well adapted to indigenous cultures.

Although the most common popular image of Native Americans may be that of a mounted Plains warrior, not all indigenous peoples made the choice to adopt equestrianism. Horses were an obvious means of increasing power, but domestic animals such as horses, cattle, or sheep also presented a series of choices. Reliance upon hunting instead of agriculture was a decision to risk greater mobility by abandoning riverine villages. Each family, band, or village had to decide what balance of horses and crops to maintain. Each option offered a different measure of reliability. Farmers balanced poor harvests with stored reserves. Horses were, for them, a potential threat to trample or consume future harvests. On the other hand, bison seemed nearly endless in number and horses provided a means to move to the herds instead of waiting for them to arrive in nearby hunting areas. The sheer size of the bison resource must have appealed to peoples in a marginal farming climate.

The increased rainfall of the Little Ice Age brought increased plant growth on the Plains and both agriculture and grazing became more reliable. As people such as Crows shifted to a High Plains strategy in the late sixteenth century, their Hidatsa cousins and other tribes along the Missouri River remained committed to agriculture. Buffalo were a seasonal resource that supplemented the crops raised in the rich floodplains. Mandans and Arikaras performed both Buffalo Calling ceremonies to ensure a good hunt and Mother Corn ceremonies to honor and ensure good harvests.

Corn was an especially important trade good throughout the northern Plains and by caching their dried corn in their fortified earth-lodge villages, women created reserves for years of poor crops or hunting. Agricultural reserves also enabled trade to continue even in what would have otherwise been tough times. On the upper Missouri, corn caches reinforced with posts and supports could be eight feet deep and hold up to thirty bushels of corn. By cooking, drying, and shelling their corn, women created a critical resource that could be exchanged for salt, hides, meat, pipestone, and other goods.

Several tribes ultimately decided to rely upon bison and left their agricultural villages. Cheyennes did so in the early 1700s and within a few years, some Sioux began doing the same, migrating from the woods and lakes of Wisconsin and Minnesota to the High Plains. Adopting horses and shifting to equestrianism, these westering Sioux crossed the Missouri River around 1750 and became the several tribes collectively known as Lakotas.

INCORPORATING THE HORSE

Spaniards brought horses ashore in their invasion of Mexico but the animals remained relatively rare until Spanish ranches grew in size and number. Despite their scarcity, Indians acquired horses as early as the 1540s, and equestrianism spread northward from there. Chichimecans in northern Mexico raided ranches and mines and by the 1550s were using horses to fight back against the Spanish presence. By the time Spaniards encountered Jumanos and Caddos north of the Rio Grande, they were already among the first peoples in what is now the United States to make the transition to equestrianism. Apaches and Navajos also encountered horses well before the 1598 colonization of New Mexico. When Spaniards did move their culture to north, it simply provided more direct access to horses and horse know-how. The outpost colony placed blacksmiths, saddle makers, breeders, and other people with intimate knowledge of the world of horses in the midst of peoples hungry for new technology. For millennia, people and dogs had been the only beasts of burden, and Native Americans quickly perceived the potential utility of horses.

Steady contact gave Pueblos, Apaches, and Navajos an edge in understanding every aspect of the equestrianism that Shoshones, Utes, and Comanches soon joined. The horses left behind during the Pueblo Revolt may have been less important than the motivation for tribes to solidify their capabilities or intensify their raiding. Even as many peoples fled the slave raiding zones near European colonies, other tribes including Pimas, Kiowas, Wichitas, and Tunicas relocated to be closer to colonial trading and raiding opportunities.

By the late 1500s, several areas served as distribution points for horses and other European goods through nearby tribes. Indians traded and raided for the new animals on the lower Rio Grande, the Plains of west Texas, the mining frontier of northern Mexico, the isolated colony of New Mexico, and the *ranchos* of northern Florida. By the early seventeenth century, Numic-speaking Shoshones well to the north of New Mexico provided another node of horse distribution. Through raid and trade networks extending into northern Mexico, Shoshones and Utes acquired a few animals from the Spanish outposts and nearby tribes. Once they were able to relocate horses into the grasslands of the Snake River Plain of southern Idaho, they quickly became the northernmost peoples to make horses central to their lives. The Great Plains was the primary area for equestrian expansion, but other grassland regions such as the Snake River Plain, the Palouse in the Pacific Northwest, and California's Central Valley also sustained vast numbers of horses. Eastern North America held fewer bison and the peoples there tended to continue as horticultural villages instead of shifting to equestrianism. There, horses remained prestige goods and were valuable in trade with Europeans, but dense woods reduced horses' utility in hunting and canoes provided the best way to travel.

The investment in horses in much of the west led to a reordering of many tribal societies. Many tribes reached their political, economic, and military peak in tandem with their herds of horses and good bison hunting. With horses, hunting became more efficient and regular. Peoples could follow bison year round rather than wait for migration to bring the herds in proximity to villages. Hunters racing alongside herds could bring down more meat, resulting in more hides, sinew, and bone for women to process. Workloads increased as there were more hides to dress and successful hunters multiplied the number of wives to keep up.

At the same time, the larger hunting territories brought greater conflict. Tribes clashed as they contended for prime hunting grounds. Exacerbated by raiding, a culture developed in which warriors rose to prominence. Men's individual prestige increased with their abilities, as warriors, hunters, and horsemanship became the primary routes to individual power. The more horses a man could steal from enemies, the more people he could feed with his hunting, and the more prowess he demonstrated in battle were critical measures of his abilities. For equestrian tribes, horse herds became measures of wealth and raiding became the norm for the Great Plains.

Horses also enabled people to access trading centers from farther afield, increasing the economic reach of Indian trading fairs and Euro-American trading posts alike. Trade networks stretched across much larger areas as tribes bypassed middlemen to make better trading deals. This gave tribes some immediate advantages, but also made friendly relations with agricultural trading villages less necessary. However, even those Plains tribes who became fully equestrian maintained relationships with riverine agricultural villages along the Missouri River. Some of those villages continued in their older role as trade centers while others suffered raids from equestrians. The appeal of sedentarism and cities was stability, but village life also made their occupants targets for nomadic raiders.

Tribes with horses also became better trading partners for Europeans seeking beaver pelts and buffalo hides. Since horses allowed people to carry more possessions, heavy trading goods such as kettles could be added to the travois. Equestrian tribes became mobile villages with larger teepees of up to a dozen hides.

Ultimately, those tribes that could bring both horses and guns to bear gained advantages over their neighbors. Guns flowed from French and British traders east and north of the Plains as horses came from the south and west. For a time, tribes with either horses or guns were able to leverage their increased power over neighboring peoples. Both horses and guns leaked out over time and tribes slowly equalized the earlier disparities. Another round of advantage came when peoples on the Plains were able to combine horses and guns over peoples more remote from British or French traders who had horses, but no guns.

The equestrian shrinkage of space also meant that disease traveled more quickly, spreading epidemics over a greater area, to more peoples. Sedentary villages continued to suffer more from diseases than mobile peoples who could avoid hard-hit vectors along the waterways. A 1780–1782 outbreak of smallpox on the Great Plains also ravaged much of the continent, in part because the addition of horses to almost all Plains tribes enabled the disease to follow trade networks more efficiently. Though the epidemic hit many tribes, killing as many as 40 percent of all indigenous people on the Plains, the agricultural villages suffered the worst losses. In the years immediately following the outbreak, the balance of power had clearly shifted to the mobile equestrians.

Adopting horses required all kinds of new knowledge. Care and feeding, dealing with equine diseases and injuries, and making saddle and tack all required new ways of teaching and required subtle shifts in culture. Keeping horses away from crops became a new task and continual access to grass and water became new constants in village life. Riparian areas in arid regions offered forage as well, but were far more restrictive than larger grasslands. In arid regions such as the Great Basin and the Southwest, animals' competition with people for food was even more direct and intense.

The increased number of horses on the Plains also led to direct competition with buffalo for feed and critical wintering-over in the river valleys. With newly mobile tribes and their horses seeking shelter from wind and weather, they displaced buffalo. When disaster struck, buffalo suffered in ways they had not in prehorse times. And as buffalo moved, so too did tribes. When horses exhausted the grazing near a campsite, camp had to move. Only after the summer hunts could tribes lay in enough food to see them through the winter.

Counter-intuitively, the shorter grasses of the High Plains provided more sustenance through the winter than the lush tall grass prairies of the eastern Plains. Tall grass died off in the fall and stored energy through the winter in underground rhizomes. However, bison and horses could continue to graze on short grass species wherever snow did not bury them. In deeper snow, boys harvested cottonwood bark to see horses through the winters. Over time, this reduced the availability of firewood and feed and riverside camps had to move in order to survive through the harsh Plains winters.

Areas with colder winters saw greater numbers of animals die each year; grass buried under deep snow, weeks of subfreezing temperatures, and shorter growing seasons directly affected the animals' survival. Whether through trading or raiding, Crees, Assiniboines, Blackfeet, and other peoples living in harsher northern climates had to regularly acquire more animals to replace losses. The ripple effect of raiding emanating from the northern tribes reached peoples across the continent.

Buffalo hunters had long understood the relationship between animals, grasses and fire. Where they burned off the old grass, sun warmed the exposed ground earlier in the spring. In these areas, grass sprouted and grew earlier than elsewhere and drew grazing animals to feed. Such burning was not unique to the Plains, but there it created the hunting grounds that provided relief from long winters. Indians may not have had enough time to completely incorporate horses into a sustainable ecological balance. Many of the effects of horses were gradual and nearly invisible, but tribes did disperse into smaller groups in winter months at least partly to distribute grazing in the leanest months of the year.

As historian Elliott West has pointed out, horses allowed peoples to capture the enormous reserve of energy stored in grasslands. By consuming grass, buffalo transformed this energy into a form that people could use and equestrianism allowed consistent access to the herds. Equestrian peoples expanded their populations and became powerful military and trading forces, partially eclipsing the sedentary villages. As those villages continued as important trading centers, they also became targets for raiding.

SNAKES AND COMANCHES

Shoshones were relatively isolated from Europeans and while they could not play European powers off of each other in the same way, they too were able to build power from horseback. When Cheyennes met French explorer Pierre de la Verendrye in 1742, they refused to escort him further west, fearing *les Gens du Serpent*, the "Snakes." The Cheyennes had good reason to fear these Snakes since they were still reeling from a series of raids the previous year. The Snakes had killed many of the men and the old women, but took the young women captive and sold them off for more horses.

Horsemanship made Snakes the most feared power of the Rocky Mountains and western Plains in the early eighteenth century. At times those Snakes were Shoshones, and at others may have been Utes or Comanches. In any case, Snakes' power reached its peak in the mid-1700s. Shoshones displaced their Blackfeet, Cheyenne, Crow, and Ute neighbors, acquired greater territory, additional hunting grounds, and ever more horses. Once they acquired horses, mounted Shoshone warriors embarked on long-distance raiding expeditions, sometimes lasting years.

Peoples to the west of the Great Plains and Rocky Mountains such as Nez Perces and Cayuses had to travel across the mountains or to the Snake River Plain to access buffalo, and horses allowed them to do so. Their societies relied upon a mix of salmon migrating into the Columbia River watershed and seasonal buffalo hunts. Like Plains tribes, they hunted in the late summer in order to lay in provisions for the winter. They used bison hides for tipis and also fished for salmon, or traded at centers such as The Dalles on the Columbia River.

Paiutes in the eastern and northern Great Basin desiring to take advantage of an equestrian strategy shifted eastward into the grasslands of the Snake River Plains and took up residence near Shoshones. These Paiutes became Bannocks and joined other tribes of the region in using the Bannock Trail across the mountains to tap the High Plains bison herds. Nez Perce, Salish, and other tribes of the Columbia Plateau and northern Rockies invested in horses and were able to draw upon the bison herds as a resource alongside salmon and other foods closer to home.

With the proliferation of horses, other peoples of the Plains and Rockies equaled Shoshone equestrianism. Tribes able to control territory while maintaining connections to English and French gun traders became powerful. The combination of horses and guns turned the tide against Shoshones. By the time Lewis and Clark encountered the Lemhi Shoshones in 1804, they had become a beleaguered people. Running horses in relays, they chased down pronghorn antelope instead of crossing the mountains to hunt bison. Sacagawea's appearance as a Hidatsa slave at the Mandan Villages a thousand miles east of her homeland was a prime example of the changed power dynamics. By then, Hidatsas, Arikaras, Lakotas, Crees, and Blackfeet all raided Shoshones regularly, taking captives and horses.

In the southern Great Plains, an even more powerful people were on the rise. As they increased their horse wealth, some Shoshones elected to remain closer to Spanish raiding targets in New Mexico and Texas. Spaniards soon

An Osage Indian Pursuing a Camanchee [Comanche] by George Catlin, ca. 1861–1869. The arrival of the horse on the Great Plains enabled greater hunting and trading but also intensified raiding between tribes. Comanches, Lakotas, and other nations rose to power as equestrianism became central to their cultures. (National Gallery of Art)

identified them as Comanches. Though the first Spanish record on contact with Comanches came in 1706, they had likely been in the region for much longer, still conflated with Utes and Shoshones. By the 1720s, they also came into contact with French traders and from that point their rise was rapid. Comanches were representative of the many peoples who moved closer to European outposts in order to better take advantage of European goods, foods, and animals. Being located between Spaniards, Pueblos, and Apaches to the west and the French, Osages, Caddos, and Quapaws to the east made Comanches a key link between rival European empires and tribes. As brokers for the region, Comanches were able to concentrate the combined resources of these colonies into what historian Pekka Hämäläinen has called "the Comanche Empire."

By the early 1700s, Comanches were well-horsed and well-armed. New Mexico's governors rightly feared that Comanches could overwhelm them, being far better armed than the European colony. French guns and Spanish horses allowed Comanches to displace Lipan Apaches and Kiowas in west Texas, and strike at the European colonies as well. Comanches raided northern Mexico and Texas for resources, but only strategically sought to destroy European outposts. From Spaniards and their Indian allies' perspectives, Comanche raids were terrifying. With little means to defend themselves against such powerful foes, the villages of northern Mexico and Texas bore the burden of Comanche raids.

Comanches also became important trading partners for the isolated European colonies. As early as the 1720s, New Mexico's governors declared truces over the summer months so that Comanches could trade with colonists, especially at Taos and Pecos. Raiding continued as a way of life, alternating with periods of peace in which Comanches brought Indian captives into the colony in order to sell them under the guise of rescuing or ransoming prisoners. With slavery illegal in New Spain, Comanche sellers and colonial buyers both had to engage in a *rescate* system in which colonial funds would pay for *indios de depósito* and place the "saved" Indians with Christian Spaniards. The rescued Indians, usually women and children, then worked in homes and fields as servants.

The smallpox epidemic that struck in 1780 weakened all peoples of the southern Plains, including Comanches. Shortly after, Comanches engaged Spaniards in peace talks. Ecueracapa made peace with New Mexico in 1786, allowing for more commerce with less threat of violence. However, Apaches continued their raiding and the economic fortunes of Pueblos continued to decline. Indeed, having Comanches and Utes as allies against raiding Apaches was a strong motivation for Spaniards to seek peace. From the mid-1700s forward, Spaniards feared angering either Utes of Comanches by entering into trade with the enemy of the other tribe. Comanches sought peace as much to lift trade restrictions as to expand the influence of their Comanche Empire deeper into New Mexico.

In Texas, the Comanche Peace of 1785 increased trade with those Spanish settlements but also included a specific provision that Comanches first offer Spanish captives to Spaniards. Texas officials were concerned about the number of Spaniards sold off to other tribes, especially to Wichitas. Though Comanches were disappointed by the low level of goods available from both of their Spanish partners, the trade from Texas was so meager that a lower level of raiding continued into the nineteenth century.

Increasing European encroachment crumbled many indigenous trading arrangements. By the 1820s, Americans had joined the Shoshone trading fairs in the north. On the southern Plains in the late 1700s, the upper Arkansas River Comanche trade center began to decline in influence but persisted until about 1830. Pecos, the longtime link between the Pueblos and the Plains, ceased to hold its annual trading fair in 1815 and Pueblos abandoned Pecos altogether by 1838.

THE MANDAN VILLAGES

The agricultural villages of the Mississippi and Missouri River valleys continued to be important trading and production sites. Arikara, Hidatsa, Ioway, Kansa, Mandan, Omaha, Oto, Pawnee, and Ponca women farmed the floodplains, growing several varieties of corn and squash suited to the short growing season. In the spring, they cleared the ground of brush and weeds, repaired willow fences, built low mounds, planted seeds in May, then raked and weeded into the summer. Girls often had the job of scaring away birds and boys watched for enemies and kept horses out as women worked the fields. Some tribes abandoned their established crops and pursued buffalo before returning to harvest in August and September.

The 1804 Louisiana Purchase marked the extension of American policies to the Great Plains. The Lewis and Clark Expedition conducted a series of ceremonies, gifting peace medals to tribal leaders while delivering messages that the "Great Father" President of the United States now presided over his "Indian children." Such language was patently belittling, but reflected Jeffersonian concepts of indigenous peoples as wards of the state. While many tribes welcomed the opportunity to trade, it was not always clear that the United States intended to extend its sovereignty over western tribes.

For some tribes, the Americans threatened to disrupt supply routes or bypass entire peoples. Thus, previously isolated tribes such as Shoshones and Crows welcomed traders even as Lakotas and Blackfeet attempted to thwart them. Although Europeans and Americans had hoped to direct indigenous economies to their advantage, they did not always understand the dynamics of the worlds they had entered. Meriwether Lewis and William Clark seem to have genuinely not understood Sioux motives for attempting to turn Americans back as they approached the Mandan Villages. Nor did they fully understand Shoshones' desperation for American trade and instantaneous friendship as a reaction to being cut off from trade goods by Plains tribes. By their very presence, traders could displace middlemen tribes who had controlled trade through their lands. Horses (and later, steamboats) allowed indigenous and non-indigenous traders alike to reorder the economic geography of North America.

The arrival of Americans also followed a severe reduction in the populations of the Missouri River villages. Smallpox epidemics in the 1730s and again in the 1780s devastated Arikaras, Mandans, and Hidatsas. An outbreak that ran from 1800 to 1803 left villages reeling when Lewis and Clark passed through in 1804. Omaha chief Blackbird, who had acted as a conduit of Spanish goods into the Missouri River, was one of the more famous victims. Another wave of disease in 1806 extended for years, eventually taking the life of Sacagawea along with thousands of others. In 1815, given their reduced numbers, the Arikaras, Hidatsas, and Mandan Villages on the upper Missouri River gave up their usual summer hunts in the face of continued Sioux raiding.

The final demise of the federal factory system in 1822 allowed for private traders to move into the markets of the Great Plains. Traders moved up the Missouri River, striving to reach the Mandan Villages trade center. Americans sought the pelts of the Missouri River watershed, but trappers pressing deep into Indian Country threatened tribes such as the Arikaras who sought to maintain their role as middlemen between Euro-Americans in the east and tribes farther upstream on the High Plains to the west. When an American trapper killed an Arikara chief's son, it triggered an outbreak of violence. In June 1823, a party of 600 Arikaras attacked the Rocky Mountain Fur Company as they moved up the Missouri River. Twelve trappers died and the Americans retreated back downstream. Messengers carried the news to St. Louis, where Henry Leavenworth set out with reinforcements. Leavenworth led a force of 1,000 men (three-quarters of whom were eager Sioux raiders) into the Arikara campaign and in the first confrontation, over fifty Arikaras died. The Sioux burned an Arikara village and the U.S. Army took advantage of the situation, building a fort on the site as a clear signal to tribes opposing the United States. However, the alliance dissolved and Leavenworth ended his campaign without further engagements. Arikaras relocated and joined alliance with their Mandan and Hidatsa neighbors, but most Americans understood that the upper Missouri was a dangerous place to attempt to force their way. The Rocky Mountain Fur Company abandoned their upper Missouri hunting grounds and turned to the Rocky Mountains to hunt furs in Crow and Shoshone territory.

One result of the brief Arikara War was a series of treaty negotiations between the United States and Plains Tribes in 1825. Cheyennes, Crows, Dakota and Lakota Sioux, and Pawnees all signed. Along the Missouri River, Mandans, Hidatsas, Arikaras, Poncas, Omahas, and Otos also signed. The commonality of the treaties was an acknowledgment that tribes were part of the United States and subject to trade regulations

Indians removed from their homelands in the east began to arrive on the Plains in numbers beginning in the 1800s. They quickly outnumbered some tribes hit hard by disease. Osages resisted the incursion of eastern Indians and Americans alike, only to have restrictions placed on their purchase of gunpowder while other tribes continued to buy. William Clark forced Osages to separate from the Americans by ceding their eastern lands in 1808, and again in 1818. In 1825, Congress designated the lands between the Platte and Red Rivers as Indian Territory and Osages were forced to cede all of their claims in the state of Missouri. Eastern Indians and the Osages would join Pawnees, Poncas, and other diminished tribes on lands facing pressures from multiple tribes contending for a shrinking bison resource.

The predictable response to the scramble for survival was violence between tribes. As peoples from the eastern Plains shifted westward, they came into closer proximity to their raiding enemies form the High Plains. These tribes (Cheyennes, Comanches, and Kiowas) had also suffered from epidemics, but with fewer deaths and continued access to horses and guns. At the same time, the new eastern peoples, especially the numerous Cherokees, engaged in a series of clashes to defend their people in their new lands.

LAKOTAS AND THE 1851 TREATY OF FORT LARAMIE

As Shoshones expanded into the Plains from the west, Lakotas moved in from the east. In a lengthy sequence, the agricultural canoe peoples of the upper Great Lakes who met French explorers in the upper Great Lakes and Mississippi River Valley in the early 1600s shifted westward to the heart of bison country. Lakota stories about White Buffalo Calf Woman, a mysterious figure from the west who greeted them with gifts and turned into a white buffalo calf as she departed, are at the foundation of ties between the strength and plenty of bison herds and the strength of the Lakota people. Connections between bison and the people who relied upon them were both spiritual and practical. For Lakotas, their people's continued success and bison became inseparable.

By 1750, the Lakotas had shifted their territory across the upper Missouri River onto the High Plains and brought with them guns acquired from British and French Canadian traders. A generation later, they added enough horses from western tribes to their holdings that they became fully equestrian. As they increased their power and commitment to the High Plains in the west, they maintained contact with their Dakota cousins and traders to the east. Dependence on bison drew Lakotas to contest the prime hunting grounds surrounding the Black Hills. Drawn by the larger herds to the west, Lakotas continued their long westering trend and pushed out Crows, Kiowas, and Shoshones. Lakotas had the advantage of a steady supply of guns, an increasing population, and an alliance with Cheyennes. By the early 1800s, the Lakota tribes had secured the lands from the Missouri River west to the Black Hills, and afterwards pressed into the Powder and Yellowstone River valleys. This gave them a critical geographic position in the richest lands of the northern Plains and made them an important economic and military power. Dependence on bison drew Lakotas to contest the prime hunting grounds surrounding the Black Hills. Lakotas continued their warfare against Crows and Shoshones to defend territory stretching across Black Hills and pressed west into the Powder River and Yellowstone River valleys.

On the south, they regularly battled Pawnees in central Nebraska. On the Missouri River, they carried out raids against the agricultural villages of Arikaras and Mandans.

Several tribes suddenly encountered large numbers of American overlanders traveling through their territory in the 1840s. The Oregon, California, and Mormon Trails all brought people through the heart of Pawnee, Lakota, and Shoshone lands. The zone extending along the trails quickly became destitute of game and surprisingly little conflict occurred between overlanders and Plains peoples. In part, because the Platte River was no longer a valuable resource for Lakotas, they tended to stay away from the wagon trains.

Representatives of most of the Lakota tribes met with government agents near Fort Laramie in 1851. Other tribes included Arapahos, Assiniboines, Cheyennes, Crows, and Shoshones from the Plains and Rockies and Arikaras, Hidatsas, and Mandans from the Missouri River. In all, more than 10,000 Native Americans camped in what may have been the largest ever gathering of Plains people. The resulting treaty prescribed boundaries and selected a single leader, Conquering Bear or Frightening Bear, a Brulé Lakota as the head chief through whom the United States would conduct further business. Lakotas protested against both the imposition of limits on their lands and the structure of government relations that had no validity among the multiple Lakota tribes and leadership. Under pressure, the other tribes present eventually agreed to the head chief provision, but Lakotas, whose delegation included Brulés, Hunkpapas, Mineconjous, Oglalas, and Two Kettles, could not. The U.S. negotiators simply overruled these protests and selected Conquering Bear as Lakota head chief anyway. Frightening Bear himself appealed to the American agents that he was not a senior enough chief to assume such a position and only six chiefs signed from the entirety of the Sioux nations. These chiefs did not have absolute authority over even the Brulés, Two Kettles, and Yanktons they represented and much less over the Oglalas, Hunkpapas and others who had no chiefs signing the treaty. This attempt to force the various Lakota tribes and bands to act as one, answering to a single leader doomed any chance for real cooperation between Lakotas and the United States from the beginning. Lakota decision-making had long been based in consensus, with lengthy discussion and agreements among many leaders. The U.S. model in which individuals could speak for a nation and commit them to a specific agreement was not simply foreign, but antithetical to Lakota ways. Any documents signed by a single or even a handful of chiefs without consensus would have little effect.

Many, perhaps most, Lakotas did not know the provisions of the treaty, much less agree to its terms. Congress demanded a reduction in the costs of the treaty and cut the terms for annual payments from fifty years to ten years. They sent the revision to the treaty to the tribes in 1853 and met with even less enthusiasm and participation. Only four of the original Sioux signers agreed to reduce the annual distribution of goods required under the treaty.

When an Army unit under John L. Grattan set out to demand compensation for the killing of a cow that had wandered away from a Mormon wagon train near Conquering Bear's camp only three years after the Fort Laramie Treaty of 1851, they found that the head chief was powerless to compel a visiting Mineconjou Lakota named High Forehead to surrender. Conquering Bear offered any of his horses as compensation instead, but the cow's owner refused. One of the soldiers shot Conquering Bear in the back as the negotiations were breaking up, triggering what newspapers and politicians called the Grattan Massacre and others have called the Grattan Fight. The mixed Brulé-Oglala camp immediately struck back against the inexperienced Grattan and all twenty-nine of his men were killed in a matter of minutes.

The Grattan Fight sparked a series of battles in which the U.S. Army attempted to simultaneously punish Sioux and force them into compliance with the Fort Laramie Treaty. Lakota bands harassed travelers along the Oregon Trail and when the U.S. Army struck on September 3, 1855, it was at Brulé chief Little Thunder's camp near the trail on the North Platte River. During the Battle of Ash Hollow, mounted Lakota warriors attempted to pull troops into a running fight away from the village, but only some troops pursued them. Others fired into caves sheltering women and children. In what many Lakotas understood as retaliation for the Grattan Fight, eighty-six Sioux lay dead and seventy surviving women and children were taken as prisoner. Crazy Horse, then a young man who had been out hunting during the attack, vowed to lead his people in revenge in the aftermath. Spotted Tail and four others surrendered to the Army in order to end the killing. After a year in the prison at Fort Leavenworth, Spotted Tail became an advocate for a diplomatic solution.

In April 1856, Sioux gathered at Fort Pierre to negotiate peace. The United States again insisted on its head chief system and appointed Hunkpapa chief Bear Ribs as the head chief and eight other subchiefs. Mineconjou chief One Horn surrendered the cow killer as an additional peace gesture and the Sioux representatives agreed to the modified system that at least partially recognized the more dispersed authority, including additional designations of chief soldiers under the subchiefs. However, Congress rejected the new treaty and the older Fort Laramie Treaty remained in force. Many Lakotas continued to reject the terms of that agreement and vowed to defend the lands north of the Platte River against encroachment and refuse any treaty-related payments. When Bear Ribs accepted a June 1862 shipment of goods, he was murdered. Hunkpapas tried to explain to the U.S. Indian Agent that Bear Ribs had been warned, but had not listened to the will of the people. Bear Ribs was the last of the U.S.-appointed head chiefs.

Lakotas, Cheyennes, Comanches, and others whose cultures centered on equestrianism found that defending grasslands against encroaching Americans became even more difficult. Over the course of the nineteenth century, American hide hunters decimated bison herds to feed the demand for durable belts to run eastern factory machinery. By the 1870s, buffalo numbers plummeted as railroads delivered hunters into the heart of the Great Plains.

PROFILE: BUFFALO HUMP

The Penateka Comanche war chief Buffalo Hump led his people in both negotiations and fighting with the fledgling Republic of Texas and the United States. With their independence from Mexico, Texans had demanded the return of all captives held by Comanches but did not recognize that leaders of one band could not force others to follow any agreement. The many Comanche bands made negotiating a comprehensive peace difficult, but Buffalo Hump and others sought recognition of Comanche sovereignty over their territory from the newly formed government of Texas. When eastern Comanches under Muguara arrived in San Antonio in 1840 for talks accompanied by their families, Texans attempted to imprison them in order to force other bands to release captives. When the Comanche leaders attempted to flee from confinement inside the Council House, Texans opened fire. More than thirty Comanche leaders died in the Council House and nearly as many family members died outside.

To avenge the massacre of the Comanche delegation and the betrayal of the peace council, Buffalo Hump gathered more than 400 warriors and struck out on a raid that was far larger than any previously undertaken. Comanches struck the town of Victoria on August 6, en route to the coastal village of Linnville on August 8. Most Linnville residents fled to a schooner in the harbor as Comanches sacked the port's warehouses, killed penned cattle herds, and burned the town before fleeing.

Three years later, Texans and Comanches again met to discuss peace. By early 1844, Amorous Man, Buffalo Hump, and Old Owl agreed to return captives and end raiding against Texas targets in exchange for formal recognition of the boundaries of Comanche territory. The Texas Congress eliminated the boundary that would have kept settlers east of the Edwards Plateau before approving the treaty, and Buffalo Hump rejected that version. However, once Texas became a state, Buffalo Hump again returned to negotiations and signed the Treaty of Council Springs in 1846.

Buffalo Hump moved to the Comanche Reservation in 1856, but only stayed two years before moving his band to the Wichita Mountains to hunt and feed their families. There, U.S. troops attacked the Comanches and forced them back to the reservation. Living a long life in which he transitioned from warrior to farmer, Buffalo Hump died in 1870 on the Kiowa-Comanche-Apache Reservation in Oklahoma.

PROFILE: SACAGAWEA

Though she is among the most famous of Native Americans, even the matter of her name is a matter of controversy. Three versions are popular: Sacagawea (as recorded by Lewis and Clark), Sakakawea (which reflects Hidatsa spelling), or Sacajawea (as preferred by some modern Shoshones). In 1800, when she was thirteen, a Hidatsa raiding party captured Sacagawea, her friend Otter Woman, and several other Shoshones near the Three Forks of the Missouri. The beleaguered Shoshones suffered raids from many northern Plains tribes in the early nineteenth century and venturing into buffalo country had become dangerous.

As the second Shoshone wife of French-Canadian Toussaint Charbonneau, Sacagawea's experience reflected a pattern of western tribes with little access to guns being raided by tribes closer to European trading sources. When the Lewis and Clark expedition hired Charbonneau, a pregnant wife stayed at the Mandan Villages, but Sacagawea and her infant Jean Baptiste accompanied the men to the west. The presence of a woman and baby among the well-armed men may have signaled to others that this was not a war party and the Americans were already conscious of Shoshones' reputation as a horse-rich tribe.

One of the ironies of the initial American encounter with Shoshones was that Sacagawea was not present. When the Corps of Discovery arrived in Shoshone territory, they had divided into two groups. Cameahwait welcomed Meriwether Lewis and three other men to his village at Lemhi, Idaho and through the Plains Indian sign language, they were able to communicate. When Sacagawea arrived several days later, she found that Chief Cameahwait was her "brother." It remains unclear whether he was a literal brother as many historians have asserted, but he was clearly a close relative who recognized and welcomed the girl from five years earlier. Her brief return to her people and the promise of American trade made Lewis and Clark very popular. Shoshones guided the Americans across the Rocky Mountains and welcomed them on their return journey.

Sacagawea's death is another matter of controversy for some who believe that she lived till the age of 100 and died on the Wind River Reservation in Wyoming. However, the historical record indicates that she died only a few years after the expedition's end at Fort Manuel in 1812. William Clark became the guardian of both her children, Jean Baptiste and Lisette, the following year in St. Louis. Well after her death, Susan B. Anthony anointed her as the greatest woman of American history at the 1905 unveiling of a Sacagawea statue in Portland, Oregon and she continues to serve as a symbol of female strength and leadership.

REFERENCES AND FURTHER READING

Binnema, Theodore. *Common and Contested Ground: A Human and Environmental History of the Northwestern Plains*. Norman: University of Oklahoma Press, 2001.

Fenn, Elizabeth A. *Encounters at the Heart of the World: A History of the Mandan People*. New York: Hill and Wang, 2014.

Flores, Dan. "Bison Ecology and Bison Diplomacy: The Southern Plains from 1800 to 1850." *Journal of American History* 78, no. 2 (1991): 465–85.

Hämäläinen, Pekka. *The Comanche Empire*. New Haven: Yale University Press, 2008.

Holder, Preston. *The Hoe and the Horse on the Plains: A Study of Cultural Development among North American Indians*. Lincoln: University of Nebraska Press, 1970.

Isenberg, Andrew C. *The Destruction of the Bison: An Environmental History, 1750–1920*. New York: Cambridge University Press, 2000.

Liberty, Margot. "Hell Came with Horses: Plains Women in the Equestrian Era." *Montana: The Magazine of Western History* 32, no. 3 (1982): 10–19.

McGinnis, Anthony. *Counting Coup and Cutting Horses: Intertribal Warfare on the Northern Plains, 1738–1889*. Reprint ed. Lincoln: University of Nebraska Press, 2010.

Ostler, Jeffrey. *The Plains Sioux and U.S. Colonialism from Lewis and Clark to Wounded Knee*. New York: Cambridge University Press, 2004.

Smith, F. Todd. *From Dominance to Disappearance: The Indians of Texas and the Near Southwest, 1786–1859*. Lincoln: University of Nebraska Press, 2008.

West, Elliott. *The Contested Plains: Indians, Goldseekers, and the Rush to Colorado*. Lawrence: University Press of Kansas, 1998.

White, Richard. *The Roots of Dependency: Subsistence, Environment, and Social Change among the Choctaws, Pawnees, and Navajos*. Lincoln: University of Nebraska Press, 1983.

_____ *Chapter 6* _____

California and Tierra Despoblada, 1760s–1840s

California Indians saw a gradual movement of European goods and settlements northward from Baja California and across the Mojave trade routes from Arizona and Sonora as the Spanish frontier crept northward. However, they were likely only vaguely aware of the far off Russian settlements in Alaska. When Spaniards heard rumors of an imperial rival encroaching on their claimed (but largely unexplored) territory, they launched an effort to secure Alta California against the Russians. It was immediately apparent that California would be a remote colony that was both difficult and expensive to provision. However, by using missions as the primary tools of colonization, the Spanish Crown hoped to reduce costs by using converted Indians as the primary bulwark against foreign invasions. Building a mission-centered colony, the Spanish Empire thought to secure California's ports with a minimum investment.

Spaniards had expelled the Jesuit order from Baja California just a year before the 1769 Spanish settlement of Alta California. The Franciscans led by Junipero Serra were more conservative and zealous than the Jesuits who struggled to support missions in the arid lands to the south. Serra in particular sought martyrdom and increased his personal suffering through self-flagellation and wearing hair shirts. In 2015, Pope Francis canonized Serra for his work in extending Catholicism to California, but many indigenous leaders and scholars protested that the missions he established were the means to cultural genocide for California Indians.

THE MISSIONS

Establishing twenty-one missions extending from San Diego in Kumeyaay territory in the south to Sonoma in Coast Miwok lands north of San

American Indian women at a mission near San Francisco, California, by Louis Choris, 1822. Spanish California relied upon the labor of Mission Indians and Indian women were often the targets of village raids and sexual violence. In spite of indigenous rebellions, raiding from the interior, and high indigenous death rates, 21,000 Indians lived in missions by 1821. (Library of Congress)

Francisco Bay, the Spaniards created a coastal colony of mission towns approximately one day's journey apart from each other. Presidios at San Diego, Santa Barbara, Monterey, and San Francisco housed small garrison of soldiers to back up the missionary effort with force. The missions' success depended on turning as many as possible of California's more than 300,000 Indians into Spanish subjects in order to spare the few Spanish soldiers and settlers available. Missions thus had the twin charge of converting California's Indians to Catholicism and turning them into Spaniards as quickly and efficiently as possible. The padres understood that Indians could be starved into submission and noted that conversions often came on the heels of game disappearing or harvest failures. Once one family member was converted, the pressure to keep families together often meant the remainder of the family would soon convert as well.

Coastal peoples faced continual pressure to move to the missions, where they became laboring neophytes for the Franciscan enterprise. Each mission required dozens of skilled and unskilled laborers to operate, essentially forming self-contained small towns. Indians dug and maintained ditches; erected buildings; cleared, planted, and harvested grain fields; and herded animals. Workers in mission workshops made shoes, saddles, candles, soap, and blankets. Settlers on *ranchos* also vied for Indian labor to move cattle, sheep, and horses and any number of general tasks. They too resorted to raiding, but usually with less thought of coerced work as a route to learning Christian morality.

California's Indians faced a series of decisions regarding their colonizers. As elsewhere, European arrival brought numerous changes. Some of the foods and goods benefitted Native Americans, but the impacts of disease countered those advantages. The sheep, cattle, and horses that soon grew to the tens of thousands grazed carefully tended gathering grounds and competed with game. To protect their investment, Spaniards actively destroyed animals they thought competed with their cattle and sheep, killing elk, deer, and even wild horses. Spanish officials also banned Indian burning as they believed that it destroyed the grasslands that their grazing economy relied upon. Ironically, Indian burning had instead created and maintained the vast grasslands. Without burning, chaparral slowly encroached on grazing areas and the zone extending inland from the coastal Spanish missions and ranchos emptied of game, replaced by sheep and cattle. Indians lost access to the seeds, acorns, and wild plants that formed a central part of their diet.

As in New Mexico, Texas, and Florida, priests' claims of the numbers converted may have been inflated. However, there is no question that Indians from the coastal zone bore the brunt of Spanish policies. As an effort to prevent sexual assaults and prevent runaways, padres soon confined all Mission Indians to gender segregated barracks. In those crowded conditions, diseases spread rapidly, resulting in a horrific death rate. By about 1800, the populations between the sea and the Coast Ranges had been exhausted, and soldiers began crossing more often into the Central Valley to take captives and force them into the coastal missions. Forced marches brought interior Yokuts and Miwoks into the lands of coastal Luiseños and Ohlones. At their peak in the early 1800s, the missions housed 21,000 Indians, only a quarter of the number of those who had been baptized.

Indians' main means of protest was faking illness or misunderstanding. However, at several points, protest became outright violence. At Mission San Diego in November 1775, an estimated 800 Kumeyaays (Diegueños) rose up against their Spanish colonizers. Kumeyaays had resisted the initial arrival of Spaniards in 1769 and several smaller attacks had occurred. Padres moved the mission inland in 1774 and launched a much more intensive conversion effort in the midst of Kumeyaay villages. Soldiers raped and murdered Indians, cattle destroyed Kumeyaay crops, and as more Indians were baptized, the threat of Christianity to native traditions became clear. One of the reasons padres had moved the mission was to distance themselves from the bad influence of the soldiers, but that did not prevent violence. Runners sent to tribes to the east failed to win those Indians over to the revolt, but fifteen Kumeyaay villages, including several that the Spanish padres considered to be fully Christianized, rose up to kill three padres and burn the mission. The other Spaniards fled back to the presidio nearer the coast. Such resistance against the Spanish usually resulted in disproportionate retaliation. However, in the initial years of Spanish colonization, California Indians usually remained divided against the strength of Spanish organization, horses, and guns.

By 1778, the California colony was essentially self-sustaining, with nearly 100,000 cattle and well over that number of sheep. Cattle became the central economic resource of the colony as a trade in hides and tallow commenced with Spanish ships returning to Mexico from Asia called to refresh water and food. This trade brought a few imported staples and luxuries to Californios, but fell far short of driving a robust economy. Few women traveled to the colony, and the Spanish settlement of California continued as a relatively feeble effort, thwarted by isolation from New Spain, and the colony's failure to generate wealth.

A 1781 Quechan uprising led by Quechan headman Olleyquotequiebe on the Colorado River expelled Spaniards from two nearby missions and cut off overland routes to California from Mexico. Peoples beyond the reach of Spanish missionization did not factor into their imperial schemes, but indigenous people continued to interact across these regions between European frontiers. Spaniards labeled the vast interior between California and New Mexico *tierras despobladas*, or empty lands. These lands, of course, were populated, but not by peoples that Spaniards considered to be Christianized *gente con razon*.

Reliant on indigenous labor to run their ranching economy, one of the most successful aspects of their cultural teaching was to create indigenous equestrian raiders. By 1800, Miwoks, Yokuts, and others regularly struck at the very strength of the Spanish colony. They killed ranch and mission animals, seized horses, and then used them to run off other animals. The missions had established a foothold, and California's ecology continued to change, but indigenous resistance halted Spanish expansion. Spaniards never reached the gold fields of the Sierra and failed to incorporate themselves into the indigenous trade network.

Historian Natale Zappia argues that the indigenous world away from the coast continued to function as Cocopahs, Mojaves, Quechans, and Yokuts used trading and raiding to maintain their power. An older trade in *pook*, or shell beads formed from *olivella* shells from the southern California coast, extended into Arizona and beyond. Later, horses and other Californio goods followed the same routes as indigenous trade persisted well beyond colonization. However, Spaniards and Mexicans were excluded from this indigenous trade network and thus failed to redirect Indian economics.

ALEUTS IN CALIFORNIA

The initial trigger for Spanish colonization of California was the rumor of Russian expansion into North America. Vitus Bering reached the Aleutian Islands in 1741 and in the decades that followed, the Russian American Company extended their practices from Siberia. In Alaska, they would sweep into a village armed with guns, took hostages, and demanded that men meet a quota of furs to secure the release of their family members. As they moved southward, they began to take Aleuts captive and deployed them in their kayaks to fish the rough waters of the Pacific coast. Traveling as far south as Baja California, Russian ships dropped Aleuts off on rocky headlands and offshore islands with the charge of trapping sea otters in order to be returned home. Aleuts faced starvation and other hardships. Some fell to their death while collecting seabird eggs on the steep rocks where they had been marooned. Others disappeared while working the offshore kelp beds.

In 1812, the Russian-American Fur Company established a southern outpost north of Bodega Bay dubbed Fort Ross. Hundreds of Aleuts, Hawaiians, and Pomos served as labor in the wheat farms and cattle ranches in the Russian River valley intended to feed their Alaskan hub. However, these did not produce well enough to meet the Russians' needs and illegal trade with nearby missions and ranches provided a necessary margin. Once the missions were secularized, and with the Hudson's Bay Company's Pacific Northwest farms providing the majority of the food for Alaska, the Russians abandoned California. Their final act was selling the post in 1841. Many Aleuts had intermarried with local Pomos and some at least, remained behind in the Pomo villages.

The story of Peter the Aleut is illustrative of the clash of rival Europeans and the entanglement of indigenous people in California. Russian Orthodox priests baptized a Kodiak Island native, Cungagnaq, as "Peter" before he found himself shipped to Fort Ross as part of a southern fur hunting party. Like other Aleuts, he and his companions risked capture or attack by Spaniards. In 1810, Spanish troops killed at least a dozen Aleuts as they hunted sea otters in and around San Francisco Bay. As many as sixty kayaks worked in the waters around San Francisco Bay as Spaniards occasionally opened fire or patrols surprised small hunting parties. In an effort to stave off the hunters, soldiers guarded springs and other water sources necessary for the Aleuts to carry out their extended hunts. In 1815, a patrol captured Peter and some companions when they came ashore south of San Francisco and he later died in mysterious circumstances. Accounts vary from torture meted out by padres at the Mission San Francisco to an execution for his explicit refusal to convert to Catholicism. "Saint Peter the Aleut" thus became a martyr while working as compulsory labor for the Russian Empire, dying at the hands of Spanish authorities.

Well to the south of the Russian-Pomo contact zone, Chumash Indians launched a revolt in 1824 that ousted Mexicans from three missions: Santa Inés, Purísima, and Santa Bárbara. Presidial troops skirmished with Chumash at La Purísima, but were unable to force them into submission. Many Chumash were part of a Spanish-trained military company, organized six years earlier to defend the missions against foreign attack. Trained in European armaments and tactics, Chumash disarmed the surrendering troops and forced them to return to Santa Inés as an escort for the evacuating Mexican families. For more than a month, Santa Inés and Purísima Chumash occupied the latter mission. Others led by Andrés Sagimomatsee at Santa Bárbara also defeated a small detachment of soldiers and then retreated to the Central Valley to form a new village.

Unlike earlier uprisings, Mission Chumash did not target their priests. The padre at Santa Bárbara, Antonio Ripoll, was unusual in his promotion of Chumash dancing and singing as part of church ceremonies. He also promoted the manufacture of *olivella* shell beads as money and used it to lure peoples of the interior into an expanded economic relationship with the mission. When Chumash overthrew Mexicans, they temporarily removed their oppressors, but they had also incorporated at least some Christian elements and mission culture into their lives. Chumash who had mastered skills valuable to the mission economy had gained status outside of the older indigenous structures. When Mexicans eventually persuaded most of the Chumash rebels to return to the missions, the padres were key in negotiating an end to the revolt and granting pardons.

An 1826 Proclamation on Emancipation freed Indians from the missions and made them Mexican citizens. Still, many Indians elected to remain on the missions where they had made their lives rather than relocating. A few years later, in 1833, the missions were secularized, effectively ending the role of the padres and missions in Indian's lives. The mission properties were to be reserved for the Indians, with a mix of individual acreage and a shared grazing commons. Instead the lands were sold off and Indians who had sought refuge there became landless peoples seeking refuge on nearby ranchos or among sometimes alienated tribes. Most Indians either found work and shelter on the ranches or fled to the interior to seek refuge among relatives.

Two of the more notable sites of Indian labor in the wake of mission secularization were at Mariano Vallejo's Rancho Petaluma and John Sutter's holdings stretching northward from his headquarters in what is now Sacramento. Vallejo received a land grant situated between the Russian Colony and the newest and final mission, San Francisco Solano. He used a combination of fair dealing and military force to put hundreds of Indians to work on his many projects. His younger brother rounded up Miwoks, Patwins, and other peoples north of San Francisco Bay from the surrounding area and forced them to work in building, planting, harvesting, herding, and other tasks. After secularization, Vallejo added the lands of Mission Solano to his own and many of the Mission Indians remained as labor for the growing Vallejo holdings. An alliance with Solano, a Patwin chief, and a nearby garrison of soldiers guaranteed Vallejo had his way in his relations with local Indians.

Sutter visited Vallejo's operations before he set up his own fiefdom along the lower Sacramento River. Sutter had purchased an Indian boy at the 1838 rendezvous in the Rocky Mountains, but little is known of his origins or his fate. Eight Hawaiians traveled with him from Hawaii and were critical in his initial establishment of New Helvetia. Sutter deliberately sited his fort and farms adjacent to several Indian villages to take advantage of resident Miwoks and Nisenans as laborers. He developed a system in which Indians could work to earn tokens to purchase goods such as clothing and outfitted a small Indian Army in European uniforms. Sutter's Indian force grew to ninety men in the 1845 failed defense of California governor Micheltorena. A Lieutenant Rufino was the Moquelumne Miwok leader of this force that eventually marched as far as the San Fernando Valley where Sutter and his remaining troops were captured. The Californio rebels made Rufino and the other Miwoks serve as pack bearers to carry supplies and unload ships at San Pedro. Instead of gaining horses or other goods, Sutter's Indians experienced forced servitude until their release. Sutter no longer trusted his Indians and the reverse also seems likely. Sutter and the Indian Army made their way back to their homeland separately. In the weeks that followed, Miwok raiders attacked area ranchers and threatened Sutter. In response, Sutter tracked down and killed Raphero, a leader of the Miwok raiders. In a gruesome display, Sutter had Raphero's decapitated head displayed on the wall of his palisaded fort. This act drove Rufino, formerly one of Sutter's most trusted allies, to turn against him. Rufino began actively raiding Sutter's horses and cattle. By the fall of 1845, Rufino too was captured, stood trial, found guilty of murder, and executed.

An estimated 20,000 Indians died in the Central Valley of California in the 1833 malaria epidemic. The disease came south from the Columbia River with an Hudson's Bay Company fur-trapping brigade and quickly spread to the densely populated villages. When Sutter arrived to set up his empire in 1839, Miwoks and Nisenans were still reeling from the devastating losses and subsequent outbreaks. The Miwoks in particular were amiable and willing to join forces with Sutter. Using gifts that included sugar imported from Hawaii, Sutter swayed Miwok chieftain Narciso to his side. Other Miwoks with experience in the missions followed and many relocated to Sutter's Fort. Nisenans were generally less enthusiastic, partly because they feared a buildup of Miwok strength in alliance with the Europeans, but many were willing to deal with the newcomers. Others resisted Sutter in much the same way as they had the Spaniards before him and Sutter retaliated violently, sometimes employing cannons on unsuspecting villages. In one incident, former Mission Indians raided a nearby Nisenan village, seizing women and children and killing many of the old people. Nisenans initially suspected Sutter of plotting with the raiders, but in a move that may have been as much to win over reluctant Nisenans as to protect an indigenous village, Sutter led a combined force of Europeans and Indians and captured the raiders after a brief fight. Several Indians escaped, but Sutter executed ten on the raiding Mission Indians.

OVERLANDERS

The 1820s brought fur traders into the Great Basin and in 1828 Peter Skene Ogden led a Hudson's Bay Company along the Humboldt River in northern Nevada, then southward to the Gulf of California. Ogden's charge was to carry out the HBC's scorched stream policy. They destroyed the beaver along the length of the river even as they noted Western Shoshones used the animals' pelts for clothing. Ogden also noted numerous horses being moved across this route as Shoshones transferred herds of horses from California to the Snake River Plain.

Five years later, having heard rumors of Ogden's take, an American party under Joseph Reddeford Walker made its way west from the Great Salt Lake. Frustrated by their poor returns, the men became violent and taking potshots at Indians they encountered became a regular practice. After wounding and killing several Paiutes and Shoshones along the Humboldt River, the party arrived at a large encampment near the Humboldt Sink. There, they refused to allow Indians to come into their camp and turned back several individuals. A few days later, as they made their way through grass so tall that they could not see over it on horseback, they suddenly encountered a clearing and perhaps one hundred Indians. Fearing an ambush in retaliation for their earlier acts and deciding these Indians were a threat, Walker ordered a mounted charge. It remains unclear whether these Indians were welcoming the party or indeed threatening, but the result was at least three dozen dead Indians. Walker rapidly pressed on across the Sierra into California in an effort to avoid retaliation.

The combined effect of fur trappers and Shoshone horsemen forced Humboldt River Paiutes and Shoshones to shift away from the resource-rich corridor. Dispersing into smaller bands, Paiutes became exiles in their own lands. However, the problem of encroaching outsiders became exponentially worse with the advent of the California Trail. The Paiute homeland became the most arduous section of the long journey from the United States to California, and overlanders increasingly referred to the Indians along this route west of the Rocky Mountains as "diggers." The belittling term associated impoverished people who dug roots from the ground to live and the harsh climate and lack of resources along the Humboldt.

MALARIA AND THE MEXICAN WAR

Spanish plans to expand the coastal mission system into the densely populated Yokut and Miwok interior failed at the outset. The environment of tule marshes, confusingly braided waterways, and vast shallow lakes cowed Spaniards and hid even large villages. Yokuts began raiding Spanish ranchos and retreated into their homeland. Horses, and later cattle, became targets of Yokuts and Miwoks compensating in part for the demise of an indigenous trading network. With coastal villages shattered by the mission system, interior peoples compensated by tapping the new goods of Spaniards. Among these, horses became the most valuable, especially given the growing needs of people to the east for horses.

The nineteenth century brought a series of rapid and monumental changes to California Indians' lives. The comparatively late arrival of disease in the interior made for a sudden and enormous impact. The Central Valley of California was one of the most densely populated areas in North America, but when malaria arrived with a Hudson's Bay Company trapping brigade in 1833, it spread quickly. Indian villages emptied as the epidemic swept through. Trappers found former village sites along the lower Sacramento and San Joaquin Rivers reduced to strewn bones.

Coincidentally, American troops arrived in California as part of the Mexican War just as Native Americans were at their lowest ebb. Reeling from malaria, remaining Indian raiders who had previously held Spaniards to their coastal enclaves became almost invisible. When Americans found their Mexican opponents mostly confined to coastal settlements, it fulfilled several American mythologies at once. Observers noted that Mexicans were obviously lazy, or else they would have exploited many more of California's abundant resources. Similarly, they deemed California's Indians to be cowardly "Diggers" who were subhuman specimens of poverty and disease. Americans joining old Californio Indian fighters on dawn raids against sleeping villages thus justified their practice of taking Indian captives as forced labor.

THE GOLD RUSH AND STATEHOOD

In January 1848, Indians digging the ditch for a Sutter sawmill on the American River unearthed the gold that set off the California Gold Rush.

The flood of outsiders made for more rapid change in California than any-where else in North America. Homelands known only to indigenous people saw thousands of Euro-Americans arrive in the space of months. Millennia of culture and life ways came to an abrupt halt as gold seekers displaced indigenous people. Miners hunted out the local game, destroyed the fish runs, and occupied village sites. In addition, the latecomer Forty-Niners resented Indian labor as an unfair advantage in the gold fields. Murder became regular as Indians became hunted exiles in their homelands.

One outgrowth of the Gold Rush was a codification of the new status for indigenous peoples. Under the Mexican Constitution, indigenous people and mestizos were full citizens, but with the sudden imposition of American law, Indians lost their status as citizens. Further, the state of California embarked in a genocidal policy that specifically targeted Indians.

By the eve of the Gold Rush in 1848, California's Native American popula-tion was half that of Spanish colonization eighty years earlier. A decade later, only 35,000 California Indians remained. Hydraulic mining spelled disaster for California's streams. Fish smothered in mining waste and the gravel neces-sary for salmon redds was deposited on riverbanks. These tailings deposits destroyed the streamside vegetation and buried rich riparian resources. Throughout the Sierra and into the Central Valley, one of the richest sources of food for indigenous people rapidly disappeared. Conflict with miners also forced peoples to withdraw from streams to ever more remote hiding places and tenuous existence. Miners' hunting reduced another entire category of food and clothing as deer, elk, and many birds became scarce.

In answer to urging from newspapers and white constituents, Governor Peter Burnett's 1851 address to the California Legislature announced a war of extermination with the end goal being the extinction of California Indians. The Legislature followed up with $500,000 for a state militia cam-paign against Indians. Towns and counties raised money to pay bounties for Indian scalps or other evidence of killing.

California law also prohibited Indian testimony in court, regulated most traditional hunting and gathering through a system of licenses and limits, and rarely punished any kind of wrongdoing by whites against Indians. Though California entered the Union as a free state, it effectively legalized the enslavement of Native Americans

The 1851–1852 treaty commission signed eighteen treaties with the vari-ous tribes of California. More than 500 Native American leaders signed these treaties to reserve 8.5 million acres of land, divided into parcels larger than 25,000 acres. Though these were often less desirable reserves, they did hold some land aside for exclusive Indian occupancy. However, Congress passed none of those treaties and by then, almost all of California's Indians had removed from their homelands.

Instead, the United States established five reservations in California, but failed to fund them. One of these, the Nome Cult Farm, was eventually renamed the Round Valley Reservation. This single reservation became the *de facto* home of many of the peoples of the northern Coast Range and Central Valley. When treaties failed, whites claimed Indian land and forced Indians out again. From 1855 to the mid-1860s, a series of forced marches removed California Indians from temporary reservation lands to Round Valley. As settlers and loggers pressed into Indian lands, conflict increased. Volunteer militia waged intermittent war against the peoples of Northern California and federal troops moved into attempt to reassert control. The outbreak of the Civil War shifted federal troops to the eastern Unites States and left Indians to fend for themselves against militias patrolling the region.

The federal government established the Nome Lackee Military Reservation in 1854 and as many as 3,000 Indians gathered there over the next few years. No funding or supplies arrived for the gathered people at Nome Lackee for the first years of the reservation, but they managed to survive by growing wheat and other produce. When supplies meant for the Indians did finally arrive, Vincent Geiger, the agent at Nome Lackee, sold them to nearby farmers instead. An investigation eventually found that Geiger had also indentured Indians on the reservation.

In February 1861, a group of Confederate sympathizers attacked Nome Lackee and destroyed it. These Indians also made a march to Round Valley and Geiger escaped to Canada. Survivors of California's genocidal Indian policies found themselves crowded onto a small slice of the Yuki homeland among a mix of friends, enemies, and strangers. Other Indians who were not consolidated into Round Valley remained outside of the federal recognition process. In order to survive, many assumed Hispanic identities to hide their Indian origins. Although this did not grant Native Americans equal treatment, it was a means to avoid violent attacks.

PROFILE: ESTANISLAO

Born around 1800, Estanislao was a Yokut whom Spaniards captured and brought to the Mission San José as a young boy. He became a neophyte and the priests must have regarded him as one of their most promising converts. He rose through the ranks of his fellow Mission Indians and became an *alcalde*, the highest position to which an Indian could be appointed. As *alcalde*, Estanislao was an official boss, directing at least some of the work of his fellow Mission Indians. That role also allowed him access and the opportunity to plan amongst Indians outside of priest observers.

In 1828, Estanislao and several other Mission Indians secured passes to travel into the interior to visit Indian villages there. However, Estanislao refused to return, even writing a note to the lead padre that he did not fear the Mexican troops and that the Indians would rebel against them. A new policy that allowed married Indians to leave the missions and rumors of the imminent demise of the institution may have fueled the revolt. Cipriano, a neophyte *alcalde* from Mission Santa Cruz, soon joined Estanislao and Mission Indians from across the region fled to their encampment on the San Joaquin River.

By transitioning from trusted convert to resistance leader, Estanislao fit a recognizable pattern. Three of the four leaders of the 1775 Tipai Revolt at San Diego were supposed converts as well. It seems that the missionaries were almost always surprised by such backsliding but rarely attributed it to any fault of their own or of the mission system. Instead, they saw the Devil at work as Estanislao led raids on the missions and ranchos around San Francisco Bay. Like others before him, he used his intimate knowledge of the colonizers' world to aid indigenous raiders. Understanding how the ranchos operated and when animals were most vulnerable, Estanislao led raiders to strike at horses when they were unprotected, then to return to take slower cattle and sheep.

Rancheros protested that they did not have enough horses to mount a pursuit and demanded that the military do more to protect them against the growing party of raiding Indians. Volunteers twice attempted to crush Estanislao, but in both fights, the rebels turned back the Californios. In 1829, a third expedition of presidial troops and Indian auxiliaries faced Estanislao's followers who by then numbered nearly 1,000. Three days of fighting caused most Indians to flee, but the Californios declared victory after setting fire to the undergrowth surrounding the Indian stronghold. In the aftermath, captured Indians faced tortures and impromptu executions. Estanislao escaped to Mission San José where the priest pardoned him. Perhaps fulfilling a promise, he occasionally aided the San José authorities in their efforts to halt Indian raiding, but died of smallpox only a few years later.

PROFILE: JUANA MARIA, THE LONE WOMAN OF SAN NICOLAS

An American sea captain, George Nidever, rescued "The Lone Woman of San Nicolas Island" in 1853. She was the sole inhabitant of the island more than fifty miles off the California mainland. Though San Nicolas Island was described as densely populated in 1602 when Spaniards briefly stopped there, and archaeological evidence indicates at least 8,000 years of occupation, only about a hundred Nicoleños remained in the early 1800s. Russians left Aleut sea otter hunters there in 1811 and the Russians attacked the Nicoleños—at least once—in 1814. Spanish missionaries from Santa Barbara rounded up the survivors in 1835 and forced them to the mainland mission. However, one woman escaped to look for a missing child and could not be found. Eighteen years later, Nidever and his crew landed and found a woman about fifty years old dressed in a cormorant feather dress, skinning a seal.

The Lone Woman became an instant celebrity upon her arrival in the village of Santa Barbara and such novel items as a horse-drawn wagon surprised her. The missionaries baptized her as "Juana Maria" and she performed songs and dances that none of the other Mission Indians could interpret. Some have speculated that the years alone had taken her language. Others assert that none of her people remained alive to translate. Through sign language, she made it clear that she was the woman who had been left behind eighteen years earlier and had never found her baby. However, after less than two months ashore, Juana Maria contracted dysentery and died.

Juana Maria's story became the basis for *The Island of the Blue Dolphins*, one of the most popular young adult novels of California. The 2012 discovery and partial excavation of the cave where Juana Maria lived for those years alone triggered controversy. The Pechanga Band of Luiseño Mission Indians asserted a cultural affiliation with the site and demanded that the U.S. Navy (who operate a missile testing base on the island) cease all archaeological work. Gabrieliño-Tongvas have contested the Pechanga claim, but the fate of archaeology on San Nicolas—and much of Juana Maria's story—remain unresolved.

REFERENCES AND FURTHER READING

Gamble, Lynn H. *The Chumash World at European Contact: Power, Trade, and Feasting Among Complex Hunter-Gatherers*. Berkeley: University of California Press, 2008.

Haas, Lisbeth. *Saints and Citizens: Indigenous Histories of Colonial Missions and Mexican California*. Berkeley: University of California Press, 2013.

Hackel, Steven W. *Children of Coyote, Missionaries of Saint Francis: Indian-Spanish Relations in Colonial California, 1769–1850*. Chapel Hill: University of North Carolina Press, 2005.

Hurtado, Albert L. *Indian Survival on the California Frontier*. New Haven, CT: Yale University Press, 1988.

Jackson, Robert H., and Edward Castillo. *Indians, Franciscans, and Spanish Colonization: The Impact of the Mission System on the California Indians*. Albuquerque: University of New Mexico Press, 1995.

Lightfoot, Kent G., and Otis Parrish. *California Indians and Their Environment: An Introduction*. Berkeley: University of California Press, 2009.

Lindsay, Brendan C. *Murder State: California's Native American Genocide, 1846–1873*. Lincoln: University of Nebraska Press, 2012.

Madley, Benjamin. *An American Genocide: The United States and the California Indian Catastrophe, 1846–1873*. New Haven, CT: Yale University Press, 2016.

Margolin, Malcolm. *The Ohlone Way: Indian Life in the San Francisco–Monterey Bay Area*. Berkeley: Heyday Books, 1978.

Mayfield, Thomas Jefferson. *Indian Summer: Traditional Life among the Choinumne Indians of California's San Joaquin Valley*. Edited by Malcolm Margolin. Berkeley: Heyday Books, 1993.

Phillips, George Harwood. *Indians and Intruders in Central California, 1769–1849*. Norman: University of Oklahoma Press, 1993.

Sandos, James A. *Converting California: Indians and Franciscans in the Missions*. New Haven: Yale University Press, 2004.

Zappia, Natale A. *Traders and Raiders: The Indigenous World of the Colorado Basin, 1540–1859*. Chapel Hill: University of North Carolina Press, 2014.

_____ *Chapter 7* _____

Pacific Northwest Trade and Treaties, 1770s–1860s

Indigenous communities across the Pacific Northwest were connected by water and overland trails in a network of trade and family relations. The Columbia River remains the central feature of the region, but the wetter lands west of the Cascade Range and the drier lands to the east make for different ecological and cultural regions. Densely populated, multilingual plankhouse villages characterized the lower Columbia River and Puget Sound. Cedar canoes were a primary means of travel and cultural identity. To the east, people were more mobile and many adopted horses to pursue buffalo across the Rocky Mountains. Kutenais, Nez Perces, and other eastern peoples were also adept in using canoes on the rivers and lakes and continued to do so even after the adoption of horses. For many people, salmon, lamprey, and sturgeon were important food sources alongside berries, roots, elk, and deer.

Along the Lower Columbia, fish were an obvious and important resource. Smelt arrived in spring, often just as winter stores were running low and the oil-rich fish were a protein and fat-rich food. The trade in eulachon may have given rise to a mispronounced "Ouregan" and thus "Oregon" applied to the region. The Eulachon Trail connected British Columbia and the Columbia River region. The Columbia itself was a trade route between coastal people harvesting shellfish, sea mammals, and other fish to interior people who brought buffalo and hides from the east. Obsidian from the Cascade Range and beyond met *dentalium* shells from Vancouver Island.

Salmon fishing in a river as large as the Columbia was difficult except in places where the river narrowed and the fish were forced to move upstream through falls and rapids. The Dalles was one of the richest fisheries in North America and families from tribes across the Pacific Northwest had fishing platforms that extended over the roaring waters there. Other fishing sites, such as Sherars Bridge on the Deschutes River, Willamette Falls near Oregon City, and the now drowned Celilo Falls on the Columbia still see continued use by tribal fishermen.

INTERACTION WITH OUTSIDERS

Although the Pacific Northwest was geographically distant from some of the early contact points with European colonists, diseases may well have reached the region many years before the arrival of strangers themselves. There is some speculation that the early sixteenth-century diseases that swept over Mexico may have reached all corners of the continent. Whether the population estimates of 200,000 people in the precontact Pacific Northwest reflect earlier waves of disease, it is clear that people suffered terribly with the arrival of smallpox in the 1770s. The disease also lowered fertility and birth rates across the region and sparked a pattern of Euro-American settlement following in the aftermath of epidemics led to a simultaneous reduction of indigenous population and a flood of newcomers.

Native Americans from the region also played a key role in connecting Japan to the rest of the world as Ranald MacDonald, the son of a Hudson's Bay Company (HBC) trader and Raven, a Chinook woman, became the first English speaker to come ashore in Japan in 1848. There, indigenous Ainu rescued him and delivered him to Japanese authorities. MacDonald became an instructor in English and his pupils included the translator for the first American-Japanese treaty. After nearly a year in Japan, MacDonald boarded a passing whaling ship and returned to the Americas.

As elsewhere, the arrival of Europeans brought change to the Pacific Northwest. The late eighteenth century brought a wave of ships to the area, many of them seeking the soft gold of sea otter pelts and hoping to engage in trade with Asia. Vancouver Island became an exotic port of call for Europeans convinced that securing trade from the Nuchahnulth homeland was the key to making a fortune in Canton or Hong Kong. As American, British, French, Russian, and Spanish vessels scoured the area, contact between coastal people and sailing ships became regular. By the 1790s, ships regularly visited the Columbia River, Puget Sound, and Vancouver Island. As trade goods made their way inland, the furs of beaver, mink, martens, and more came to the coast. Thus, inland people understood newcomers to be in almost every direction by the nineteenth century, even if they remained far away.

Contact with outsiders included both long-distance journeys to colonial outposts and sailors who washed ashore aboard storm-damaged ships. One Japanese vessel, the *Hojun-maru*, carried three survivors into Makah territory at Cape Flattery in 1834. Makahs rehabilitated the men, feeding them and allowing them to recuperate until they could join in work as slaves. One of the Japanese men drew a picture of their ship surrounded by Indians and the message eventually made its way to Fort Vancouver where Chief Factor John McLoughlin saw it. In two separate exchanges, the Makahs freed the men to the HBC. Though relatively rare, nearly three dozen Japanese sailors are known to have come ashore along North America's west coast and occasional goods and rarities such as iron made their way into villages.

THE FUR TRADE ERA

The richness of the Pacific Northwest made it a densely populated region, and its long-held position in the continental trade network also made its people shrewd and experienced bargainers. When Europeans arrived to trade, they were initially encouraged by their ability to trade inexpensive goods for pelts. A few pennies worth of glass beads, needles, awls, or hatchets could garner hundreds of dollars in pelts at the Asian markets. However, as European goods became more common, the bargains became less obvious. By the 1800s, many Euro-Americans complained that the Indians drove too hard a bargain and that their dealings were often disappointing. Aside from a few specific goods, which had no effective local substitute, Pacific Northwest Indians simply did not need much of what foreign traders offered. Euro-Americans often found that they needed indigenous foods more than Indians wanted European trade goods. Native people's ability to draw upon the bounty of sea and land made it difficult for newcomers to drive unequal bargains. This more equitable trade also led to disdain from traders and trappers. Traders perceived Indians who did not abandon their traditional rounds to begin trapping beaver as lazy or petulant. It seems clear that many Indians saw no reason to submit to schemes to enrich the HBC and simply did not need the company as much as the company may have needed them.

The first decades of the 1800s would see explorers and traders pour into the Pacific Northwest from almost every direction. English and American ships coasted Oregon and Washington. Americans arrived overland in 1805 with the Lewis and Clark Expedition, followed by the Astorians in 1811. Nez Perces spent considerable time hosting Lewis and Clark and they ultimately considered amity with Americans to be a crucial step toward maintaining their place in the face of Plains tribes with better access to guns. Chinooks, on the other hand, may well have understood the opening of new trade connections as a threat to their near-monopoly on seaborne trade.

The British North West Company built posts in Salish Flathead, Pend Oreille, Spokane, and Walla Walla homelands in 1809–1810. However, by 1821, the British Parliament forced a merger of the North West Company with the HBC, extending a monopoly over trade stretching from Hudson Bay to the Oregon Country. The intervening War of 1812 dashed the American Pacific Fur Company's plans for Fort Astoria in Chinook territory, and the HBC became the *de facto* European presence in the region from 1821 to the 1840s.

As part of the geopolitical contest for western North America, the HBC operated as an arm of the British Empire. In order to secure the region's furs and ports, the HBC formulated a policy that stood in stark contrast to their earlier relationship building with indigenous people. In the Oregon Country, they sought to create a buffer against potential American encroachment by destroying the fur resource south and east of the Columbia River. Removing all of the valuable beaver from this swath of territory was meant to thwart rival trapping efforts. The HBC made no real effort to trade with Indians in this region except incidentally, even as they upset the ecosystems upon which native people relied.

Shoshone territory in southern Idaho and eastern Wyoming became the main front in this ecological warfare to create a fur desert. HBC brigades of over 100 individuals included substantial numbers of Iroquois and other eastern Indians along with native Hawaiians and Métis. These parties issued out from Fort Vancouver on the lower Columbia River to trap nearly year round. Contrasting with the HBC's resource management efforts that allowed other areas in North America to rest and recover, the orders were to kill all furbearers, including beaver pups. This kept parties in the field longer but reduced the number of beaver when most of these trappers' income depended directly upon the number of pelts they could produce. After an incident in 1825 in which a large contingent of Iroquois free trappers abandoned the HBC brigade when offered better trading terms by Americans, the HBC brigade leaders had to carry out dual tasks of ruining the fur trapping and keeping their employees happy enough to return another year. That meant ever-wider circuits for brigades that ultimately reached the Gulf of California.

The final potential entry route for American trappers was California. Annual HBC brigades heavily trapped the Central Valley of California, mirroring their Snake Country sister unit. Little trade with local Indians occurred, but the 1833 brigade was the likely vector bringing malaria from the lower Columbia to California. The disease quickly became endemic and California tribes declined rapidly. The Gold Rush accelerated many of the ecological trends begun by the fur desert as game and waterways came under assault by thousands of miners.

Though some tribes may have benefitted from increased contact with traders, the HBC strategy and competition with American trappers focused the impact of the fur trade in Bannock, Shoshone, and Paiute territory.

Blackfeet had access to British forts on the Saskatchewan and Bow Rivers and thus the HBC chose not to include their homeland in the fur desert. Indeed, the British relied on Blackfeet with a steady supply of guns to stave off any northern encroachment by Americans. But, in the Great Basin, removal of beaver led to a general decline of riparian ecosystems and the dispersal of Paiutes into smaller family bands who could no longer rely upon those resources. In Shoshone territory, buffalo had roamed as far west as the present-day Oregon border, but trappers competing for game drove the animals into local extinction. By 1840, tribes would only find buffalo herds at the end of lengthy journeys east of the Rocky Mountains. Other game declined as well as elk, deer, mountain sheep, mountain goats, and antelope sustained hungry trappers and their families.

From 1825 to 1840, Americans also essentially took over Shoshone trading fairs and transformed them into mountain man rendezvouses. Fur companies used several sites in Shoshone territory as annual resupply points for trapping parties. Bannocks, Crows, Salish Flatheads, Nez Perces, Shoshones, and Utes used these month-long summer rendezvouses as opportunities to engage in trade as well. These fairs were also an occasion for horse and foot racing, wrestling matches, drinking, marriages, disputes, and discussion. Blackfeet, who had perhaps the most to lose from increased trading connections, attacked rival tribes intermixed with American trappers at or near the rendezvous in 1827, 1828, and 1832, but did little to change the trading patterns.

Tribes important to the HBC's economic schemes fared better. Nez Perces and other Columbia Plateau tribes supplied many of the horses that enabled the lengthy brigade expeditions. Trade and travel between HBC posts also relied on Indian cooperation and Cowlitz, Chehalis, and Nisquallys both supplied western posts with game and offered labor for schemes such as the Puget Sound Agricultural Company farms at Cowlitz Prairie. The prairie openings maintained by Indian burning became the sites of farms whose produce fed both HBC employees and, after 1839, the Russians and Aleuts of the Russian American Company.

The HBC brigade system also relied upon the uncompensated families of employees. Indian women relied upon generations of knowhow to process furs and live away from the confines of the fort. Wives and children carried out innumerable camp tasks, freeing up men for hunting and trapping. In contrast to the efficiency of the multiethnic HBC brigades, American trapping parties tended to be all male and comparatively inexperienced. In essence, every American trapping party was a potential war party, while the HBC more often appeared as a mobile village of families. The HBC brigades were not immune from raiding, but Americans encountered more conflict with Indian war parties. Over time, Americans increasingly turned to hunting for beaver in Blackfoot territory and encountered stiff resistance.

Henry Warre's 1848 depiction of the Hudson's Bay Company's Oregon Country headquarters at Fort Vancouver. The headquarters was a community of Europeans, peoples from regional tribes, Native Hawaiians, Iroquois, Métis, and others. Though the fur trade offered greater opportunities for trade, it also brought devastating disease to the Pacific Northwest. (Encyclopaedia Britannica/UIG Via Getty Images)

The legacy of tribal relations with the HBC in the Pacific Northwest is mixed. As a vector of disease and environmental disruption, tribes throughout the region suffered. The Willamette Valley homeland of Kalapuyas became a primary retirement area for former HBC trappers. Many native women found advantages for themselves and their children in marrying into a fur-trading family and those ties created a French-Indian culture with connections to both the British Company and indigenous families. Children educated in the HBC colony at Red River (Winnipeg) or serving as important figures in the regional posts were important bridges to an increasingly Europeanized world.

MISSIONARIES AND SPIRITUAL CHANGE

Just as Europeans relied upon native knowledge of geography and ecology, Indians facing a changing world began to inquire more deeply about Europeans' seeming abilities to better fend off sickness and increase in number. Exchanges of spiritual beliefs were regular, but missionaries became authoritative sources for European knowledge. In the wake of devastating epidemics, Indians may have been ripe for conversion or experimentation with alternatives to tradition. New spiritual approaches offered hopes of turning the tide against the losses that devastated many tribes.

In 1826, the first two indigenous boys from the Pacific Northwest traveled east to the Red River Settlement to attend school. Together, these chiefs' sons represented the first of several families' decisions to better understand and address the problems wrought by the increasingly unavoidable interaction with Euro-Americans by sending their children into the white world. Kootenai Pelly died at the school in 1830, but Spokane Garry (Slough-Keetcha) returned to become a headman, teaching English and Protestantism while navigating the crises that faced the Spokane Tribe.

A group of four Salish Flatheads and Nez Perce traveled from their homeland to St. Louis in 1831 in order to make contact with Americans who held the power of the book. American missionaries took this to be a version of the Macedonian Call, a voice from the wilderness asking for missionaries to bring the Christian bible to them. Whether they were primarily interested religion, a solution to the plagues sweeping their lands, or literacy and writing remains unclear. However, a band of Iroquois led by Big Ignace LaMousse had settled among the Salish Flatheads and were instrumental in the spread of an Iroquoian version of Catholicism. Both Catholics and Protestants answered the call to the Northwest, creating some confusion over differing versions of Christianity.

Jason Lee established Willamette Mission near Salem, Oregon in 1834 but primarily addressed his efforts to nearby French-Canadian and American families. Malaria had decimated Kalapuyas and Lee seems to have been uninterested in ministering to Indians in any case. In contrast, Marcus and Narcissa Whitman loom large over Pacific Northwest history due to forcing their way into Cayuse territory more than 200 miles east of Fort Vancouver. Nearly forgotten with the focus on the tragic melodrama of the Whitman Massacre is the far more mutually respectful relationship between the Henry and Eliza Spalding and their Nez Perce neighbors. Part of the same 1836 mission, the Spaldings chose to locate among Nez Perces in part because of the positive relationship between the HBC and the tribe.

The Whitmans entrenched themselves, uninvited, on a Cayuse gathering area. That Cayuses spoke a language not shared by other neighboring tribes also exacerbated the relationship. Narcissa Whitman, in particular, became more antagonistic toward the Indians she was supposed to be serving after the accidental drowning of her daughter. Her high handedness, including injecting emetics into melons grown on the Whitman farm so that anyone who stole from them would be overtaken by diarrhea—a symptom of many deadly diseases then sweeping over the villages—may have been a final straw. What was clear was the Whitmans' role in assisting the overlanders who came through their farm. The Whitmans adopted, at least temporarily, many children who had lost their parents along the trail and Cayuses could not but wonder at the deaths of their own children and the steady stream of children entering the Whitman home.

By 1847, Cayuses had enough, and sought to eject the Americans from Waiilatpu. When Cayuses rose up against the Whitmans, it triggered an immediate response from whites. Peter Skene Ogden, a former leader of the HBC's Snake Country brigades, negotiated for the release of captives from Cayuses and the surrender of five Cayuses. A large crowd watched the 1850 hanging in Oregon City, even though it was clear that these Cayuses saw themselves as martyrs staving off all-out war against their people.

Fathers François Blanchet and Modeste Demers were among the most influential of the Catholic missionaries, and it seems clear that French-Canadians, Metis, and Iroquois all brought various levels of Catholic beliefs to Pacific Northwest Indians well before the arrival of formal missionaries. Blanchet established a mission at Cowlitz Prairie in 1838 using a Catholic Ladder to aid in delivering Catholic doctrine. This wooden carving was a graphic depiction of several key biblical events and *saghalie* sticks, a portable ladder on a smaller scale, became a widespread means for Indians to understand the new religious ideas of both Catholics and Protestants. Demers established another Catholic outpost to the north at Nisqually and traveled widely and used the Chinook Jargon to interact with many tribes throughout the region.

If the Whitman Massacre was a symptom of the increasing friction between the world wrought by American emigrants and indigenous culture, so too were the series of decisions that almost every village faced by the 1830s. An almost endless procession of wagons continued to deliver more whites to the Pacific Northwest. Cholera was nearly endemic to wagon trains and malaria swept the lower Columbia and Willamette valleys. Thousands died and villages collapsed as survivors relocated and sought ways to reverse the sudden decline in fortune.

Syncretic religious practices began to spread among many Columbia Plateau tribes, perhaps in part due to the large number of shamen who perished in these years. Whites' comparative ability to stave off disease was not lost on Indians and the new missionaries apparently offered alternative strategies for how to best interact with the spiritual world. Many Pacific Northwest Indians had already incorporated elements of Christianity into older practices.

By 1850, a Wanapum spiritual leader from the mid-Columbia River named Smohalla rose to prominence as he spread his vision of the Dreamer religion. This retained many elements of the older Seven Drums *washat* ceremonies, but rejection of white culture was one of the central new elements.

Revealing schisms over the strategies to deal with the increasing demands of a growing white population, Walla Walla chief Homli and Smohalla clashed over the treaty-making process. Smohalla and a band of followers eventually left his homeland to relocate at Priest Rapids on the upper Columbia River in Sinkiuse territory. There, he came into conflict with Chief Moses over similar issues. Smohalla then made a lengthy journey to California and the Southwest before returning to a more receptive community. As elsewhere, fundamental disagreements over what strategy to pursue in the face of the ongoing crisis created schisms in Native communities. It simply was not clear whether working toward better agreements with whites or a more radical path of rejection was the better way forward.

AMERICAN RULE, TREATY-MAKING, AND RESISTANCE

The new settler culture brought another unique aspect of Indian policy to the Pacific Northwest. The Oregon Donation Land Act of 1850 extended the policy of the Oregon provisional government to give every male over the age of eighteen 320 acres, and 640 acres to every married couple. Reflecting the reality of families in the Oregon Country, the law extended this policy to specifically include "American half-breed Indians" as eligible for these lands. The wording was deliberate in excluding British former trappers and requiring that applicants for land not include the indigenous inhabitants. Only those individuals who were part of the Pacific Northwest's American community were included. Both Acts preceded any efforts to secure title to the land through treaties with tribes. Instead, in the Oregon Country, the federal government encouraged even greater migration by giving Indian land to settlers without any consultation.

The Oregon Donation Land Act was also responsible for a sudden rush of settlers into southern Oregon. The initial claims to the Willamette Valley bottomlands extended southward into other river valleys and in the early 1850s, the discovery of gold in the Klamath Mountains brought a surge of would-be miners and farmers into the region. As settlers and miners flooded southward to California and then back to southern Oregon, violence became regular. By 1855, 2.8 million acres of land claims had been entered under the Donation Land Act.

Only in 1851 was there an effort to secure land through legal means. Anson Dart and three subagents negotiated several treaties, but Congress rejected the agreements and revoked Dart's authority. A few years later, Oregon Governor Joel Palmer negotiated nine new treaties with tribes from 1853 to 1855. Between late 1854 and early 1856, Washington Territory Governor Isaac Stevens negotiated ten more treaties. None of these treaties reserved specific rights to Indians until mid-1855. At the Walla Walla treaty negotiations, he agreed that the Columbia River tribes could reserve fishing rights while using threats to coerce chiefs into signing. The treaties with Walla Wallas, Cayuses and Umatilla; Nez Perce; and the "Tribes of Middle Oregon" or Warm Springs included specific provisions for fishing, hunting, and gathering. Earlier treaties that did not include these specific points created a two-tiered system of rights.

Still, some areas such as southwest Washington remained entirely without ratified treaties. Congress also rejected the Willamette Valley Kalapuya treaty and another with Oregon's coastal tribes. This meant that the decimated people whose homeland had become the center of settlement in the region were increasingly ignored. They also joined dozens of other people as landless tribes with an unclear federal status. Their struggles to maintain and regain the federal recognition indicated by the 1850s treaty councils continue into the twenty-first century. Cowlitz, for example, only regained federal acknowledgment in 2000. For Chinooks, the people who aided Lewis and Clark in securing the U.S. claim to the region over the winter of 1805–1806, the irony of not being federally recognized is deep. Although the tribe briefly gained recognition in 2001, the Bureau of Indian Affairs rescinded this in 2002.

The Palmer and Stevens treaties became something of a template for later treaty negotiations. Across the border in British Columbia, Governor James Douglas consulted regularly with Stevens as he arranged a series of treaties meant to resolve the British Crown's title for the settled areas of southern Vancouver Island. Ultimately, those treaties were the basis for dealings with people elsewhere in the British Empire, as far away as the Maoris of New Zealand. These Pacific Northwest treaties were also used as a framework for the many subsequent Plains treaties of the 1860s and 1870s.

The provision that Pacific Northwest Indians universally insisted upon for hunting and fishing in their "usual and accustomed places" guaranteed that the richness of indigenous culture in the region remained intertwined with resources. Even given their diminished numbers and difficulty in negotiating fairly as tribal nations under strict deadlines, these explicit rights have remained important aspects of the treaties. Though many factions did not agree with the result of the treaties, these agreements between the federal government and tribal nations have continued to be fundamental to both tribal identity and their roles in much of modern politics. In issues ranging from game management to clean water to energy policy, tribes often have senior standing due to their grandfathers' insistence on the tribal right to their traditional resources.

Disagreements over the Stevens Treaties are intimately connected to the outbreak of warfare in Washington as well. Pro- and antitreaty factions fractured indigenous communities and fighting broke out on both sides of the

Cascade Range by late 1855. The Puget Sound War and the Yakama War often appear as two separate but loosely related events, but it is clear that familial ties and alliances connected the two. Prospectors violating the new Yakama Reservation triggered violence when two men raped a Yakama woman. Qualchin killed the men in retribution, and when the Indian Agent, Andrew Bolon, attempted to approach him another Yakama, Mosheel killed Bolon. The situation rapidly became a full-blown conflict between the U.S. military and Yakamas led by Kamiakin. Oregon governor George Curry led a volunteer militia in attacking neutral Indians of eastern Washington, bringing Cayuses, Palouses, Umatillas, and Walla Wallas into the conflict.

West of the Cascades, Leschi, a Nisqually headman whose mother was Yakama, began consolidating a coalition of tribes to fight and briefly threatened the Puget Sound settlements. Seattle evacuated and Stevens, who remained Washington's governor, urged a war of extermination. Further, he detained several white farmers he suspected of collaborating with Leschi and Kamiakin. A small party of Snoqualmie and Snohomish men joined Stevens' efforts and attacked enemy Indians as well. As the war turned against the Yakamas, Kamiakin escaped to Canada.

The Coeur d'Alene War followed on the heels of the Yakama settlement in 1858 and was an extension of earlier fighting. This phase began when some Spokanes broke with Spokane Garry to join Coeur d'Alenes, Palouses, and Yakamas in a battle with American soldiers near Steptoe Butte. In retaliation, a punitive expedition into Spokane territory captured the tribal horse herd and slaughtered them. Garry worked to secure a reservation for his tribe in their homeland for nearly thirty years, but ultimately signed a treaty to move to the Coeur d'Alene Reservation to the east.

The 1860s brought a renewal of treaty making. However, the new treaties were almost exclusively a process meant to reduce Indian claims and reservations. For example, Nez Perces signed a treaty in 1863 to reduce the size of their reservation by 90 percent, ceding land to gold miners and sowing the seeds of a future war. The same year, the fraudulent Huntington Treaty attempted to end Warm Springs Indians' rights to off-reservation fishing and hunting. The treaty submitted to Congress was not the one that tribal leaders had agreed to which simply required a pass system to leave the reservation. Once it was revealed, Warm Springs Indians rejected the treaty and continued to fish, and it would take over a century for courts to rule that the restrictions of the 1865 treaty were illegal.

PROFILE: COMCOMLY

Comcomly was a headman of the Chinook Indians who lived at the mouth of the Columbia River. Known as a shrewd trader who maintained good relations with outsiders, his repeated interactions with Euro-American visitors played a large role in shaping outside perceptions of the Pacific Northwest. The Lower Chinooks became a primary conduit for trade and Comcomly managed the coastal trade by funneling furs and pelts through his village. Moving from subchief to become the preeminent leader of his people in the first decade of the 1800s, Comcomly had several wives and many slaves.

It is unclear whether Comcomly reported a real threat or manipulated American traders when we told them in 1812 of large numbers of Indians from the north bent on destroying the outpost at Fort Astoria on the south side of the Columbia. The Americans rewarded him with gifts and Comcomly solidified his position as both trading partner and ally. Marriage between traders and Comcomly's daughters further cemented the alliance. However, the mid-1810s brought changes to the Chinook position. Other people from the interior began traveling to the fort in order trade, weakening but not eclipsing the Chinooks' middleman status. The War of 1812 also removed Americans and replaced them with British traders whom Comcomly seems to have initially rejected. Eventually another of his daughters, "the Princess of Wales," married Alexander McKenzie, a prominent British trader. (S'Klallams later killed McKenzie and took Comcomly's daughter hostage to force a change in trading policies with enemy tribes and in a possible effort to redeem their relatives held as slaves in Chinook villages. A punitive expedition by the HBC attacked two S'Klallam villages and rescued the Princess of Wales as cannon-fire from a nearby ship rained down.)

Comcomly's fortunes changed with the 1824 removal of the HBC post from the mouth of the Columbia to establish Fort Vancouver farther inland. The death of two of his sons soon after sparked changes of sorcery against a neighboring Chinook band and intermittent violence stretched on for years. Chinooks may have been divided in their loyalties in these years, but they shared in the horrific effects of an 1830 outbreak of malaria. Comcomly and hundreds of other Chinooks succumbed as the people of the Lower Columbia experienced the most deadly round of disease to that point in the Pacific Northwest.

PROFILE: LESCHI AND QUIEMUTH

Leschi and Quiemuth were both Nisqually headmen and they represented the tribe in the council resulting in the Treaty of Medicine Creek in 1854. Leschi spoke out about his dissatisfaction with the treaty imposed upon Nisquallys and Puyallups, especially in regard to the size and location of reservations. Other Indians in the region felt the same and war broke out in the aftermath of the treaty negotiations. By October of 1855, fighting had broken out in across Washington. In a brief skirmish between volunteer militia and Puget Sound Indians on October 31, 1855, Colonel Abrams Moses was killed. Governor of Washington Territory Isaac Stevens placed the blame for Moses's "murder" on Leschi, the Nisqually chief he saw as the architect of native opposition. However, Leschi was miles away from the battle site and only one man placed him at the scene. In addition, the U.S. Army recognized the engagement as a battle and informed Leschi that he could not be tried for any crime. Leschi was captured in November 1856 and shortly after, his older brother, Quiemuth, turned himself in to Stevens in hopes of ending the fighting. However, while staying in Stevens' home, an unknown assailant murdered Quiemuth, shooting and stabbing him in Stevens' guest bed. Stevens believed the murderer to be the son-in-law of a man killed in the recent fighting, but all of the men on guard testified that they had seen nothing and Quiemuth's executioner went free.

Stevens then pressed for Leschi's prosecution and the single supposed eyewitness chaired the Grand Jury that indicted Leschi. In spite of this, the first trial ended in a hung jury with at least two white jurors believing the eyewitness account to be an invention. Subsequent trials resulted in Leschi's conviction and the State Supreme Court upheld the charge, reasoning that Leschi was the leader of the people responsible for the death of Moses and others in the Puget Sound War.

The Nisqually Tribe has long held that Leschi was not responsible for Moses's death. In 2004, following the Washington Supreme Court's refusal to follow a recommendation from the state legislature to hear Leschi's case, a historical court composed of active judges convened to retry Leschi. The court ruling that no crime existed in Moses's death during a time of war exonerated Leschi but not issued any statement about his presence.

REFERENCES AND FURTHER READING

Beckham, Stephen Dow. *Requiem for a People: The Rogue Indians and the Frontiersmen*. Northwest Reprint ed. Corvallis: Oregon State University Press, 1996.

Blee, Lisa. *Framing Chief Leschi: Narratives and the Politics of Historical Justice*. Chapel Hill: University of North Carolina Press, 2014.

Boyd, Robert. *The Coming of the Spirit of Pestilence: Introduced Infectious Diseases and Population Decline among Northwest Coast Indians, 1774–1874*. Seattle: University of Washington Press, 1999.

Cebula, Larry. *Plateau Indians and the Quest for Spiritual Power, 1700–1850*. Lincoln: University of Nebraska Press, 2003.

Douthit, Nathan. *Uncertain Encounters: Indians and Whites at Peace and War in Southern Oregon, 1820s–1860s*. Corvallis: Oregon State University Press, 2002.

Fisher, Andrew H. *Shadow Tribe: The Making of Columbia River Indian Identity.* Seattle: University of Washington Press, 2010.

Furtwangler, Albert. *Bringing Indians to the Book.* Seattle: University of Washington Press, 2005.

Harmon, Alexandra, ed. *The Power of Promises: Rethinking Indian Treaties in the Pacific Northwest.* Seattle: University of Washington Press, 2008.

Jetté, Melinda Marie. *At the Hearth of the Crossed Races: A French-Indian Community in Nineteenth-Century Oregon, 1812–1859.* Corvallis: Oregon State University Press, 2015.

Peterson, Jacqueline. *Sacred Encounters: Father DeSmet and the Indians of the Rocky Mountain West.* Norman: University of Oklahoma Press, 1993.

Pinkham, Allen V., and Steven R. Evans. *Lewis and Clark among the Nez Perce: Strangers in the Land of the Nimiipuu.* Washburn, ND: Dakota Institute Press, 2015.

Reid, Joshua L. *The Sea Is My Country: The Maritime World of the Makahs.* New Haven, CT: Yale University Press, 2015.

Whaley, Gray H. *Oregon and the Collapse of Illahee: U.S. Empire and the Transformation of an Indigenous World, 1792–1859.* Chapel Hill: University of North Carolina Press, 2010.

_____ *Chapter 8* _____

Removal and Reservations, 1820s–1860s

Many tribes went through a process of removal from their homelands. Some peoples fled their homelands under the pressure of increased colonization and conflict and others faced forced removal by federal troops. The Cherokee Trail of Tears in 1831 may be the most well-known aspect of Indian Removal, but a similar process uprooted others from the American South, the Old Northwest, and from across the West. New, often radically different geographies awaited removed tribes. In many cases, the newcomers crowded alongside other relocated tribes in other people's homelands. As Indian Country shrank, competition for limited resources increased as Plains Indians found ever more tribes arriving to government-designated reservations.

Removal was far from being a simple or uniform process. Each people and each relocated village or family experienced their own hardships of being torn from their homeland. Some were quite effective in their abilities to negotiate around removal and remain in their lands. Most were less fortunate and the rampant disease and starvation, violence and cruelty, and loss continue to affect Native Americans today. The ability to overcome the horrors of this era and persevere as a people is a testament to the resilience of indigenous culture.

Many removed peoples found themselves in the new Indian Territory of Oklahoma. Other reservations extended northward in a swath through Kansas, Nebraska, and into the Dakotas. These lands were largely beyond white settlement in the 1820s and 1830s in an area thought to be unfit for an agrarian nation such as the United States. Associating soil fertility with trees, Americans had made the mistake of seeing the Great Plains as a "Great American Desert," unfit for farming. However, Caddos, Osages, Poncas, Pawnees and others provided evidence that Native Americans could not only live, but also thrive in those same lands.

Federal policies relied on a willful fallacy that all Indians were essentially the same. Thus, removal followed in the pattern of other governmental processes that gave little consideration to cultural differences, ecological knowledge, or economic and political relationships. Placing Eastern Woodlands peoples on the Great Plains seems not to have generated much concern in the face of an ideology that indigenous peoples must not inhabit lands desired by white citizens.

Ignorance combined with antipathy to create a widespread policy of removal. Some may have truly believed that removal was the only hope for survival of Native Americans. However, many whites were indifferent about Indians' fate. They believed removal was simply a stage in the inevitable disappearance of Native Americans.

THE ROOTS OF NORTHERN REMOVAL

The early 1800s brought a surge of settlers into the Ohio River Valley and beyond. The Old Northwest from Ohio to Illinois and Minnesota became the new frontier for an expanding United States. New farms connected to the transportation network of the rivers flowing to the Great Lakes and the Mississippi could connect with a larger commercial world as farming towns and new cities sprang up. As we have seen in earlier chapters, this resulted in increased conflict between the United States and tribes across the region. The warfare that forced land cessions upon tribes created a pattern of withdrawal to the west in the face of a rising tide of white farms supported by the American military. By the 1820s, Tecumseh's confederacy had been defeated on the battlefield and few large tribes remained near the new American settlements.

The Indian Civilization Fund Act, passed by Congress in 1817, explicitly joined governmental and religious efforts. Federal funding went to schools run by Protestant missionary societies teaching academic skills such as reading, writing, and mathematics, but also actively stripped students of their culture. This was the seed for boarding schools and reservation schools established over the following century with much the same mission, including among peoples to be removed. By 1824, Congress decided that it needed an agency to administer the funds attached to the program and in a renewal of the Act created the Bureau of Indian Affairs to do so.

Northern removal was no less systematic or consolidated than the more familiar southern removal. In both cases, broadly applied removal policies and practices collided with individual and tribal decisions. In Illinois, Indiana, Michigan and Ohio, Kickapoos, Lenapes, Meskwakis (Foxes), Miamis, Ojibwas, Potawatomis, Sauks (Sacs), Senecas, Shawnees, Wyandots, and others continued to live in much reduced territories. Many lived in multitribal villages composed of the survivors of earlier conflict and forced removals. This gave rise to observations that the Indians of the region were somehow less cohesive or weaker than southern tribes. Several tribes remained on lands scattered across the region, intermixed with newly arrived settlers who paid little heed to Indian claims or territories. Many whites argued for the further forced consolidation of peoples on reservations to the west even as Indians protested that farmers took lands, chased away the game, and began plowing before treaty councils could address any conflicts. Tribes also protested that crossing the Mississippi River into Dakota Sioux territory put them closer to enemy raiding parties. An 1830 agreement by multiple tribes ceded land to the United States and created a forty-mile wide Neutral Ground buffer between Dakota Sioux and several tribes, including the Sauks and Meskwakis.

BLACK HAWK'S WAR AND AFTERMATH

In the wake of the War of 1812, Americans still saw the hands of their British rivals behind indigenous resistance. Many communities simply moved west to avoid confrontation but many Sauks, Meskwakis, and Potawatomies remained in their homeland. The final steps toward removal in the North hinged upon the Sauk leader Black Hawk's refusal to move west in 1832. As word spread of Black Hawk's intentions, many Indians from across the region joined his followers, swelling their ranks. The presence of so many Indians frightened white communities, leading them to call for military action. After a confrontation with ill-disciplined militia that led to the death of eleven soldiers, Black Hawk and his "British Band" followers retreated and sought to escape west to Iowa.

The violence reached a climax at the Battle of Bad Axe River, where hundreds of Sauks and Meskwakis died as the U.S. Army pinned the tribe against the river and opened fire. Those who made it to the other side met a party of Sioux who coordinated their attack with the U.S. officials. Only 200 of an original 2,000 members of Black Hawk's band survived. A few weeks later, Black Hawk surrendered and was imprisoned. On orders of President Jackson, Black Hawk and several other leaders were sent east to Washington, D.C. before being imprisoned again in Virginia. Sent west again months later, authorities released Black Hawk into Keokuk's custody in Iowa where he dictated his autobiography and settled among other Sauks and Meskwakis.

The 1850s brought a second northern removal as Indians who had resettled in Kansas, and Nebraska encountered the familiar situation of whites settling on or near reservations agreed to less than a generation earlier. The Kansas-Nebraska Act, usually appearing in historical texts as a failed experiment in popular sovereignty and a step on the road to the Civil War, also brought a flood of settlers to the tall grass plains.

Some tribes or portions of tribes decided that a better option was to leave the United States entirely. Kickapoos faced the same process of removal as all other eastern tribes. They were initially sent to Missouri and then relocated to Kansas in 1832. Portions of the tribe continued to move south, eventually settling in Texas and Mexico. A second migration occurred in 1864 during the Civil War, when around 700 Kickapoo moved south to Texas and Mexico. After the war the United States and Mexico agreed to remove the Kickapoo to Indian Territory, though some Kickapoos remained behind, making Mexico their new home.

THE ROOTS OF SOUTHERN REMOVAL

The United States presented a contradictory program that stands at the root of later actions by Andrew Jackson and the State of Georgia. Partly because so many tribes had allied with the British in the American Revolution, the new American government understood Indians to be enemies that they needed to either sway into allegiance or push beyond any zone of settler contact. Federal Indian policy focused on civilizing peoples they understood to be uncivilized, with the possibility of eventual citizenship. At the same time, the federal government moved to extinguish Indian land claims where settlers encroached. In an 1802 agreement with the Jefferson administration, Georgia ceded its claims to western lands that became Alabama and Mississippi in return for a guarantee that the federal government would purchase the remaining Cherokee and Muscogee lands within the state.

After completing the Louisiana Purchase, Jefferson encouraged further voluntary removal of Indians to the newly acquired Trans-Mississippi territory. The land swap would separate settlers and Indians while making more land available for his Empire of Liberty composed of white yeoman farmers. In 1808, a party of Cherokees applied to Jefferson for citizenship in order to avoid removal. In response, Jefferson encouraged the Cherokees to fully adopt agriculture before they could be considered as equals to American citizens. Protestant missionaries advocated for these policies and encouraged Western dress and food in their schools as well as a near reversal of traditional Cherokee roles. To become Americans, Cherokee women would have to abandon their fields and connections to land, while men ceased hunting and became farmers. Many Cherokees tended toward a partial adaptation in which women carried on their role as growers of crops and men shifted to raise cattle and horses. Like their white neighbors, some wealthier Cherokees purchased African American slaves. However, Jefferson and his successors believed that Indian farmers of either type would need less land than a people who continued to engage in traditional hunting.

Whether as slaves, maroon refugees, or as partners, African-Americans had become an ever-larger portion of the peoples living in Indian villages across the South. Indian Country offered a potential escape from white-owned plantations and households beyond the effective reach of British control. By the early 1800s, "Black Indians" had become notable members of many tribes. As chattel slavery expanded into the interior with the rise of the Cotton Kingdom and white settlers, the situation for those Black Indians became increasingly complicated. Some continued as slaves to Indian owners, others married into families and they and their offspring remained free. White culture and white laws forced many families to make difficult decisions about how to continue to incorporate blacks into their communities as distinctions between Indians and blacks became issues of freedom and control.

Spanish Florida was the home to many African-Americans who had escaped the United States altogether. There they joined former Muscogees and Yamasees who had withdrawn to Florida in over the 1700s. Spanish authorities tolerated and even encouraged the growth of Seminole culture as something of a buffer against British invasion from colonies to the north. In several places, communities of Black Seminole *cimarróns* or maroons grew alongside other Seminole villages. However, Seminoles' stand against Americans in the War of 1812 situated them as enemies of the expanding United States. In 1823, they signed the Treaty of Moultrie Creek agreeing to a large central Florida reservation.

Also in 1823, Chief Justice John Marshall issued a key U.S. Supreme Court decision based on land sales fifty years earlier. Thomas Johnson's bought land from Piankeshaw Indians in 1773 and 1775 in the Ohio Country and William M'Intosh later obtained a patent to the same land from the federal government. Though it quickly became evident that the Johnson and M'Intosh claims were actually not the same, and in fact did not even overlap, both parties pursued the case to force a ruling. The *Johnson v. M'Intosh* decision stated that individuals could not purchase land from tribes. However, Marshall recognized that Indians were the original inhabitants of the land and that following the logic of the Doctrine of Discovery, the United States had inherited sovereignty and the right of preemption over indigenous lands. In essence, Indians could occupy lands, but could not own them. Only the federal government could transfer indigenous people's title to land.

CHEROKEE REMOVAL

Cherokees attempted to stop land sales to the United States even as political power shifted away from clans to the Tribal Council. In their 1827 Constitution, Cherokees declared themselves a sovereign nation as part of

Portrait of John Ross, Cherokee leader. Like other eastern tribes forced into removals, the Cherokee were split over the decision of whether or not to cooperate with federal and state authorities. Ross, as the elected chief, led the opposition to removal but ultimately moved west with his people over the Trail of Tears. (Library of Congress)

their strategy to hold on to their land. The following year, the *Cherokee Phoenix* newspaper began publication in both English and in Cherokee, using the alphabet developed by Sequoyah to press a nationalist perspective. The Tribal Council revoked tribal citizenship from Cherokees who moved west and in 1829, added a death penalty for any Cherokees attempting to sell Cherokee land. The effort to force a nation-to-nation relationship with the United States by developing a Western-style constitution and concentrating power centrally did not change the fundamental relationship with the states. Encouraged by Jackson's election, the State of Georgia unilaterally annexed Cherokee lands in direct contradiction of the *Johnson v. M'Intosh* ruling.

Led by Chief John Ross, a group of Cherokees pressed their case against Georgia and in 1831, Marshall and the Supreme Court again made a foundational ruling in Indian Law. Though Marshall declared in *Cherokee*

Nation v. Georgia that Cherokees were a "domestic, dependent nation" and thus had no standing as U.S. citizens before the Court, he also went on to rule that the Cherokee Nation was a ward of the federal government. Their status as native nations reaffirmed that the responsibility for all negotiation was through the federal government. Though this decision stands as the foundation of the principle of tribal sovereignty and the federal relationship today, both the Jackson administration and the state of Georgia continued to harass the tribes.

The following year the Supreme Court issued yet another decision of critical importance to the tribes resisting removal. *Worcester v. Georgia* focused on the State of Georgia's attempt to enforce a law making it illegal for whites to enter Indian lands without a state license of residency. Samuel Worcester was one of several white missionaries who had come to Cherokee lands to assist in education and worked closely with Elias Boudinot to translate materials into Cherokee, including the Bible. Worcester and a handful of other missionaries refused to leave and they found themselves at the heart of the ongoing clash between Georgia's state's rights arguments and the unpopular opinion of the Marshall Court. The Cherokee Nation hired lawyers to defend the missionaries sentenced to hard labor. Reiterating his earlier statements, Marshall wrote that Indian nations retained "their original natural rights" and that States could not interfere or revoke the rights of a sovereign nation. Even after the Supreme Court ruled, Georgia Governor William Lumpkin only released Worcester after several months and a coerced promise that he would not revisit Cherokee lands.

Andrew Jackson effectively ignored the court rulings and is said to have responded to Marshall's opinion with the retort, "Let him enforce it!" Though likely apocryphal, the statement summed up Jackson's actions as the Supreme Court had no means with which to impose their consistent assertions that Georgia was in violation of federal law in their coercion of Cherokees. Jackson had long believed that Indian nations were a fiction and that there was no reason to negotiate with them. Congress and Jackson had acted together to pass the Indian Removal Act in 1830. Small groups had moved west since the 1810s, but the majority had remained. The Act gave President Jackson the authority to negotiate a new round of treaties requiring Indians to give up their homelands and move west.

Many Cherokees prepared for the worst and began to sell their property and goods to nearby whites. In 1834, Georgia ordered the survey of Cherokee lands and initiated a lottery to distribute land to white settlers after the Cherokee removal. As white settlers began a mad rush to claim Cherokee land and property, the tribe itself was in the midst of political crisis and split that would have repercussions for decades to come. One group, the Treaty Party, led by Major Ridge, John Ridge, and Stand Watie, believed the best course of action at that point was removal. Principal Chief John Ross and his followers opposed this removal and the federal government used this split to facilitate their plans. In December 1835, the Treaty Party led by Major Ridge signed the Treaty of New Echota, committing the entire tribe to removal west of the Mississippi River. The United States Senate quickly ratified the treaty, and with Jackson's signature the federal government rapidly moved to compensate Cherokees for their land and organize their removal.

The removal process took nearly three years. At first nearly 2000 Cherokees, mainly members of the Treaty Party, moved west to Indian Territory. This left about 16,000 Cherokees under the leadership of John Ross who resisted removal. Initially sent in to maintain the peace between settlers and the Cherokees, the U.S. Army eventually rounded up the remaining Cherokees, sending them to camps for enrollment and then removal west. The trip was an arduous one made worse by bad weather and tough terrain. Sickness, depression, exposure, poor food, and little medical care caused the death of many Cherokee people. It is estimated that one quarter or nearly 4,000 Cherokee people died en route to Indian Territory. The tribe called this suffering "Nunna daul Tsunyi" or the Trail of Tears.

Not all Cherokee people left their homeland and removed west. Some hid in Georgia and other places, often living on the fringes of white society. One group coalesced in North Carolina and with the assistance of whites and the state government purchased land and began a new life there. Around 10,000 Cherokees remain in western North Carolina today.

OTHER RESISTANCE TO SOUTHERN REMOVAL

The experiences of Cherokees were mirrored in many other native communities throughout the southeast portion of the United States. Seeking stay on their homelands, Choctaw, Chickasaw, Muscogee and Seminole people sought to accommodate newcomers while retaining their heritage and culture. Unfortunately, white settlers, state officials, and the federal government worked to remove these communities despite their best efforts to remain in their homelands. Each state government enacted laws that discriminated against Indian communities and offered enticements and threats to encourage removal.

In 1830, the Choctaw Nation signed the Treaty of Dancing Rabbit Creek, which ceded millions of acres of land to Alabama and Mississippi. While promised cash, goods, and protection, the federal government failed to live up to its promises, and between 1832 and 1839, Choctaws removed to Indian Territory. Again the trek was difficult with many people succumbing to disease and poor treatment along the way. Once in Indian Territory, Choctaw people sought to rebuild their lives the best they could in light of the circumstances.

Chickasaws also faced similar circumstances in northern Mississippi and southern Arkansas. Pressure mounted on their homelands after Choctaws signed their treaty in 1830. By 1837, Chickasaws began the process of removal facing many of the same challenges as the Choctaws and Cherokees. Chickasaw removal was completed by 1840. The Muscogee also came under increasing pressure to remove in the early 1830s, and Opothleyoholo, their leader, eventually signed the Second Treaty of Washington in 1832, agreeing removal from their homeland in Alabama. Once again, the federal government rounded up Muscogees, placing them in concentration camps, and then forcing them to march to Indian Territory. By 1837, nearly 15,000 people, the bulk of Muscogees were removed from their homeland with 3,500 losing their lives on the trail. One important aspect of these removals is that African-Americans, whether slave, free or of mixed heritage, often accompanied these southern tribes on removal. These were some of the first African-Americans to enter into the territories west of the Mississippi River.

The same year that Muscogees signed the Treaty of Washington, the Seminole Nation agreed to the Treaty of Payne's Landing, stipulating their removal to Indian Territory. Nearly 3,000 Seminoles made the journey to Indian Territory but the bulk of the tribe remained in Florida and resisted removal. Under Osceola (Asin Yahola) and other leaders, Seminoles attacked agents and soldiers attempting to enforce removal. Seminoles ambushed the U.S. Army at Fort King, killing over one hundred soldiers. This was the spark that ignited a seven-year war between the Seminole Nation and the United States. Some Seminoles continued to Indian Territory but as a result of the war the tribe has members in both Florida and Oklahoma.

SEMINOLE WARS

Many of the Muscogees who refused removal escaped to Spanish Florida where they joined other refugees including runaway slaves. American warfare against Seminoles began as a series of Andrew Jackson–led invasions in 1817. These attacks were a continuation of warfare against Muscogees who escaped across the border and American raids and expressly targeted former Muscogees and runaway slaves. Black Seminoles faced enslavement if captured, but when Florida became part of the United States in 1821, Seminoles joined other southern U.S. tribes facing removal to Indian Territory west of the Mississippi River.

Following the 1832 Treaty of Payne's Landing, a delegation went to Indian Territory and approved of the land they found there. However, when they returned, most Seminoles refused to leave their central Florida reservation and open warfare resumed. Osceola and several other Seminole leaders

Lithograph of Seminole warriors attacking a Florida blockhouse in December, 1835. A majority of Seminoles rejected the 1833 Treaty of Payne's Landing, which called for removal of Seminoles from their central Florida reservation and sparked the Second Seminole War (1835–1842). What followed has been called the most expensive of America's Indian Wars. (Library of Congress)

refused to sign a new treaty ceding their remaining lands in Florida and violence escalated. The Second Seminole War was characterized by regular deception and violence as each side used truces and parleys to their own advantage. Micanopy's December 1835 attack on a column of troops under Major Francis Dade killed all but three of the 110-man column. During the Dade Battle, Osceola executed Indian Agent Wiley Thompson forty miles away at Fort King.

The Seminole population in Florida fell as individuals were either captured or killed. Osceola and Coacoochee met with U.S. troops under a flag of truce in 1837, but the Americans captured and imprisoned them along with several other Seminole leaders. Coacoochee escaped but Osceola was moved to Fort Moultrie in Charleston, South Carolina where he died in custody. Some 3,000 Seminoles moved west under military escorts by 1842. Others remained hidden in the swamps of south-central Florida. Warfare erupted again in the 1850s and Billy Bowlegs's band of Seminoles eventually removed to Indian Territory in 1855. The few remaining Seminoles continued living deep in Big Cypress Swamp and their descendants continue to press claims to Seminole land within Florida.

PROFILE: KEOKUK

In an attempt to bring peace to the Midwest, Sauk chief Keokuk led a delegation to Washington, D.C. in 1824. He had made a grand tour of eastern cities only three years earlier and had come to the conclusion that his tribe could not withstand warfare with the United States. He appealed directly to Secretary of War John C. Calhoun to hold a grand treaty council for the tribes of the region to clarify Indian claims and to delineate boundaries between various tribal and U.S. lands. In August 1825, nine tribes gathered at Prairie du Chien.

Superintendent of Indian Affairs William Clark had warned Keokuk to end his raiding against Sioux, but Keokuk's mistrust continued. In the treaty council, Keokuk refused to recognize Sioux claims and nearly derailed the proceedings because Dakota Sioux were included. However, he eventually signed a treaty that included specific language guaranteeing peace among the tribes, including Sauks and Sioux.

While Keokuk negotiated with the United States in order to secure lands and peace, even if removal was an eventual result, Black Hawk hoped to lure British support in a renewed war against Sioux and U.S. enemies. Black Hawk did not attend the Prairie du Chien treaty council and rejected the terms of the treaty. Though he restrained his warriors for a time, raiding by Meskwaki chief Morgan in 1828 set off a series of raids and counter-raids between Sioux and the allied Sauks and Meskwakis. During this renewed warfare, American settlers seized Indian land and forced Sauks and Meskwakis to encroach more regularly on Sioux hunting lands. Keokuk again appealed to Black Hawk and others arguing that removal was the only solution that would allow their people's culture to continue. The majority of Sauks and Meskwakis moved west of the Mississippi River with Keokuk in 1831. However, a large group led by Black Hawk crossed back east of the Mississippi in 1832, marking the outbreak of the Black Hawk War. Keokuk later led his people on a second phase of removal to Kansas in 1842 and died six years later.

PROFILE: COACOOCHEE (WILD CAT)

Coacoochee was one of twenty men who escaped U.S. troops at Fort Gibson, Florida in late 1837. He had been one of several military leaders in the Seminole resistance who rejected the 1833 Treaty of Payne's Landing, which they argued was fraudulent and that the coerced signers held no authority over the Seminole people. The Second Seminole War broke out in 1835 and is often cited as the most expensive of all U.S. wars against tribes. After Coacoochee's father, Emathla, and Osceola both died in American custody in 1838, Coacoochee was the most influential Seminole head man remaining and he carried on the fight against the United States through the spring of 1841. However, by May of that year, most Seminoles understood that their people could no longer continue war. Coacoochee's followers moved west to Oklahoma, arriving in November 1841 where they found temporary homes in Cherokee Territory.

The reordering of tribal leadership; the clash of removed tribes with both white Texans and other removed tribes; and the ongoing shifts in policies, payments, and settlements within Indian Territory made an era of chaos. In 1845, in the wake of flooding, which left many Oklahoma Indians hungry, Seminoles, Muscogees, and the United States signed another treaty designed to stabilize Indian Territory. However, under the terms of the treaty, Coacoochee's Seminoles would be subject to the Muscogee Creek Tribal Council. Seminoles who had lost their homes and crops to flooding moved once more to take up temporary residence in Muscogee Territory.

By late 1849, Coacoochee's people began to move south into Texas. They joined a band of Kickapoos in central Texas for a time, but moved on during the following spring, crossing into Mexico. Over the course of 1850–1851, they established a new village at El Nacimiento, Mexico. A treaty with Mexico granted Seminoles and Kickapoos roughly one hundred square miles of land and the right to continue their culture under Mexican law. There, they functioned as buffers against Comanches, Mescaleros, and Lipan Apaches and their descendants remain there to this day. Coacoochee, known by then to Mexican authorities as *Capitán Gato*, died during a January 1857 smallpox outbreak.

REFERENCES AND FURTHER READING

Anderson, William L., ed. *Cherokee Removal: Before and After*. Athens: University of Georgia Press, 1991.

Black Hawk. *Life of Black Hawk, or Ma-ka-tai-me-she-kia-kiak*. Edited by J. Gerald Kennedy. New York: Penguin, 2008.

Bowes, John P. *Exiles and Pioneers: Eastern Indians in the Trans-Mississippi West*. New York: Cambridge University Press, 2007.

Bowes, John P. *Land Too Good for Indians: Northern Indian Removal*. Norman: University of Oklahoma Press, 2016.

Garrison, Tim Alan. *The Legal Ideology of Removal: The Southern Judiciary and the Sovereignty of Native American Nations*. Athens: University of Georgia Press, 2002.

Green, Michael D. *The Politics of Indian Removal: Creek Government and Society in Crisis*. Lincoln: University of Nebraska Press, 1985.

Hauptman, Laurence M. *The Tonawanda Senecas' Heroic Battle Against Removal: Conservative Activist Indians*. Albany, NY: Excelsior Editions, 2011.

Miller, Susan A. *Coacoochee's Bones: A Seminole Saga*. Lawrence: University Press of Kansas, 2003.

Perdue, Theda, and Michael D. Green. *The Cherokee Nation and the Trail of Tears*. New edition. New York: Viking, 2007.

Robertson, Lindsay G. *Conquest by Law: How the Discovery of America Dispossessed Indigenous Peoples of Their Lands*. New York: Oxford University Press, 2005.

Rockwell, Stephen J. *Indian Affairs and the Administrative State in the Nineteenth Century*. New York: Cambridge University Press, 2010.

Saunt, Claudio. *Black, White, and Indian: Race and the Unmaking of an American Family*. New York: Oxford University Press, 2006.

Smithers, Gregory D. *The Cherokee Diaspora: An Indigenous History of Migration, Resettlement, and Identity*. New Haven, CT: Yale University Press, 2015.

Wallace, Anthony F. C. *The Long, Bitter Trail: Andrew Jackson and the Indians*. New York: Hill and Wang, 1993.

Watson, Blake A. *Buying America from the Indians:* Johnson v. McIntosh *and the History of Native Land Rights*. Norman: University of Oklahoma Press, 2012.

_____ *Chapter 9* _____

American Indians and the Civil War

Through the 1840s and 1850s, native people in the West faced greater and greater incursions into their homelands from whites seeking land, resources, and wealth. During this period, the federal government sought to concentrate and confine Indians into Indian Territory and onto reservations, opening land for white settlement and exploitation. Each Indian community was faced with decisions about the survival of their people and way of life.

The Civil War era was once again a watershed moment in the ongoing domination or death choice faced by native people throughout their long and troubled history with Europeans and Anglo-Americans. Even before the Civil War, Indian communities in Kansas, Nebraska, and Indian Territory were caught in the bloody conflict between anti- and proslavery forces seeking to control these territories for their cause. As the United States and the Confederate States of America battled over the fate of the Republic and slavery, Indian communities continued to be caught in the maelstrom of these opposing forces. While most historians of the Civil War focus primarily on the eastern theater of the war, tremendous upheaval and conflict occurred along the Mississippi River, affecting Indian tribes in Indian Territory, Kansas, Minnesota, New Mexico, and beyond. Agents from both the Confederacy and the United States sought to entice Indian people to their side. Whether choosing sides or attempting to stay neutral, these choices carried risks and placed Native Americans once again in the position of making a choice about their futures and struggling to maintain their sovereignty and way of life.

Even in areas not directly impacted by the war itself, Native Americans continued to face pressure from settlers, miners, and trespassers on their land. When the U.S. Army withdrew from posts across the Great Plains, the Southwest, and Far West, the void left by these forces could be filled by

Confederate forces or local militias that had little interest in protecting Indian communities or honoring previous treaties and agreements. When federal troops abandoned these posts, many native communities interpreted this as the U.S. government losing power and as an opportunity to exert greater control over their traditional homelands. During the war, settlers and miners continued to pour into the West, further increasing tensions and conflict in these regions.

While it is impossible to detail the full story of American Indian involvement in the Civil War, this chapter will provide a picture of the desperate struggle of many native people to maintain control over their homelands and negotiate the treacherous divide between the United States and the Confederacy. From Minnesota and the Great Plains to Indian Territory and the desert Southwest, American Indians struggled over the implications of this conflict, sometimes joining the fight and many times hoping to stay neutral and protect their families and land.

THE CIVIL WAR IN INDIAN TERRITORY

Native people throughout the United States were affected by the onset of hostilities in 1861. Even before the start of the Civil War, Indians dealt with the conflict between pro- and antislavery forces in the United States. Many communities had been removed to what would become the Kansas and Nebraska territories, and they experienced firsthand the violence that occurred in "Bleeding Kansas."

With the election of Abraham Lincoln as president of the United States, southern states started the process of secession and forming a new nation. Tribal leaders and their people feared what this meant for their communities, in particular many wondered what the federal government might do to their land since William Seward, a staunch supporter of Lincoln and his future secretary of state, called for opening of Indian Territory to white settlers. It seemed like a repetition of the same experience under Andrew Jackson and the federal government in the 1830s. Fear of government action and theft was heightened because of the struggle over slavery and the threat of secession after the election of 1860. Native people had survived removal, rebuilding their lives and improving the land they lived on in the Territory, building farms, homes, granaries, and new government and civil institutions. In addition, some prosperous families owned slaves and had established plantations in Indian Territory, carrying the institution with them from the South during removal. Most tribes also had greater geographical affinity with the South, since most were from that region and their traditional homelands were located there and many friends and relatives still lived in the South.

The events surrounding the beginning of the Civil War also reinvigorated old disputes between various factions among the tribes in Indian Territory. Those who supported removal, often the wealthiest in the tribes and owners of slaves, sympathized with the South and supported secession and the formation of the Confederacy. Antiremoval factions, which included full-blood Cherokee, Creek (Muscogee), Choctaw, and others, urged their followers to remain neutral or actively supported the United States. These choices were often based on long-standing political, factional, and individual disputes among communities and tribes, leading to complicated and very personal choices during the war.

Indian communities in Indian Territory also remembered the broken promises, malfeasance, and theft they experienced during their long history with the United States and European powers in North America. Once the Confederacy was formed, Confederate officials used this legacy of distrust to their advantage. After federal troops withdrew from Indian Territory, Confederate troops occupied the abandoned posts. In 1861, President Jefferson Davis dispatched Albert Pike, an Arkansas lawyer and supporter of the Confederacy, to negotiate new treaties with tribes and gain their support for the Confederate war effort (Trafzer, 204).

Pike's efforts to negotiate new treaties exposed preexisting divides in many communities, as the Cherokee, Creek, Choctaw, Seminole, and other tribes decided whether to stay neutral, side with the new Confederacy, or support the United States. Concentrating on the larger tribes in the Territory, Pike eventually negotiated new treaties with many of the most influential and powerful tribes like the Cherokee, Choctaw, Chickasaw, Seminole, Comanche, and Kiowa. These agreements stipulated that the tribes end their relationship with the United States and enter into a new treaty relationship with the Confederacy. Part of the new agreements required the tribes to recruit troops to fight for the Confederacy.

The treaties caused tension and bloodshed in these communities, as factions split over their allegiance to the Confederacy. For example, Stand Watie, a pro-removal Cherokee who raised a regiment for the South and was commissioned a colonel, pressured John Ross, the leader of the Cherokee, to support the South and eventually forced Ross to flee after he abandoned his support for the South. Among the Creek (Muscogee), Opothleyoholo, a powerful leader in the tribe who had opposed removal to Indian Territory, urged his people to remain neutral and refused to support either side.

Unfortunately, it was difficult for native people in Kansas and Indian Territory to stay out of the war. Confederate Indian troops attacked Opothleyoholo and neutral Muscogee in November and December 1861, forcing them to flee north to Kansas where they sought aid from Union forces. Facing desperate conditions, many people died from exposure, disease, and malnutrition. Many Creek joined the United States in the fight after this experience.

The fighting continued in Indian Territory and Kansas, culminating in March 1862 with the Battle of Pea Ridge in northwest Arkansas. In this battle, Confederate forces, including Stand Watie and his regiment of Cherokee Rifles and other Native American units, were defeated by U.S. forces. Indian troops fought on both sides, further illustrating the deep fissures unveiled by the war. In July 1862, Union forces invaded Indian Territory, occupying much of the Cherokee Nation and capturing Tahlequah, the political center of the nation. John Ross surrendered to Union forces, and many of his followers joined the United States in its fight against Confederate forces in Indian Territory (Trafzer, 205).

After Union forces retreated north to Kansas, the conflict in Indian Territory devolved into a bloody, internecine guerilla war that devastated much of Indian Territory. Often settling personal scores and focusing on civilian populations, this guerilla warfare was conducted by both Indian and non-Indian irregular units and led to the emergence of some of the most infamous and notorious criminals in U.S. history like William Quantrill, Jesse James, and the Younger Brothers. Unlike the guerilla irregulars, Stand Watie and the Cherokee Rifles continued operations against military targets. Watie and his regiment continued to fight even after Lee's surrender at Appomattox Courthouse. He eventually surrendered in June 1865, nearly two months after the official end of the war.

The physical devastation of the war in Indian Territory was enormous and contributed to death and misery in Indian communities, both during and after the war. Farms, outbuildings, and other structures were burned and destroyed. Livestock and crops were decimated, and most of the infrastructure in the Territory was damaged or destroyed. At the end of the war, Cherokee, Seminole, and Creek losses reached nearly one-third of their prewar population, and almost 25 percent of Cherokee children were orphaned during the war. Indian communities in Indian Territory suffered a greater casualty rate than any other region or state in the United States (Edmunds, Hoxie, and Salisbury, 272).

CONFLICT AND RESISTANCE IN THE WEST

While fighting occurred between Confederate and Union forces in Indian Territory and Kansas, other Indian communities were faced with many trials and decisions during the Civil War that set the stage for further conflict after the war. Conflict occurred throughout the West, but native people on the Plains and in the Rocky Mountain West faced increasing trespass from whites traveling through their territory to reach points further west, especially places where gold had been discovered. These travelers disrupted food supplies, killing animals and disturbing or destroying plant resources and crops. They also used these resources without regard to the people who inhabited the region. Conflict often arose between native people and transient whites, low-key at first and then boiling over after prolonged abuse and exploitation of Indian homelands.

Prior to the outbreak of the Civil War, miners and settlers streamed into lands west of the Mississippi River. Numerous conflicts and wars occurred just prior to the Civil War, often resulting from the actions of miners and settlers eager to exploit the mineral resources and land of native people. Two examples of these conflicts are the Rogue River War in Oregon and the Northern Paiute War in Nevada and Idaho. In 1855–1856, hostilities erupted between native communities along the Rogue River, as settlers and miners attacked Indian villages, desiring revenge and access to land. Raids and attacks continued through 1856 when the Rogue River Indians were defeated by the U.S. Army and were removed to various reservations throughout Oregon. In early 1860, prospectors and Northern Paiute, Shoshone, and Bannock fought for four months over treaty breaches and increasing violence and incursions by whites in the region. While an uneasy truce was negotiated in 1860, tensions simmered in the region, exploding once again with the Bannock War in 1878.

Once secession occurred and the Civil War erupted, the U.S. government recalled most troops from the West and concentrated forces in the East to counter Confederate armies near Washington D.C. The void in military presence was often filled by militias comprised of inexperienced local recruits with small contingents of regular army soldiers. These units were frequently undisciplined and used the situation to move against Indian communities and force them from their homelands. Despite the fighting in the East, settlers, miners, and other emigrants continued to stream West, increasing pressure on native communities and raising the potential for conflict in many regions in the West. When confronted with Indian resistance, they repeatedly called on territorial governments and the federal government to protect them. This protection most often came in the form of poorly trained militias and military forces that only added fuel to the fire. Local officials and military officers responded to these demands, since the Lincoln administration was preoccupied with the fighting in the East and the problems of administering conquered Confederate territory.

CONFLICT ON THE NORTHERN PLAINS

Resentment over past treatment and removals fueled conflict in Indian Territory during the Civil War, but these feelings were also strong among many other Native American tribes. In the early 1850s, the Santee Sioux, who lived in Minnesota and Iowa, negotiated a treaty with the United States, relinquishing their traditional homelands for two reservations in western Minnesota. The two reservations were known as the Lower and Upper Agency. Resentment toward the government, Indian agents, and traders increased throughout the 1850s, culminating in 1860–1861 with disputes over land annuity payments and Indian trader fraud that siphoned off a significant portion of annuity payments to pay off the alleged debt of individual Santee. Growing resentment and anger was stoked when the federal government failed to deliver annuity payments in spring 1862, forcing many Santee Sioux families into starvation and desperation during the summer. In August 1862, a hunting party of young Wahpeton (Lower Santee) warriors attacked a farmhouse and killed five settlers. The Lower Santee decided that they most certainly would be punished and decided to attack the Lower Agency, killing Indian traders and agency workers, and then moved against settlers in the region. As with many of these conflicts, some Santee joined in the raids while others declined, sometimes protecting white settlers from harm. The Upper Santee, upon hearing of the conflict, also divided in their response. Some joined the uprising, attacking the Upper Agency, while others opposed the violence (Edmunds, Hoxie, and Salisbury, 278).

After attacking the agencies, Sioux Warriors under Little Crow attacked Fort Ridgely and when unsuccessful in capturing the fort, moved on to the town of New Ulm. After repulsing two attacks, the residents fled, abandoning the town. The residents of western Minnesota panicked and supported Governor Ramsey's deployment of Colonel Henry Sibley's 1,400 troops against the Lower and Upper Santee Sioux. After brief skirmishes around Fort Ridgely, Sibley raised more troops and defeated nearly 1,000 warriors under Little Crow at Wood Lake in September 1862.

After the defeat, Sibley and his forces arrested 2,000 Santee Sioux. Many others, like Little Crow, fled to the Great Plains to join relatives and friends among the Sioux. Four hundred Santee were tried for murder, rape, and theft. Included in this group were many Santee who helped protect settlers during the conflict. Sibley's court sentenced 306 people to be hanged, including several who had helped settlers. In December 1862, thirty-nine prisoners were publicly hanged, the largest mass execution in American history. As punishment for the uprising, the U.S. government liquidated the reservations in Minnesota and removed the remaining Santee Sioux to a reservation in Nebraska. Many other Santee moved to the Great Plains or to Canada. Little Crow moved to Canada but was killed by whites on a return trip to Minnesota in 1863 (Edmunds, Hoxie, and Salisbury, 280).

The Santee Sioux uprising set the stage for further conflict on the Great Plains and started the process of militarization of the region by the United States in preparation for warfare against native people of the region.

CONFLICT ON THE SOUTHERN PLAINS

The Civil War affected the southern Great Plains region as well. Cheyenne, Arapaho, Kiowa, and Comanche controlled much of this area and also resented the increasing incursions of whites on their territory. As raids and attacks on both sides increased, settlers and territorial governments in Colorado and New Mexico pressed the federal government for troops and protection from Indians. Since much of the regular army was engaged in the East, volunteer units and militias were used against Indian communities on the southern plains.

According to the treaty of Horse Creek and the first treaty of Fort Laramie in 1851, the Cheyenne and Arapaho controlled much of the land east of the Rocky Mountains in present-day Colorado. To their consternation, emigrants and miners continually crossed their territory, and new settlements like Denver grew quickly to support mining in the region. In addition, ranching operations also trespassed on Cheyenne and Arapaho territory (Trafzer, 210).

In February 1861, U.S. representatives negotiated a treaty with peace chiefs from the Southern Arapaho and Cheyenne that created two small reservations along the Arkansas River and Sand Creek in exchange for much of their traditional homeland. Most Cheyenne and Arapaho leaders, including Black Kettle and White Antelope, did not know what the treaty said but signed it anyway. Powerful Southern Cheyenne and Arapaho groups, including the Dog Soldiers, an influential warrior society, denounced the treaty and refused to move to the reservations. The Northern Cheyenne and Arapaho also refused to comply with the treaty. At stake were the rich traditional hunting grounds of these tribes, which the treaty stipulated that the tribes must give up while going to the reservations.

The U.S. Senate ratified the treaty and shortly thereafter created the Territory of Colorado. Incidents continued between whites and Indians, and in 1863, Indian leaders from the region traveled to Washington D.C. and pledged peace with the United States. Most settlers and members of the new territorial government, including the new territorial governor, John Evans, believed the federal government was being too lenient on Indians. Among them was Colonel John M. Chivington who commanded the Colorado District. Chivington was a notorious Indian hater and wished to see the Cheyenne, Arapaho, and Kiowa punished for attacking whites and resisting the government (Trafzer, 211).

Resistance to encroachment was occurring along the whole eastern slope of the Rocky Mountains, encompassing the Lakota, Cheyenne, Arapaho, Kiowa, Kiowa-Apache, and Comanche. As raids and conflict increased, in early June 1864, Governor Evans demanded that all Cheyenne and Arapaho withdraw to the reservation created by the 1861 treaty. Evans blustered that

An oil painting illustrating the Sand Creek Massacre in Colorado. On November 29, 1864, U.S. troops attacked the peaceful encampment of Cheyenne and Arapaho at Sand Creek, Colorado. One of many such attacks in the American West, it would be known as the Sand Creek Massacre. (DeAgostini/Getty Images)

any Indian not on the reservation would be considered "hostile" and would be attacked.

Several peace chiefs, including Black Kettle (Cheyenne) and Left Hand (Arapaho), met with Governor Evans in September and "agreed" to go to the reservation. They asked for protection, but the governor did not promise any. In November, Colonel Chivington and Evans lobbied to have the commander of Fort Lyon, Major Edward Wynkoop, removed because he was too "friendly" to Indians. His replacement joined Chivington at Fort Lyon, moving out to attack Black Kettle and Left Hand's villages at Sand Creek near the reservation.

Early in the morning of November 29, 1864, one of the worst atrocities of the long history of abuse and depravation between whites and Native Americans occurred. As Chivington's troops approached the village, Black Kettle raised an American flag and a white flag over his tipi, and Left Hand approached the troops to tell them that they were peaceful. The 700 troops under Chivington, many of them drunk, shot every man, woman, and child in sight as they attacked the village. Left Hand was shot while he sang his death song. As the slaughter continued, many Indians ran up Sand Creek and offered little resistance since they did not have firearms and most were women and children. Colorado militiamen slaughtered indiscriminately and then took trophies of ears, genitals, and scalps, which they proudly displayed in Denver to cheering crowds after the battle (Trafzer, 213).

Counts of the dead vary. Most historians estimate the death toll between 150 and 200. Present-day Cheyenne and Arapaho estimates are as high as 400. The immediate effect of the atrocity was a tremendous increase in raids and attacks on white emigrants and settlers by Cheyenne, Arapaho, Lakota, Kiowa, and Comanche. Many Cheyenne and Kiowa moved north to join the Lakota or fled to Indian Territory. For Chivington the attack did not bring the fame and fortune he craved. Congress investigated the attack and determined it to be an illegitimate use of force, but Chivington and his soldiers were not prosecuted since they had resigned from the military and were no longer under military jurisdiction. Many Americans in the eastern United States responded to the violence with revulsion and disgust.

RESISTANCE IN THE SOUTHWEST

Just like in the northern and southern plains, the coming of the Civil War influenced tensions between settlers and Indians in the desert southwest. Long-standing conflicts were reinvigorated, and many native communities were faced with decisions to either allow their domination by whites or resist their encroachment.

THE APACHE

The Apache are a diverse grouping of bands that included Mescalero, Jicarillo, Mimbres, and many others. These bands were led by local leaders that had limited control over members of a village, like many other native communities in the West. As discussed earlier, the Apache bands generally maintained their autonomy during the Spanish and Mexican period in the Southwest, but violence flared after Mexican Independence in 1820 as Mexican officials instituted a brutal bounty system for Apache scalps, hoping to stem violence against settlers in the region by escalating violence. At first happy to see the American military during the Mexican-American War, the Apache quickly were disillusioned as miners and settlers flooded the Southwest after 1850.

With the onset of the Civil War, the Apache, just like many other native communities, believed that the power of the federal government was disappearing. Unfortunately, this was not true. In 1861, Confederate forces invaded New Mexico from Texas. By 1862, these forces retreated back to Texas but not before inflaming the situation. The Confederate commander ordered his troops to lure Indians to their camps, murder them, and sell their children into slavery. While denounced by President Jefferson Davis, this attitude illustrates the hatred of Indians by white Americans during the period.

After the Confederate withdrawal, Union forces from California, under General James Carleton, advanced through Arizona toward New Mexico. After an attempt to capture Cochise, one of the leaders of the Chiricahua, warriors harried Carleton's column, culminating in a pitched battle at Apache Pass in Arizona. Apache forces withdrew after Mangas Coloradas, another important leader of Chiricahua bands, was wounded. Carleton and his troops built Fort Bowie near Apache Pass and reoccupied Union posts throughout New Mexico and southwest Texas.

Apache from numerous bands continued to harass Carleton's troops, and Carleton, who believed that negotiating with Indians was pointless, raised a large force of New Mexican volunteers and recruited Kit Carson to lead the fight against the Apache and other Indians in Arizona and New Mexico. Carleton and Carson implemented a strategy where they singled out individual bands, like the Chiricahua and the Mescalero, and began a campaign to decimate and pacify the Apache. Carson and the New Mexican troops destroyed crops and houses, killing any Indian who resisted. Some Apache surrendered to Carson and Carleton, while others fled to the mountains of Mexico. During the campaign, Carleton established the Bosque Redondo Reservation in eastern New Mexico, where he prepared to place Apache and Navajo, building Fort Sumner to guard the reservation.

In January 1863, Carleton sent another expedition against the Apache. This operation was unsuccessful, as most members of the Chiricahua and Mimbres fled from their villages to the mountains. After the campaign, Mangas Coloradas was captured by a group of miners under a flag of truce and handed over to the military. He was killed in a staged escape attempt and then beheaded. His skull was later sent to New York for study. The death of Mangas Coloradas did not end resistance by the Apache. Cochise and his people continued to resist the U.S. Army from their mountain strongholds. Warfare and resistance continued in Arizona and New Mexico until 1886.

DINÉ (THE NAVAJO)

The Navajo (Diné) were also targets of military campaigns during the Civil War. The Diné were of Athabaskan descent like the Apache. Organized into a number of bands led by headmen, the Navajo traditional homeland spreads across New Mexico, Arizona, and Colorado. Very much like the Apache, the Navajo retained their autonomy during the early nineteenth century despite increasing pressures from Mexican and American settlers. During the Mexican-American War, the Navajo successfully held off U.S.

forces and protected their sacred Canyon de Chelly from invaders. Despite signing treaties, the Navajo continued to experience incursions and depredations by whites while at the same time resisting government domination. By 1851, the U.S. government built Fort Defiance as a key installation to control the Navajo who increasingly resented the use of their land and water by whites and the government for grazing. In 1860, the Navajo attacked Fort Defiance in Arizona and nearly overwhelmed the fort. They were led by Manuelito, an important headman among the Navajo, and Barboncito, a revered medicine man. The fort was abandoned in 1861 at the beginning of the Civil War. This battle though started the policy of total war against the Navajo by the U.S. Army.

During the Civil War, General Carleton intended to subdue both the Apache and the Navajo, sending Kit Carson first to attack and subdue the Apache. In 1863, Carleton commanded Carson to take the fight to the Navajo and force them to move to the Bosque Redondo Reservation. Using a scorched earth policy, Carson and U.S. troops destroyed homes and crops and killed livestock, making it difficult for Navajo people to resist and survive. This was a common strategy used against native communities. By 1864, many Navajo were making the Long Walk to Hweeldi (Bosque Redondo). By this point, Carson and his troops had scoured the canyons where the Navajo took refuge, and approximately 10,000 surrendered to Carson. Many others fled to the Pueblos. Life at Bosque Redondo was difficult for the Navajo, with many people dying from disease and malnutrition.

After Carson defeated the Navajo, Carleton authorized an expedition against the Kiowa and Comanche in New Mexico. In November 1864, the same month that Chivington and his men massacred Cheyenne and Arapaho people at Sand Creek, Carson's forces attacked a large Kiowa and Kiowa-Apache camp in southwestern Texas. After a day-long battle, Carson retreated to Fort Bascom in New Mexico. Sporadic fighting continued along the Arizona, New Mexico, and Texas borders, as Comanche, Kiowa, Arapaho, and Cheyenne raided along the Santa Fe Trail and harassed settlers. A fragile peace was established in 1865 but would soon be broken as conflict continued in the region.

CONCLUSION

The Civil War affected native communities with long-term consequences. Indian Territory was devastated, taking years to rebuild as more and more tribes were forced into the Territory when conflict reignited in the West after the Civil War. On the Plains, tribes continued to face incursions from whites and the erosion of their culture and land through forced removal and treaties. Whether Indian communities and individuals fought for the North and the South or attempted to stay neutral, they found their situation ever more precarious, often facing decisions of life and death or domination.

PROFILE: STAND WATIE

Stand Watie was born into the Cherokee Nation in 1806. His family was politically influential and included Elias Boudinot, the founder of the *Cherokee Phoenix*, and John Rollin Ridge who was a well-known late nineteenth-century Cherokee poet-author who lived in California. During the fight over removal, Watie and some of his relatives, including Elias Boudinot, Major Ridge, and John Ridge, were part of a small group that favored removal. Watie signed the 1835 Treaty of New Echota, which was considered invalid by the majority of Cherokee. This action split the tribe into pro- and antiremoval factions and influenced Cherokee history through the Civil War.

In 1837, Watie and many of the signers of the New Echota Treaty moved to Indian Territory before the formal removal of the antiremoval faction by the Trail of Tears in 1838. The two factions clashed in the Territory, and in 1839, some of Watie's relatives were executed by the antiremoval faction. Conflict between the two factions continued, only ending when peace was made between the two factions and the United States in 1846 through the signing of a new treaty.

Before the Civil War, Watie started a law practice and a family. As the secession crisis emerged in late 1860–1861, he organized the Cherokee Regiment of Mounted Rifles. Watie used the regiment as a tool to force John Ross, the leader of the tribe, to side with the Confederacy. In 1862, Ross fled Indian Territory, and Watie was elected principal chief of the Confederate Cherokee. During the war, Watie was the only Native American to hold the Confederate rank of brigadier general. He and his troops took part in numerous battles, and Watie was known for his guerilla tactics during the war. Resisting long after the war ended, Watie was the last Confederate general to surrender, nearly two months after the cessation of hostilities at Appomattox Courthouse. After the war, Watie returned to Indian Territory and died in 1871.

PROFILE: ELY PARKER

Ely Parker was born in 1828 to William and Elizabeth Parker. The Parker family lived on the Tonawanda Reservation, where the Seneca lived, one of the six members of the Iroquois Confederacy. Parker was educated at the local missionary school and went to college, eventually reading law and taking the bar examination in New York State. He was not allowed to practice law because he was not considered a U.S. citizen. He later attended Rensselaer

Polytechnic Institute and worked as a civil engineer until the outbreak of the Civil War.

Parker used his bilingual abilities to help negotiate land and treaty rights, and he was made a sachem of the Seneca in 1852. It was during this period that Parker met Ulysses S. Grant in Galena, Illinois, while he worked for the U.S. government.

At the outbreak of the war, Parker attempted to raise a regiment of Iroquois soldiers and volunteer for the Union Army, but he was denied because he was an Indian. He contacted Ulysses S. Grant and through his influence was commissioned as a captain and set to work as an engineer during the siege of Vicksburg. When Grant became the commander of the Military Division of the Mississippi, he chose Parker as his adjutant. He would serve in this post until 1865 when he was promoted to lieutenant colonel and named Grant's military secretary. At Appomattox Courthouse, Parker drafted the surrender documents. In April 1865, he was promoted to the rank of brigadier general, only one of two Native Americans promoted to this rank on either side of the war.

After the war, Parker continued to serve Grant as his military secretary. He left army service in 1869 after serving as a member of the commission that renegotiated treaties with tribes that sided with the Confederacy during the war. In 1869, newly elected President Grant appointed Parker commissioner of Indian affairs, and he served in this post until 1871. As the first Native American to serve in the post, he was the principal architect of Grant's Indian Peace Policy. Unfortunately, the Indian Ring, a group of corrupt contractors and Indian agents, resisted Parker's efforts to reform the Office of Indian Affairs and eventually forced him out of office.

After leaving the post of commissioner of Indian affairs, Parker was hired as a desk clerk for the New York City Police Department in 1876, a post he held until his death in 1895.

REFERENCES AND FURTHER READING

Anderson, Gary Clayton. *The Conquest of Texas: Ethnic Cleansing in the Promised Land, 1820–1875*. Norman: University of Oklahoma Press, 2005.

Confer, Clarissa W. *The Cherokee Nation in the Civil War*. Norman: University of Oklahoma Press, 2007.

Edmunds, R. David, Frederick E. Hoxie, and Neal Salisbury. *The People: A History of Native America*. Boston: Houghton Mifflin Company, 2007.

Franks, Kenny A. *Stand Watie and the Agony of the Cherokee Nation*. Memphis, TN: Memphis State University Press, 1979.

Gibbon, Gay. *The Sioux: The Dakota and the Lakota Nations*. Malden, MA: Blackwell Publishing, 2003.

Josephy, Alvin M. J. *The Civil War in the American West*. New York: Knopf, 1992.

Trafzer, Clifford E. *As Long as the Grass Shall Grow and Rivers Flow: A History of Native Americans*. Fort Worth, TX: Harcourt College Publishers, 2000.

West, Elliott. *The Contested Plains: Indians, Goldseekers, and the Rush to Colorado*. Lawrence: University of Kansas Press, 1998.

Westerman, Gwen, and Bruce M. White. *Mni Sota Makoce: The Land of the Dakota*. St. Paul, MN: Minnesota Historical Society, 2012.

Chapter 10

Resisting Outsiders

In the aftermath of the Civil War, most Indian communities were confronted with the stark question of whether their societies could continue as they had in the past. After the war, military and settler pressure increased on these communities, heightening tensions and increasing conflict throughout the Great Plains and the western United States. While violence regularly accompanied these encounters, Indian communities were also split into various factions, differing in their approach to solving the vexing problem of white incursion on their lands and culture. These differences often led to bitter divisions and intratribal conflict, with one faction helping the U.S. military in their fight against other tribal factions. These divisions frequently festered for long periods of time. An example of this is the events that occurred around the signing of the Nez Perce "Thief Treaty" of 1863.

As the presidential election of 1860 approached and the specter of secession rose in the South, two miners, Ellias Pierce and Seth Ferrell, ignored the boundaries of the 1855 Nez Perce Reservation and discovered gold in the Bitterroot Mountains of Idaho. Gold rushes attracted numerous miners, speculators, and businessmen seeking to find wealth and prosperity. Nez Perce communities complained bitterly to the U.S. Army and government about these activities and illegal incursions on the reservation, especially about the illegal towns of Lewiston and Elk City that sprang up to support the gold rush. In 1863, Superintendent of Indian Affairs Calvin Hale and other peace commissioners met with Nez Perce leaders at the Lapwai Council. Meeting with prominent leaders like Old Joseph, White Bird, and Eagle from the Light, Hale proposed to reduce the size of the reservation to one tenth of its original size. Nearly all of the leaders opposed this, refusing to cede any land to the federal government. After most of the leaders left the council, Hale negotiated with Chief Lawyer, and on

June 9, Lawyer and fifty-one members of his band signed a treaty that ceded nearly 7 million acres of land to the federal government (Trafzer, 259–260).

Government negotiators often played factions off one another and negotiated treaties with small factions within tribes, setting the stage for conflict in the future. For the Nez Perce, it split the tribe between treaty and nontreaty factions, with many of the nontreaty communities renouncing Christianity and resisting white incursions on their land. These divisions and disputes set the stage for the Nez Perce War in 1877.

The "Thief Treaty" is only one example of many during this period of federal, state, and local government officials pressuring native communities to renegotiate treaties and give up land, as more and more settlers streamed into the West. The period from the end of the Civil War to 1880 is filled with reduction of Indian Territory, armed conflict, and the concerted effort of the U.S. government to solve what they called "The Indian Question."

RECONSTRUCTION AND THE PEACE POLICY

The experiences of many whites during the Civil War led numerous people to question the use of military force against Native Americans. Important reform efforts occurred directly after the Civil War. One of the most important of these was the work of the Doolittle Commission, named after Senator James R. Doolittle, chair of the Senate Committee on Indian Affairs. The investigators researched the condition of tribes within the United States. The "Doolittle Report," issued in 1867, created a national debate over Indian policy, pitting advocates of Force Policy against those for a Peace Policy. The U.S. Army was the chief proponent of the Force Policy, but Presidents Andrew Johnson and Ulysses S. Grant favored a Peace Policy that focused on negotiations and efforts to "civilize and assimilate" native people. In 1867, Congress created the Peace Commission to deal with the "Indian Problem" and attempt to mitigate problems between whites and Indians. Both Johnson and Grant appointed advocates of the Peace Policy to the Bureau of Indian Affairs, to the Peace Commission, and as Indian agents. President Grant granted control of Indian agencies to Christian missionaries and denominations. This was in response to Congress passing a law forbidding army officers from holding the post of Indian agent. At the same time, Congress appropriated $100,000 for the education of Indians and to support the first industrial schools for Indians. These new Indian agents were ministers and members of Christian denominations that had long sought to convert and "civilize" Indian people. Whether Quakers, Methodists, or Presbyterians, these Indian agents and bureaucrats sought to change Indian culture and life (Trafzer, 230–231).

By 1869, Congress created the Board of Indian Commissioners, charged with regulating agents and reservations and attempting to end corruption in the Bureau of Indian Affairs. The Board of Indian Commissioners operated alongside the Peace Commission. Unfortunately, the budget for the board was too small and the problems it faced were too great to tackle with its meager resources. The Peace Commission, after touring and meeting with tribes in the western United States, advocated for the end of treaty making with all Indian tribes in the United States. In 1870, the Supreme Court also weighed in on treaty making, ruling in the *Cherokee Tobacco* decision that federal law was superior to treaties. In addition, the case also ruled that treaties with foreign countries were superior to those negotiated with Indian communities. In 1871, Congress, in an appropriations bill, declared that no further treaties would be signed with Indian nations. From this point forward all agreements between tribes and the United States would be through executive order from the president or by an act of Congress (Trafzer, 232).

INDIAN TERRITORY AND RECONSTRUCTION

During the debate over the Doolittle Report and the establishment of the Peace Commission, the United States began the process of reconstructing and punishing Indian communities in Indian Territory for their treaty and relationship with the Confederacy. Despite the fact that many native people from Indian Territory fought for the Union, numerous politicians, bureaucrats, military officers, and citizens of the United States saw this as an opportunity to gain the land and resources of the tribes in Indian Territory. Thousands of Indians were removed from Kansas into Indian Territory onto land taken from the Five Civilized Tribes. The U.S. government negotiated new reconstruction treaties with the tribes that stipulated loss of land for the tribes and grants of right-of-way for roads and railroads through the Territory.

In the midst of dealing with new treaties and rebuilding their shattered homelands, tribes in Indian Territory continued to face the threat of violence from outlaws and former soldiers who raided towns and farms, carrying off livestock and valuables and threatening native and nonnative populations in Indian Territory and beyond. Tribal leaders sought help from the federal government, and in 1871, Isaac Parker was appointed to the Arkansas Federal District Court, which oversaw Indian Territory. "Hanging Judge Parker," as he became known, utilized U.S. Marshals to bring order and peace to the Territory. As the situation in the Territory stabilized, tribal governments reformed and attempted to reassert sovereignty in the Territory, often working against Indian agents and government officials who constantly attempted to undermine that sovereignty (Trafzer, 235).

One step that the tribes vehemently opposed was the formation of a unified territorial government that would undermine tribal sovereignty and eventually lead to admission as a state. Indian leaders recognized that this would mean the loss of land, resources, and right-of-ways to railroads and local governments. In 1870, Senator Benjamin Rice from Arkansas introduced a bill to organize the Territory of Oklahoma. Intertribal meetings occurred in Indian Territory, and native communities moved quickly to counter this threat by drafting the Okmulgee Constitution, which they sent to Congress for approval. Congress rejected the Constitution, but these actions set the stage for the eventual merging of Indian Territory with Oklahoma Territory to form the state of Oklahoma in 1907.

RESISTANCE ON THE PLAINS

Whether through the Peace Commission or the U.S. Army, the goal of the federal government was to force native people onto reservations, thereby freeing up land for settlers and lessening conflict between whites and Indians. These pressures from settlers, miners, government officials, and the military contributed to profound cultural changes for Native Americans on the Great Plains. Traditional leadership among tribes on the Plains had always focused on two distinct roles—peace chief and war chief. Peace chiefs tended to be older men who had once been warriors who later became diplomats and political leaders for their people. Before the 1860s, peace chiefs exerted the most influence, as they led people in hunting, settling disputes, and negotiating with neighboring tribes. In times of conflict, war chiefs led parties of warriors for brief periods of time, and their leadership role was relinquished once the conflict ended. During the 1860s and 1870s, as the role of warfare became a nearly daily reality for most native communities on the Plains, war leaders exerted greater influence.

In addition to the change in political structure, many native communities on the Great Plains struggled with changes in their subsistence and resource economies. As white populations streamed into the region, tribes found that they competed for limited food resources. In particular, the trade in buffalo robes that emerged after the Civil War began to significantly impact buffalo numbers and threatened a food source that was central to many tribes on the Plains. As the herds diminished, many Indian communities and families were forced to rely on government annuities and those that did not participate in annuities often found themselves hungry.

Some tribes shifted from buffalo hunting to stock raising, either cattle or horses to cover the deficit of buffalo. The Comanche and Kiowa were particularly adept at the livestock trade, trading with whites and maintaining large herds. Native people also slowly immersed themselves in trade with whites, purchasing goods, weapons, ammunition, and trade goods. The procurement of weapons and ammunition was very important because of the threat of warfare and increasing tensions with whites in the region.

CONFLICT ON THE SOUTHERN PLAINS

In 1865, treaties were negotiated with Kiowa, Kiowa-Apache, Cheyenne, Comanche, and Arapaho people at a council on the Little Arkansas River near present-day Wichita, Kansas. Under the terms of the treaty, Kiowa and Comanche would remove to one reservation and Cheyenne and Arapaho to another. All Indian land north of the Arkansas River would be relinquished to the U.S. government. While the leaders of these communities negotiated in good faith, the U.S. Senate did not ratify the treaties, and the U.S. military was unable to stem the tide of settlers who trespassed on Indian land, often appropriating property for ranches and farms.

In 1867, General Winfield Scott Hancock ordered a military expedition to confront Indian attacks on settlers. Raids and skirmishes erupted between the Army and Indians, with Kiowa, Comanche, Arapaho, Cheyenne, and Kiowa-Apache parties attacking whites throughout the region. Throughout the summer and early fall of 1867, the Army campaigned against these groups, but the pressure on native communities eventually led to negotiations for peace. In October, over 7,000 native people gathered at Medicine Lodge in southwestern Kansas to negotiate with a U.S. peace delegation. Under the terms of the treaty, Kiowa, Comanche, and Kiowa-Apache would move onto a reservation in the southwestern corner of Indian Territory, and the Cheyenne and Arapaho would occupy a reservation in the original Cherokee Outlet. The tribes also negotiated for continued hunting rights and promised to let settlers use roads and trails and for federal troops to build forts in the region.

The Medicine Lodge Treaty did not end raiding or hunting outside of reservation land. Raids continued into Kansas, Texas, and Nebraska, provoking the U.S. military to send out scouting parties and units to track down the raiders. In the summer of 1868, fifty scouts attempted to track a large party of Cheyenne, Lakota, and Arapaho, ending up surrounded on Beecher Island on the Arikara Fork of the Republican River. The scouts repulsed numerous attacks, and the battle had relatively few casualties except for Roman Nose, the most famous of the Cheyenne war chiefs. His death discouraged the Cheyenne and was an omen of things to come.

During the winter, the Army continued its pursuit of the tribes, hoping to confront warriors when they were more closely tied to their villages. George Custer and the Seventh Cavalry tracked warriors responsible for the summer raids to Black Kettle's camp on the Washita River in Indian Territory.

An illustration from *Harper's Weekly* depicts the meeting between the U.S. Peace Commission and Kiowa and Comanche leaders at Medicine Lodge, Kansas. The Medicine Lodge Treaty, signed in 1867, brought a tenuous peace to the Great Plains. (Library of Congress)

On November 23, troops attacked the village, killing 100 warriors, including Black Kettle, many women and children, and over 800 horses belonging to the Cheyenne. The Army continued its campaign, eventually establishing Fort Sill where many native people surrendered and accepted the offer of rations to stave off starvation. The Dog Soldiers refused to acquiesce and in July 1869 fought a fierce battle with the Army led by the scout Buffalo Bill Cody. The Battle of Summit Springs was a disaster for the Dog Soldiers, as their most prominent war chief, Tall Bull, was killed and many of their horses were killed or captured, forcing them to split up and retreat back to the reservation where Quaker Indian agents were able to maintain an uneasy peace until 1874 (Trafzer, 242–243).

The Kiowa and Comanche also continued hunting excursions and raids outside of the reservation. Sometimes raiding as far south as Mexico, Kiowa and Comanche parties often fought with the Texas Rangers, hunted buffalo, and raided farms and ranches along the way. In May 1871, a large Kiowa war party left the reservation headed to Texas for raids, starting what would be known as the Red River War. Along the way, they raided an army wagon train that happened to have General William Tecumseh Sherman on board. Sherman escaped but the Kiowa party killed twelve teamsters. When the war party returned to the reservation, they were arrested by the Army, and the leaders were sent to Texas to be tried for murder. The imprisonment of many prominent chiefs split the Kiowa into peace and war factions, but the raiding continued.

Conditions on the reservation and at villages across the region deteriorated, and by 1873–1874, many people were struggling to survive, as buffalo nearly disappeared from the region due to their indiscriminate slaughter by white hunters. A large group of Kiowa, Arapaho, Comanche, and Cheyenne attacked a group of hunters in the summer of 1874, suffering twenty killed with only two hunters killed. Events such as this convinced the government that the Peace Policy had failed on the southern plains and that the Army should move against noncompliant Indians and force them onto the reservation. The Army, using scorched earth policies of killing horses, burning lodges, and destroying food, pursued nonreservation Comanche, Cheyenne, Kiowa, Arapaho, and Kiowa-Apache, eventually forcing most to surrender by the fall of 1874. Many of the leaders of these tribes were imprisoned at Fort Marion in Florida. The end of the Red River War finished the struggle of southern plains tribes to maintain their culture and homelands unmolested by the U.S. government and white settlers. The tribes were confined to the reservation and forced to give up hunting buffalo and raiding, a way of life that had sustained them for thousands of years.

CONFLICT ON THE NORTHERN PLAINS

The Santee Sioux War and continual conflict on the northern plains created a state of constant warfare in the northern plains after the Civil War. Most Lakota lived free during this period and were not confined to a reservation. In 1865, government representatives approached some Lakota and Cheyenne communities about renewed peace negotiations. By 1866, enough leaders were convinced to attend a council and met federal representatives at Fort Laramie. The Lakota and Cheyenne refused to discuss issues of peace and relinquish a right-of-way through their land until the federal government agreed to withdraw troops from the Bozeman Trail and stop its use by settlers and miners traveling to Virginia City, Montana, where gold had been discovered in 1863. Red Cloud, one of the important leaders of the Lakota, warned the government that whites should not use the trail.

Hostility continued in the region as the Army sought to protect settlers and miners, and Lakota warriors defended their homeland and harassed the interlopers on the Bozeman Trail. In December 1866, Crazy Horse and a large group of Lakota warriors sought a confrontation with soldiers at Fort Phil Kearny. Eighty troops under the command of Captain William J. Fetterman rode out of the fort directly into an ambush, ending with the deaths of the entire detachment. The Fetterman Fight or Massacre led to a vigorous debate about Indian policy with the military advocating decisive military action against tribes like the Lakota, while civilian reformers advocated for negotiation and accused the military of fomenting violence and conflict.

Sporadic violence continued in the region until the spring of 1868 when the leadership of the Lakota agreed to meet at Fort Laramie once again to discuss peace. Meeting with representatives of the Peace Commission, leaders from the Lakota and Cheyenne successfully argued for the closure of the Bozeman Trail and the withdrawal of troops from the region. The tribes agreed to move onto reservations but could use traditional hunting grounds outside of the reservations in Montana, Wyoming, and the Dakota territories. A provision of the treaty also provided for roads, surveys, right-of-ways, and railroad construction. Historians believe that this portion of the treaty was added very late and was not well understood or translated for the tribes.

The Fort Laramie Treaty did not end conflict or tension in the region, as settlers, railroad workers, and miners continued to flood the region. Whites shot buffalo, used resources, and trespassed on land held by the tribes, increasing enmity and sparking cycles of reprisals and violence. This continual low-level violence was changed by the discovery of gold in Black Hills in 1874. Known as Paha Sapa by the Lakota, it was considered sacred land and was the center of the Sioux Reservation that was established by the Fort Laramie Treaty of 1868. In the summer of 1874, General Custer led a large force that accompanied miners and explorers to discover whether rumors of gold were true. Gold was discovered, and Custer used the national press to publicize the discovery, causing a rush to the area by miners.

The government pressured the Lakota to sell the Black Hills for $6 million, but the Lakota refused, defending their homeland and bitterly complaining of the duplicity of the government. By November 1875, the Grant administration decided to violate the Fort Laramie Treaty, withdrawing troops from the Black Hills and allowing unrestricted access to the area. In addition, the administration ordered the military to force the Lakota onto the reservations by February 1, 1876.

This was the last straw for the Lakota and the Cheyenne. Essentially the U.S. government had declared war on the native communities in the region in order to gain access to valuable mineral rights and to construct transportation routes through the territory. The deadline to remove to the reservation passed with most bands refusing to comply with the order. The Lakota, Cheyenne, and Arapaho prepared for war under the leadership of Sitting Bull, Crazy Horse, Black Moon, Lame Deer, Dirty Mocassins, Charcoal Bear, and other prominent leaders from their tribes. During June 1876, the Hunkpapa held their annual Sun Dance near Rosebud Creek. When the rite finished, the bands moved to the Little Bighorn River. On June 16, troops under General Crook attacked the encampment, but the Lakota and their allies forced Crook to retreat. Part of this larger military operation, units under the command of General Alfred Terry rushed to engage the Lakota. Under Terry's command was Custer's Seventh Cavalry, and a third portion of the force was commanded by Colonel John Gibbons. These units were to converge on the Yellowstone and Powder Rivers. After confirming that the Lakota and their allies were camped by the Little Bighorn River, Terry divided his forces, ordering Custer to bottle up Indian warriors at the south end of Little Bighorn Valley. Underestimating the strength of the Lakota and their allies, Custer divided his force into four groups and sought out a large Indian village discovered by his Indian scouts. Custer led his force of 225 men against the village that likely held between 1,500 and 3,000 warriors from the Lakota, Cheyenne, and Arapaho. Outnumbered and with his forces divided, Custer and all his command were killed. The other columns from the Seventh Cavalry also were attacked and pinned down until June 27 when reinforcements arrived and the Lakota and their allies withdrew (Trafzer, 250–251).

The Battle of Little Bighorn was a great victory that was celebrated by the Lakota, Dakota, Arapaho, and Cheyenne, but their victory was short-lived. The Army continued to pursue the nonreservation bands between 1876 and 1881. Most of these tribes eventually surrendered and moved to the reservation since they had great difficulty feeding themselves and suffered enormously from disease and malnutrition. Even Sitting Bull and Crazy Horse, the staunchest resistors of the U.S. government, ultimately surrendered to the U.S. Army. Crazy Horse was killed in 1877 when General Crook sent a party to arrest him because of fears that he might leave the reservation. After exile in Canada, Sitting Bull surrendered and was sent to the Standing Rock Reservation. In 1891, he was shot and killed by an Indian policeman attempting to arrest him during the Ghost Dance movement.

The Lakota, Dakota, Cheyenne, and Arapaho, forced onto the reservation, faced enormous challenges to their survival. No strangers to disease, starvation, and exposure to the elements, the people suffered as life on the reservation continued to expose them to death and disease. The Indian agents, government officials, military officers, and missionaries charged with their welfare often abused their charges and sought to enrich themselves in the process. Despite these challenges, these communities survived and continued to struggle for sovereignty and self-determination.

RESISTANCE WEST OF THE ROCKY MOUNTAINS

The push to move Indian people to reservations and secure land for settlement was not limited to the Great Plains. Many native communities who had already signed treaties with the United States but continued to use and traverse their traditional homelands in the Pacific Northwest, California, and the Great Basin were faced with threats of removal to the reservation. From the end of the Civil War until nearly the end of the nineteenth century, Indian communities resisted this encroachment, sometimes resorting to violence as the means to resist outsiders.

THE MODOC WAR

When gold was discovered by whites on the American River in 1848 in Northern California, the world changed for California Indian communities. Within a year after the discovery, over 100,000 miners, settlers, and people eager to make a quick buck flooded the interior portions of Northern California. These people pushed out Indians, often with brutality and violence. By 1856, the state of California offered twenty-five cents per Indian scalp, and in 1860, the price was increased to $5 per scalp. While some native people managed to live in peace with whites, the desire for land, gold, and money frequently led to violence and murder in the gold fields of California.

By 1851, miners and settlers had built the town of Yreka, not far from Tule Lake, which was the traditional homeland of the Modoc. As settlement increased, conflict between the newcomers and the Modoc heightened, leading white settlers to call for their removal to a reservation. In 1864, the federal government forced the leaders of the Modoc, Kintpuash (Captain Jack) and Old Schonchin, to agree to relocate to the Klamath Reservation in southern Oregon. The problem with this move was that the Modoc were enemies with the Klamath, who already occupied the reservation. Eventually Captain Jack and his people left the reservation and returned to Northern California. They remained in their traditional homeland until 1869 when whites in the region called for their removal once again to the Klamath Reservation. Captain Jack and his people returned to the reservation but by the spring of 1870 left the reservation once again for home.

By 1872, General Edward Canby authorized his troops to begin the forced removal of the Modoc back to the reservation. The Modoc retreated to the lava beds south of Tule Lake and held off the Army from November 1872 to April 1873. At a peace negotiation on April 11, Captain Jack, under coercion from other Modoc leaders, killed Canby, while the other leaders shot the remaining peace commissioners. Fighting continued into June 1873, but facing starvation and the deaths of their families, Captain Jack and the other Modoc leaders surrendered to the Army. The leaders of the Modoc, including Captain Jack, Schonchin John, Boston Charley, and Black Jim, were tried and hanged in October 1873. The remnants of the Modoc were shipped to Indian Territory and settled on the Quapaw Agency, remaining there until 1909. In that year some returned to the Klamath Reservation, while others remained in Oklahoma (Trafzer, 258).

THE NEZ PERCE WAR

Like the Modoc, the Nez Perce faced increasing pressure from white settlers and gold seekers both during and after the Civil War. In 1855, the Nez Perce agreed to the treaty of 1855, which secured a large portion of their traditional homeland in Oregon and Idaho. When gold was discovered on the reservation in 1860, the reservation was flooded with prospectors and settlers eager to take advantage of the new gold rush. As described at the beginning of this chapter, the U.S. government was eager to renegotiate the 1855 treaty in order to procure Nez Perce land for miners and settlers. At the Lapwai Council of 1863, Nez Perce leaders refused to negotiate, but Chief Lawyer and his followers, after other leaders left, agreed to sign a treaty that relinquished 7 million acres of land, drastically reducing the reservation. This move split the tribe into treaty and nontreaty factions.

General Miles Charging the Indian Camp—the Dash into the Ravine, from *Frank Leslie's Illustrated Newspaper*, November 3, 1877. Newspapers were fascinated by the Nez Perce War of 1877, and illustrated many scenes from it. The non-treaty Nez Perce fled their homeland after being forced onto a reservation. After a nearly 1,500-mile flight, the survivors, led by Chief Joseph, surrendered to the United States Army. (Library of Congress)

One of the most prominent leaders of the nontreaty bands was Young Joseph (Hinmahtooyahlakekht). His people lived in northeastern Oregon in the beautiful Wallowa Valley. These lands were not part of the reduced reservation, and Joseph convinced the Office of Indian Affairs bureaucrats to lobby President Grant to establish an executive order reservation for his people. Unfortunately, due to a miscommunication, the reservation set aside land that was already settled by whites and did not protect Nez Perce land. In June 1875, Grant rescinded the reservation order, leaving Joseph and his people in limbo. While General Howard and other officials in the region argued that the 1863 Thief Treaty was illegal and that the Nez Perce should be allowed to remain in the Wallowa Valley, the events on the Great Plains increased pressure to force all nontreaty Nez Perce onto the reservation.

Responding to these pressures, the War Department in 1876 ordered Howard and the Army to force the Nez Perce onto the reservation. Howard called a council at Fort Lapwai in November 1876 and informed the Nez Perce that they would be considered hostile if they did not move to the reservation. No resolution emerged at this council, and Howard held another council in May 1877 and once again issued his demand to remove to the reservation. Joseph and the other leaders appointed Toohoolhoolzote, a holy man revered by many of the people, to speak on their behalf. After a passionate speech outlining devotion of Nez Perce and Palouse to their homeland and their spiritual relationship to their homes, Howard, incensed over Toohoolhoolzote's speech, arrested the holy man and forced the remaining leaders to agree to remove to the reservation.

Reluctantly, the nontreaty bands gathered their belongings and started the long trek to the reservation. In the midst of the move, a young warrior named Wahlitits murdered Larry Ott, the man who had murdered his father, Eagle Robe, the previous year. This started a cycle of raids, with other warriors joining to kill whites in the region. Meeting to discuss what to do next, Joseph and the other leaders decided to move to White Bird Canyon, a more defensible position. Hoping to negotiate with the Army, Joseph was disappointed when the Army rode in and began firing on the encampment. The Battle of White Bird Canyon was a decisive victory for the Nez Perce, where they killed thirty-four soldiers and forced the remainder to retreat back to Fort Lapwai.

The long trek of the nontreaty Nez Perce had begun. Fleeing over the Bitterroot Mountains, the nontreaty sought to join with friends in Montana or on the Great Plains. After the Battle of White Bird Canyon, Looking Glass led the nontreaty bands and decided the best course of action was to join the Crow on the Plains. The Nez Perce traveled south from the Lolo Trail to the area known as Big Hole, a place familiar to many Nez Perce who had traveled to the Plains to hunt buffalo. The encampment was attacked on

August 9, 1877, by soldiers and volunteers under the command of Colonel John Gibbon. Nearly ninety Nez Perce were killed along with thirty-one soldiers. Chief Joseph organized the escape of the women, children, and old, while warriors fought a rearguard action to protect their retreat.

Fleeing from Big Hole, the Nez Perce traveled through Yellowstone National Park, evading the Army and hoping eventually to reach Canada safely. Pursued by at least three different Army columns, the Nez Perce made it to the Bears Paw Mountains in northern Montana by the end of September, close to the Canadian border. Exhausted, hungry, and cold, they set up camp and were attacked and surrounded by the Army on October 1, 1877. The nontreaty bands resisted until October 7 when Joseph surrendered to the Army. While many quote Joseph saying "I will fight no more forever," Joseph's cousin, Yellow Wolf, who was at the surrender disputes that Joseph said this. Historians believe that Lieutenant Charles Erskine Scott Wood made the speech up when he reported it to the newspapers.

After their surrender, many people went into captivity, while others fled to Canada. The 400 or so survivors were shipped to Fort Leavenworth, Kansas, where they spent a miserable and deadly winter. In July 1878, the survivors were sent to the Quapaw Agency as punishment for their resistance. Between 1878 and 1885, Joseph and other nontreaty leaders frequently sought to return home to the Pacific Northwest. They also gained white supporters who lobbied the government on their behalf. After nearly eight years of captivity, the Nez Perce were allowed to return home, some going to the Nez Perce Reservation, while Joseph was sent to the Colville Reservation in northeastern Washington because of threats of violence and arrest made against him and his people.

While Joseph and his people did not return to their beloved Wallowa Valley, both treaty and nontreaty Nez Perce survived and sought to preserve their culture and way of life.

RESISTANCE IN THE GREAT BASIN

At nearly the same time as the Nez Perce War, bands of Paiutes, Bannocks, Agaidikas, and Tukuarikas continued to occupy large swaths of land in Oregon, Idaho, Utah, Nevada, Wyoming, and California. As with other tribes in the West, these communities faced increasing pressure from settlers, miners, and from road and railroad construction in the region. While reservations had been established for these communities, often people hunted, fished, and moved throughout nonreservation areas. As hostility and confrontations increased, whites demanded that native people should be confined to the reservation and not allowed to exercise their treaty rights by using their traditional homelands for subsistence. After the murder of two whites in 1877, some Indians returned to the Fort Hall and Umatilla Reservations, but many followed Buffalo Horn, attacking whites and their settlements throughout the region. The Army began pursuit engaging Umatilla in northeast Oregon, Shoshone in Yellowstone National Park, and other bands throughout the region. By September 1878, the war had ended with many bands surrendering at forts and Indian agencies throughout the region.

APACHE RESISTANCE

The pattern of negotiating treaties and moving tribes to reservations occurred throughout the West, both during and after the Civil War. As Indian people tried to subsist on reservations, many refused to endure the conditions there and left to live a life free of government control. These small communities and bands were pursued constantly by the U.S. military, forcing them either back on the reservation or into violent resistance. In the Southwest, the Apache had fought for generations against the Spanish, Mexicans, and Americans, refusing to submit to outsiders. After the military action against the Apache in 1873, General Crook believed that Apache resistance was finished, but it would take another thirteen years to subdue all the Apache bands.

In 1873–1874, the federal government decided to consolidate various reservations and concentrate Indians on the San Carlos Reservation in southeastern Arizona. Forcing so many different bands and tribes of Indians onto the same reservation consistently caused problems as communities were often rivals or outright enemies. In April 1877, Indian agent John Clum, in charge of the San Carlos Reservation, arrived on reservations to remove bands of Ojo Caliente and Chiricahua from their old reservations to San Carlos. Geronimo and other leaders thought they were there to talk but instead Clum, using tribal police, arrested Geronimo and the leaders and forced their people to remove to San Carlos. While Clum resigned shortly thereafter, he set the stage for nearly ten years of conflict and turmoil in the region.

In October 1877, Victorio, who succeeded Mangas Coloradas as leader, fled the reservation and led the Army on two years of pursuit. Always attempting to return home to Ojo Caliente, Victorio and his followers negotiated numerous surrenders that placed them in their homelands, only to have the government eventually order them back to the San Carlos Reservation. In 1880, he declared war, attacking soldiers on the reservation and escaping with his followers. Fighting both Mexican and U.S. forces, Victorio rallied many Apache to his cause, raiding extensively throughout the Southwest. U.S. and Mexican forces fought the Apache under Victorio, eventually attacking them while performing a sacred rite and killing Victorio and sixty Apache. Even with this defeat, the war continued.

Until 1878, Geronimo lived on the San Carlos Reservation but left for the Sierra Madre Mountains in Mexico. During their escape, the Apache raided Mexican ranches and settlements, stealing livestock and killing anyone who got in their way. In 1880, Geronimo returned to San Carlos, but unrest continued when the Army arrested Nakaidoklini, an Apache holy man. The Apache resisted the arrest, and Geronimo and other Apache leaders fled the reservation, returning to the Sierra Madre Mountains.

In 1882, General Crook decided to crush Apache resistance. He placed the Apache on the reservation under direct military control and used Apache scouts to help attack the Apache in the Sierra Madre Mountains. The scouts were very effective, eventually leading a successful campaign that witnessed the surrender and return to San Carlos of most Apache, including Geronimo and other prominent leaders, by March 1884.

Conditions on San Carlos continued to encourage various bands of Apache to leave and return to the Sierra Madre Mountains. In 1885, the Army continued its campaign against the Apache, with the War Department arguing for the removal of all Apache from Arizona. General Crook argued successfully against this and met with Apache leaders in March 1886, telling them to surrender and informing them that they would be imprisoned in Florida for two years and then sent back to the San Carlos Reservation. Geronimo and the other leaders agreed to surrender and return to San Carlos. On the way, whiskey traders convinced the Apache that they would be hanged if they returned to the reservation, leading them to renege on the surrender agreement.

General Crook was relieved of his command on April 1, 1886. His replacement, General Nelson Miles, continued the campaign against the Apache. In August 1886, Lieutenant Gatewood with two Apache scouts managed to find Geronimo's camp and with the aid of the scouts convinced Geronimo and his people to surrender. On September 4, 1886, Miles accepted Geronimo's surrender. Shortly thereafter, the 509 Apache were loaded on trains and sent to Florida. They were imprisoned at Fort Pickens in Pensacola, Florida, where they remained until 1894 when Congress passed a bill to allow some Apache to go to Fort Sill, Oklahoma. Of the original 509 captives, only 296 made the journey to Fort Sill. Geronimo lived in Fort Sill until his death in 1909, a prisoner of war until the day of his death.

CONCLUSION

Combining a mixture of the Peace and Force Policy, the U.S. government after the Civil War sought to move Indian people and communities onto reservations in the western United States, opening up their traditional homelands to white settlement and use. While the reform movement surrounding the Peace Policy sought to find ways to do this through negotiation and peaceful means, native people, when they refused to leave their land or resisted intruding outsiders, were subjected to enormous military violence. Whether Lakota, Comanche, Kiowa, Nez Perce, Palouse, Modoc, Apache, Paiute, or Shoshone, each community and tribe faced and vigorously resisted these pressures. These pressures also fractured native communities as factions arose in response to white pressure—some groups negotiated or gave in to white demands, while others resisted using movement and violence. By the end of the 1880s, the major military campaigns against Indian people were mainly over. Now the struggle shifted to reservations where Indian people fought to preserve their culture, language, and history while facing forces that sought to erase their cultures and lives from American life.

PROFILE: KINTPUASH (CAPTAIN JACK)—MODOC

Kintpuash was born at Wa'chamshwash village near the California-Oregon border in 1837. Very little is known about his early life except that his father was killed in 1846 by whites during the Ben Wright Massacre. Little contact occurred between the Modoc and settlers until the discovery of gold along the American River in 1848. The California Gold Rush ushered in a new era of violence, disease, and dislocation for California native communities. As thousands streamed to the gold fields, miners, settlers, and businessmen trespassed on Indian land and used resources without permission or regard for the people who lived there.

Kintpuash wanted peace and argued for trade with settlers while opposing white incursion and expansion into Modoc land. He was nicknamed Captain Jack during this time because he wore a U.S. Army coat with brass buttons given to him by an army officer. During this time, Kintpuash and his people lived in the vicinity of Eureka, California. In 1864, a Modoc chief, Schonchin John, signed a treaty with the U.S. government that agreed to move the tribe to a reservation in Oregon that was located on the traditional homeland of the Klamath who resented the presence of the Modoc. Due to a lack of land and the tensions between different communities, Captain Jack and his people returned to California, asking for a reservation of their own, which was denied by federal officials.

As tensions increased between settlers and the Modoc, cries for removing the Modoc amplified. In November 1872, U.S. Army troops attacked Captain Jack's camp and forced him and his followers to agree to removal. At the meeting, some of the Modoc refused to give up their weapons, and violence broke out when the Army tried to confiscate the weapons. In the ensuing struggle, eight soldiers and fifteen Modoc were killed.

Captain Jack and his followers, fearing reprisal from the military, fled to nearby lava beds. Whites attacked the Modoc in their retreat, and the Modoc responded by killing twelve white settlers. In January 1873, U.S. troops entered the lava beds. A peace party that included Winema, Captain Jack's cousin, started talks with the Modoc. Two other chiefs, Schonchin John and Hooker Jim, accused Captain Jack of cowardice for preaching peace and agreeing to the meeting and demanded that Captain Jack kill the peace party believing that the military would retreat if successful.

At the April 11 meeting, Kintpuash agreed to the terms presented by General Edward Canby but shot Canby, while other Modoc leaders attacked the rest of the peace party. Fighting continued in the lava beds until June 1873 when the Modoc surrendered. Captain Jack and other Modoc leaders were tried by a military commission and found guilty of murder. On October 3, 1873, Captain Jack, Schonchin John, and two other leaders were hanged. The 155 Modoc survivors of the war were sent to the Quapaw Agency in Indian Territory as punishment for the war. They remained there until 1909 when they were returned to the Klamath Reservation in southern Oregon.

PROFILE: TATANKA-IYOTANKA—SITTING BULL—HUNKPAPA SIOUX

Sitting Bull was born around 1831 near the Grand River in what is now South Dakota. He had a close relationship with his mother, Her-Holy-Door, and engaged in combat at the young age of fourteen. He was married twice and was father to two daughters, a son, and an adopted son. Sitting Bull was a blotaunka (war chief) and was known for his wisdom, bravery, and generosity. He was also a holy man who participated frequently in Sun Dances.

In the 1870s, Sitting Bull was chosen as wakiconza (supreme chief) and attempted to unite the various Sioux bands to resist the incursions of white people on their land. When gold was found in Paha Sapa (the Black Hills), Sitting Bull and other leaders resisted attempts by the U.S. government to take the sacred land of the Black Hills that was guaranteed to them as hunting grounds near the reservation in the Fort Laramie Treaty. The government declared that any Indian not on the reservation by January 31, 1876, would be considered hostile and subject to military attack. Military forces soon set out to drive the Sioux onto the reservation. This was the beginning of the Great Sioux War that eventually saw the defeat of Custer and the Seventh Cavalry at the Little Big Horn River and the subsequent defeat of Indian forces, the illegal seizure of the Black Hills by the U.S. government, and the flight of Sitting Bull and many others across the Medicine Line into Canada.

Sitting Bull refused to accept a pardon if he returned to the reservation, remaining in Canada until July 1881 when he returned to the United States, was arrested, and held as a prisoner of war for two years. After his release, Sitting Bull was sent to the Standing Rock Agency where he lived with his family, caring for his children and aging mother. In 1884, Sitting Bull was allowed to take part in a traveling exhibition and would eventually join Buffalo Bill's Wild West Show for four months.

Returning home to the reservation, Sitting Bull continued to resist the United States and its unjust policies on the reservation. He bitterly denounced the land agreements of 1888 and 1889 that divided up the reservation and handed half of the land to non-Indians. By 1890, Sitting Bull participated in the Ghost Dance and the religious revival that accompanied this movement. Government officials and ordinary citizens intimidated by the Ghost Dance movement called for its suppression. On December 15, 1890, Sitting Bull was shot in the head by a Lakota Sioux policeman seeking to arrest him. His death led to the tragic events that occurred at Wounded Knee two weeks later. Sitting Bull was buried near Fort Yates, North Dakota, but his remains were later relocated to South Dakota in 1953.

REFERENCES AND FURTHER READING

Edmunds, R. David, Frederick E. Hoxie, and Neal Salisbury. *The People: A History of Native America*. Boston: Houghton Mifflin Company, 2007.

Elliott, Michael A. *Custerology: The Enduring Legacy of the Indian Wars and George Armstrong Custer*. Chicago: University of Chicago Press, 2007.

Isenberg, Andrew C. *The Destruction of the Bison*. Cambridge: Cambridge University Press, 2000.

Ostler, Jeffrey. *The Lakotas and the Black Hills: The Struggle for Sacred Ground*. New York: Viking Penguin, 2010.

Pearson, J. Diane. *The Nez Perces in the Indian Territory: Nimiipuu Survival*. Norman: University of Oklahoma, 2008.

Smoak, Gregory. *Ghost Dances and Identity: Prophetic Religion and American Indian Ethnogenesis in the Nineteenth Century*. Berkeley: University of California Press, 2006.

Sweeney, Edwin R. *From Cochise to Geronimo: The Chiricahua Apaches, 1874–1886*. Norman: University of Oklahoma Press, 2010.

Trafzer, Clifford E. *As Long as the Grass Shall Grow and Rivers Flow: A History of Native Americans*. Fort Worth, TX: Harcourt College Publishers, 2000.

West, Elliott. *The Last Indian War: The Nez Perce Story*. New York: Oxford University Press, 2009.

Chapter 11

Assimilation(s) and Reservation Life, 1880–1900

After the profound and contracted conflicts throughout the West, tribal communities were faced with confinement to reservations. These reservations varied in size and location, often occupying land that was not as desirable for white settlement. As native people arrived on reservations, they often found that the U.S. government had placed numerous bands and tribal groups on a single reservation, despite the fact that these groups may have been enemies, spoke different languages, and practiced widely divergent cultural expressions. Reservation life was precarious with many people falling victim to disease and malnutrition due to the failure of the government to provide rations and a healthy living environment. Despite these hurdles, Indian communities sought to preserve their ways of life, resisted the cultural manipulations of outsiders, and chose their own path of adaptation to this new reality rather than simply adopting the ways of white society.

THE RESERVATION SYSTEM

The history of Indian-white relations is littered with the attempts of whites to sequester native people into smaller geographic areas in order to control their movement and practice of their culture. As with most large governmental institutions related to Indian-white relations, reservations emerged from this long history of interaction between whites and Indians.

During the colonial period, two different approaches for dealing with Indian communities emerged. In New England, first the Puritans and then their successors removed tribal communities, confined them to what they referred to as "towns of praying Indians," and attempted to convert them to Christianity and control their interactions with whites in the area. Native people often saw through these efforts to control their lives and refused to move to the reservation or actively resisted colonial governments. While these were smaller experiments in the confinement of native people, they did serve as examples for later attempts to create a reservation system in the West during the nineteenth century.

The second approach was embraced by Virginia and the southern colonies. In these areas, tribal communities sought to put distance between themselves and whites, frequently moving further west, as settlers encroached on their land. Of course this created tensions between tribes and with settlers, as native communities sought safe places to avoid white contact. This pattern was played out in the nineteenth century with tribes in the West, as they used distance and movement to keep away from whites.

During the 1820s and 1830s, the United States embraced the New England method by ordering the removal of the Civilized Tribes to Indian Territory. While not a reservation, the removal and confinement of tribes east of the Mississippi River to Indian Territory served the purpose of removing Indian communities from white contact and allowed the government to annex their land for distribution to American citizens.

In 1852, the first "modern" reservation system was established in California by California Superintendent of Indian Affairs Edward Fitzgerald Beale. Seven hundred Indians were relocated to the reservation at Fort Tejon at the south end of the San Joaquin Valley. Beale intended for these communities to farm and ranch while also abandoning their culture to become productive members of society. Beale and his successor, Thomas Henley, touted the success of this system, and it became a model for the reservation system that would emerge by the end of the nineteenth century. During the Civil War, the Bosque Redondo Reservation was established using the California model. At Bosque Redondo, many different tribal communities were placed together on the reservation—Apache, Navaho, Pima, and many others, despite their differences and enmity (Trafzer, 198).

In the minds of government officials and reformers, there were two principal reasons for reservations. The first purpose was to confine native people geographically, keeping them away from whites and from nonreservation Indians who might interfere with the acculturation projects of government officials. This gave missionaries, teachers, Indian agents, and others the chance to proselytize, instruct, and control people. Indian agents and missionaries attempted to quash religious rites, dances, and music. In addition, they sought to educate Indians out of being Indian. They believed that teaching people to read and write while instructing them in Christianity and the cultural practices of white society would transform Indian people into productive members of society.

Reservations were also places designed to turn native people into farmers and teach them how to fend for themselves. This second reason for reservations was deeply embedded in the ideology of time, as whites sought to "kill the Indian, to save the man" in the famous words of Richard Henry Pratt, founder of the Carlisle Indian School in Pennsylvania. According to reformers and government officials, Indians needed to be taught self-sufficiency in order to survive in "modern" society.

In the end, reservations served white interests over and above native communities' best interests. Whites sought to control native people, destroy their culture, and take their land while simultaneously transforming individual Indians into productive members of the larger society. In the 1870s and 1880s, white reformers, Indian agents, military officials, and government bureaucrats believed that this was the only way for Indians to survive, and this belief continued into the twentieth century. These people sought to change nearly every facet of Indian life and saw reservations, boarding schools, and other means of confinement and assimilation as important means to the end of integrating native people into the larger culture.

LIFE ON THE RESERVATION

Confinement to the reservation was an enormous change for tribal communities in the western United States. Communities were forced to occupy much smaller landholding, which often made it very difficult to subsist. In addition, many reservations had more than one tribal group relocated to that location, which frequently translated into competition for resources and resentment. The main reality of the reservation was the inability to move freely. To leave the reservation, Indians often were required to obtain a pass from the Indian agents and were viewed with suspicion by the white population.

During the initial stage of reservation life, most Indian families relied on government rations for food, supplementing with hunting, fishing, and gathering when and where they could. Finding food sources on the reservation was difficult, especially as the nineteenth century progressed, as whites put enormous pressure on animal and plant populations outside of the reservation. Many tribal communities had negotiated in good faith with the federal government and had reserved fishing, hunting, and gathering rights on land outside the reservation, in "usual and accustomed places." When Indians attempted to exercise these rights, they often found white settlers occupying the land who were not interested in allowing hunting or fishing on their newly gained property, especially by Indians. Native people were frequently arrested by sheriffs and game wardens for hunting out of season or without licenses.

The inability to procure traditional foods and the reliance on rations left native people vulnerable to both pathogens and chronic diseases. Lard, sugar, white flour, and other staples wreaked havoc on people's body and were the sources of obesity, diabetes, and other diseases. Poor conditions on the reservation and inadequate health care added to this misery. Many people contracted tuberculosis, pneumonia, influenza, and other diseases. Doctors and medical workers were often overwhelmed and in short supply, resulting in poor medical care on reservations.

In addition to confronting daunting problems with food and health, Indian people also faced threats to their culture, religion, and way of life on reservations. During the Grant administration, missionaries and church workers were allowed greater access to reservations and often acted as Indian agents and teachers on reservations. The pressure to convert to Christianity increased, pitting people who had converted against groups who sought to maintain their culture and avoid white culture.

It is important to remember that there were individuals, families, and tribes that did not move onto reservations, often living on land not wanted by whites or in locations so remote that they were not often disturbed by settlers, miners, or the U.S. government. For example, there were tribes on the Columbia Plateau that were not part of the 1855 treaty negotiations who steadfastly refused to move to reservations. The most well-known of these groups is the Wanapum tribe who lived close to Priest Rapids on the Columbia River. Smohalla, one of the most influential religious prophets in the region, led this group, and their descendants still reside in the Priest Rapids area.

Refusing to move to the reservation did come with a cost. While Indian communities on reservations came under increasing pressure to assimilate, they also were somewhat protected from the white communities surrounding them. Nonreservation Indians did not enjoy this modest protection and had to find ways to live peacefully with the increasing numbers of settlers moving onto their homeland. Another problem for nonreservation tribal communities was that they were not recognized tribal entities by the U.S. government, which would have consequences later, especially in the twentieth century.

EDUCATION

Educating native people occurred in many different forms before the formal founding of Indian boarding schools in the United States. On many reservations, Indian agents and agency staff taught, with varying degrees of success, vocational and agricultural skills, especially to adult Indians. Missionaries often offered classes to children, teaching them to read and write, with a large dose of Christianity thrown in for good measure. After reservations were established, some Indian children attended public schools in their area, often facing harassment and discrimination.

Omaha boys in cadet uniforms at Carlisle Indian School, Carlisle, Pennsylvania, ca. 1880. Indian boarding schools were key instruments in the government's program to assimilate Indians into American society. Students were required to adopt western dress, cut their hair, and learn English. (National Archives)

In 1879, Richard Henry Pratt founded the first Indian boarding school in the United States at a former army barracks in Carlisle, Pennsylvania. Pratt, a former army officer, had gained experience in Indian education when, as a young army officer, he escorted Kiowa, Comanche, and Southern Cheyenne prisoners to Florida. He organized a school for the prisoners, using its success to lobby his superiors to allow him to enroll the prisoners in Hampton Institute, a private school for African-Americans in Virginia. Wanting his own educational institution, Pratt lobbied the government for a location to create the school, and the War Department offered up the former army barracks in Carlisle, Pennsylvania.

Pratt set out to recruit Indian children to the school, focusing on the Sioux, Navaho, Ojibwe, and Cheyenne. Within two decades, almost 2,000 students would attend Carlisle Indian Industrial Training School.

Pratt's model and the curriculum that he and others developed served as models as well. The main idea of the school was to control every aspect of an Indian child's life once he or she arrived at the facility. At arrival, students were given haircuts and outfitted with military-style uniforms to promote uniformity and conformity. Cultural expressions like religious rites and language were not allowed, and students who participated in these expressions were punished severely. Education was the central focus, with students learning to read and write in English. In addition, vocational, agricultural, and domestic skills were taught to girls and boys.

By the end of the 1880s, the Indian Office opened six more schools, including Haskell Institute in Kansas and Chemawa in Oregon. At the end of the 1890s, seventeen more off-reservation boarding schools were constructed. At the beginning of the twentieth century, nearly 20,000 Indian students attended government-supported schools, both on and off the reservation. Of this total, 6,000 attended off-reservation boarding schools that followed the model set up by Pratt in the 1880s (Edmunds, Hoxie, and Salisbury, 335).

LIFE AT BOARDING SCHOOL

A student's life at boarding school was often a very negative experience. From the moment students arrived, school personnel sought to control every aspect of their lives. One of the first things that was done was to cut hair and issue military-style uniforms. The idea was to strip students of any tribal identity in order to make acculturation easier. The school day was highly regimented, split between regular school lessons and vocational/agricultural training for boys and home economics or domestic skill training for girls. Even the physical space was tightly controlled. At Sherman Indian Institute in Riverside, California, Indian Office officials built the school in the new Mission Style architecture that hearkened back to the mission system in California and the attempt of the Catholic Church to convert and change Indian people. Corporal punishment was used frequently for students who broke rules or resisted the elaborate acculturation processes of the schools. This was standard practice at all schools in the United States during this period. Students were also not allowed to express themselves culturally. They were punished severely for speaking their language or attempting to hold religious or culturally significant rites or rituals. In spite of these harsh conditions, students found ways to speak their language and continue to express their unique tribal identity.

Not only did students face the harsh disciplinary environment of the school, but they also suffered from disease and death. Before the emergence of modern medicine in the early twentieth century, students contracted many diseases while at school. Tuberculosis, influenza, pneumonia, trachoma, and other diseases raced through student populations, who were often crammed into crowded living environments. Tuberculosis was a leading cause of death among American Indians during this time, and many students contracted the disease while at school, returning home to infect friends and family. It was not only diseases of the body that afflicted students, but many students also suffered from severe depression or other psychological problems.

Despite these enormous obstacles and challenges, students often used the boarding school experience as a way to help themselves and their people. Many future leaders of tribal communities attended these schools, forged friendships, continued to practice their culture as they could, and returned to their communities with skills to resist efforts to assimilate their people and rob them of their land and resources.

ALLOTMENT

It was not only Indian children who faced the challenges of assimilation and threats to their way of life. As noted earlier, white reformers were very concerned about Indian people continuing to practice their culture and way of life, even on reservations. They argued that the only way for tribal communities to survive was to abandon their "Indianness" and adopt white cultural and economic practices. One of the principal ways to do this, as many white reformers believed, was for Indians to learn to farm and ranch, thereby becoming productive members of society. Hearkening back to Jefferson and his ideas about democracy and the role of independent yeoman farmers, many white Americans believed that owning and working the land was the best way to become part of society. Intellectuals of the time argued for this as well, one of the most prominent being Lewis Henry Morgan, an anthropologist. He noted the differences between "primitive" and "civilized" cultures, focusing on how land was used by different cultural groups. He associated communal property use with primitive cultures and private ownership with more "advanced" civilized cultures. His work lent intellectual credence to the ideas of white reformers and bureaucrats who wished to change Indian land tenure (Edmunds, Hoxie, and Salisbury, 324).

As more and more whites moved into regions surrounding reservations, arguments and pressure to force change on the way Indian communities held land increased. There were not only arguments that land ownership would help assimilate Indians into the broader U.S. society, but whites were also eager to either lease or purchase land on the reservation. During this period, Henry Dawes, senator from Massachusetts, worked on passing a bill in Congress to allot land to individual Indians. Dawes's ideas drew large support from white Americans, but many native communities disapproved of these ideas and protested against the passage of Dawes's legislation. Indian communities in Indian Territory were the staunchest critics of the bill and sent numerous letters of protest to Congress. Despite Indian opposition, Congress approved the Dawes Act in February 1887, and it was signed into law shortly thereafter.

The General Allotment Act or the Dawes Act, as it was more commonly known, would change the landscape of reservations and separate millions of acres of land from tribal holdings, transferring them to non-Indians. The Dawes Act required that reservations be surveyed and then allotted. Individual heads of household would receive 160-acre homesteads, while other adult family members received 80 acres. Children, on the other hand, received only 40 acres. If an individual refused to choose his or her homestead, then after four years a site was selected for that person by the secretary of the interior, generally through the Indian agents or one of their designees. Individual allotments were held in trust by the U.S. government for 25 years. Any land that was left over after a reservation was allotted was deemed "surplus" land and would be sold to the federal government after negotiation with tribal elders and leadership. Under the original act, the "Five Civilized Tribes" in Indian Territory were excluded from allotment as well as the Seneca Nation in New York. Subsequent legislation amended the Dawes Act to include Indian Territory and dealt with taking title to the land and citizenship (Edmunds, Hoxie, and Salisbury, 325–326).

From the Act's passage until 1900, Indian landholdings decreased from 150 million acres to 78 million acres. By 1934, total land owned by Indians was down to 48 million acres. Over the course of fifty years, nearly 100 million acres was deemed surplus by the government or was sold by individual Indians after they gained title. Reservations became a hodgepodge of Indian and non-Indian landholdings, with many native people leasing their lands to white farmers and ranchers rather than working it themselves. Also, depending on the location, an allotment might not be viable for farming or ranching. On the Great Plains, a homestead of 160 acres was not necessarily a viable farm. The other problem generated by allotment was land fractionalization. Since the land was held in trust for 25 years by the United States and the rules for dividing land to heirs was confusing and problematic, many surviving heirs ended up with small parcels of land scattered throughout the reservation. Eventually many people sold their land, leaving them landless (Trafzer, 330).

Allotment occurred on nearly every reservation in the United States. On every reservation, individual Indians and tribal leadership opposed the surveys and the process of allotment. In 1889, Alice Fletcher, an anthropologist, was appointed by the Bureau of Indian Affairs to survey and allot the Nez Perce Reservation in Idaho, one of the first to undergo the process. In 1892, Fletcher finished the survey and allotment process, and the "surplus" land was sold to the U.S. government. During the four years of her work, Nez Perce people protested the process. Despite their protests, the Bureau of Indian Affairs finished the process and allotted individual holdings to the Nez Perce. In the National Archives, moving testimony of this protest and dissent is found in the records of allotment.

Two of the most dramatic episodes of the allotment and land seizure process occurred in the Dakotas and Indian Territory. After the Battle of Little Bighorn and the defeat and surrender of Plains Indian people, the U.S. government, often under pressure from settlers and local politicians, began the process of seizing land from the Sioux. The first action was to divide the Sioux Reservation into five separate reservations. The second action was Congress demanding that the Sioux cede all land west of the 103rd meridian, including the Black Hills, to the United States. Once the Dawes Act was passed, the pressure to break up the remaining reservations increased, and in 1889, General Crook coerced and persuaded enough tribal leaders to agree to sell 9 million acres of land. Soon thereafter, settlers purchased former Sioux land for homesteads and communities.

In Indian Territory, the process was also rife with protest and coercion. In 1889, Congress authorized the opening of land not assigned to tribes in Indian Territory for settlement. This was done over the protests of nearly every tribal community in the Territory. Two million acres were opened, and the first of the Oklahoma land rushes occurred with 50,000 settlers claiming land in one day. A year later, Congress recognized the Territory of Oklahoma, centered on the land opened for settlement in western Oklahoma. In 1898, Congress passed the Curtis Act, which extended the Dawes Act to the Five Civilized Tribes in Indian Territory. Following the process that had occurred on reservations throughout the West, tribes in Indian Territory had their land allotted over their objections. In addition, the Curtis Act abolished tribal governments and courts in Indian Territory, dealing an enormous blow to tribal sovereignty. From this point forward, the U.S. government would deal with individual landowning Indians (Edmunds, Hoxie, and Salisbury, 329).

STRATEGIES FOR SURVIVAL AND RESISTANCE

Confinement to the reservation, combined with subjection to the assimilation and proselytizing of missionaries, Indian Agents, and white reformers, placed enormous pressure on tribal communities and their culture. Responses to these pressures ranged from those people who fully embraced white culture to those who refused completely to adopt white practices and culture. The majority of people frequently adapted to their situation by selectively choosing elements from white culture and practice that enhanced their survival while at the same time attempting to retain their language, religion, and traditional cultural practices. For example, while Indian movement on and off the reservation was restricted, it was not unusual for families and individuals to travel around their region attending rodeos, pow-wows, or dances, visiting relatives, and working at itinerant jobs. These trips were reminiscent of the traditional seasonal round that was practiced by many native communities in the western United States and caused many a sleepless night for Indian agents who worried about children not going to school and the influence that traditional family members might exert on their charges.

This wide-ranging response to reservation life and the pressures of acculturation argues against the myth that Indians were disappearing and against the power of assimilation efforts by white society. Native people had agency in their choices, frequently frustrating government bureaucrats and missionaries by picking and choosing various parts of white culture to fit their own desires and agendas. Some people converted to Christianity but continued to have relationships with traditional, non-Christian relatives who influenced their lives and their practice of Christianity. There were parents who sent their children to boarding school, not as a means for them to lose their Indian identity but as a way to help their people by learning about white culture and using that to the advantage of their community. Each of these decisions was made by individual people who were seeking to survive in the face of enormous pressure from white society to stop being Indian and assimilate into white culture.

One of the most powerful responses to the situation on most reservations was a resurgence and reinterpretation of existing Native American religious practice. Holy people played an integral role in the resistance to whites that occurred after the Civil War. Holy men like Toohoolhoolzote, Sitting Bull, and Smohalla served as examples to their people and gave them hope and power to resist white encroachment. After their confinement to the reservation, prophets or holy men continued to help their people cope with the despair of their situation and find new avenues of hope in a desperate situation.

These prophets frequently related that they had died and traveled to the spirit world or heaven and returned with messages of hope and deliverance for their people. In the mid-1850s, Smohalla, a Wanapum warrior, began preaching that Indian people should purify themselves, reject white culture and practices, and avoid alcohol. Living at Priest Rapids along the Columbia River, Smohalla influenced many tribal communities on the Columbia Plateau with his example of resistance to white influence and adherence to traditional cultural ways. Smohalla lived and taught until 1895, profoundly impacting native communities in the region through the establishment of the Dreamer religion, which is still influential among tribes in the region.

Another Pacific Northwest prophet was John Slocum or Squaschtun, a Nisqually Indian. He experienced trances during which he communicated

A Washani ceremony in a longhouse in the Pacific Northwest, ca. 1896. Washani is a traditional Native American religion that was revived and popularized by Smohalla (ca. 1815–1895), a religious leader from the Columbia Plateau. He and other religious leaders in the Pacific Northwest were instrumental in preserving the traditional religious practices of their people and passing them to their descendants. (James Mooney, "The Ghost Dance Religion," in the *Fourteenth Annual Report of the American Bureau of Ethnography*, 1896)

with the divine, relating these messages to people on his reservation. He was the founder of the Indian Shaker religion, teaching his followers to believe in aspects of Christian belief, like heaven and hell as well as God and Jesus Christ. He also taught that his divine messages should shape religious life for his followers. The religion got its name from followers shaking to remove sins from their body. The Shaker religion quickly spread down the Pacific Coast, eventually resulting in the incorporation of the Indian Shaker Church in 1910. Like many of the prophets of this period, Slocum and his followers were closely watched by Indian agents, the military, and the surrounding white communities, especially as their influence spread. Slocum, Smohalla, and the other prophets suffered through harassment, arrest, and white opposition, since they often included teachings that prophesized the eventual disappearance of whites if Indian people committed themselves to their teachings.

One of the most influential prophets of this time was Wovoka, a Paiute man who lived on the California-Nevada border. Wovoka traveled extensively in the region as a young man, becoming acquainted with the teachings of the Shaker and Dreamer religions. In January 1889, Wovoka had a near-death experience and returned from it with messages from God that focused on people loving one another, practicing good deeds, living in peace with whites, working and not stealing or lying, and putting away violence. A very important part of his revelation was that if Indian people faithfully practiced these things, then they would be reunited with loved ones in the next world and live in a place without death and disease. These were powerful messages of hope to people living under duress on reservations throughout the western United States.

As part of Wovoka's divine revelation, he said that the Creator instructed him about a dance that he was to teach to his people. According to Wovoka, they were to dance for five consecutive days in order to bring about the reunion of Indian people with their friends and loved ones in the other world Wovoka preached about. It was whites that named the dance "Ghost Dance." Dancers were so exhausted and worn out after five days of dancing that whites believed they looked like ghosts.

Native people from all over the western United States traveled to Wovoka's residence to listen to his teachings and learn the new dance. Wovoka urged people to dance every six weeks and prepare a feast at each dance, followed by ritual bathing. Traveling by train, a Lakota delegation led by Kicking Bear visited Wovoka in 1889 and helped to spread his message and the dance to the Plains. By the summer of 1890, many Lakota and other Plains tribes participated in the Ghost Dance. For the Lakota the dance was a sign of resistance to incredible pressures placed upon their culture by whites during this period.

White settlers and government officials responded to the Ghost Dance with predictable hostility. Fearing that the dancers were preparing for war, Indian agents and the Army outlawed the dance on some of the Sioux reservations. Refusing to comply, the people continued to dance and in response the Indian agents and soldiers moved to arrest prominent leaders in the dance movement. Among these was Sitting Bull. On December 15, 1890, Indian policemen arrived to arrest Sitting Bull, shooting and killing him during the arrest. This event sent shock waves of grief and anger through the reservations.

WOUNDED KNEE

Rumors spread that the Army intended to arrest or kill anyone participating in the dance, and many dancers left the reservation to avoid this, led by Big Foot, a leader among the Minniconjou. As the band was returning to the Pine Ridge Reservation, the Seventh Cavalry met the group and ordered them to surrender. The soldiers moved the people to Wounded Knee Creek and surrounded the camp. The next day, as Lakota men were surrendering their firearms, a scuffle broke out and a weapon discharged, killing the officer in charge of the surrender. The soldiers immediately fired from all directions killing nearly 300 Indians, mainly women and children. Many of the wounded were left in the elements to slowly die from their wounds. Charles Eastman, a Sioux trained as a doctor and serving as agency doctor on Pine Ridge, treated the wounded, describing the brutality and inhumanness of the slaughter. In the end, he had difficulty reconciling this violent episode with his experiences in the white world.

CONCLUSION

The massacre at Wounded Knee did not stop the Ghost Dance or keep people from singing their songs and practicing their religion. Despite the incredible obstacles placed in their way, native people across the United States faced these challenges and preserved in their desire to remain Indian. In the decades to come they continued to see ever greater challenges to their way of life and to their culture. As white Americans appropriated their history and culture and tried desperately to acculturate Indians, tribal communities found ways to circumvent these actions, developing organizations, skills, and creating allies for the struggle ahead.

PROFILE: QUANAH PARKER—COMANCHE

Quanah Parker was born between 1845 and 1863 near Cedar Lake, Texas. He was the son of Cynthia Ann Parker, a captured white woman, and Peta Nocona, a Comanche warrior from the Quahadi band. Parker was often ridiculed for his mixed heritage by other Comanches. Before confinement to the reservation, Parker fought as a warrior in the Comanche resistance to white encroachment on their lands after the Civil War, taking part in the Second Battle of Adobe Walls and the Red River War. The Quahadi Comanche band surrendered to the Army in 1875 and was settled on the Kiowa-Comanche-Apache Reservation in southwest Indian Territory.

Once removed to the reservation, Quanah Parker was named a chief by Indian agents. In 1886, he was named tribal judge, and then in 1890, he was appointed principal chief. In these roles, Parker advocated for leasing tribal land and cooperating with white ranchers in the area, amassing a significant fortune for himself in the process. During his life, he had eight wives and twenty-five children. His practice of polygamy aggravated Indian agents and officials, since they advocated for the end of traditional Comanche cultural practices. Parker was a tireless advocate for his people, traveling to Washington D.C. twenty times, participating in the 1900 inaugural parade for Theodore Roosevelt, and traveling to Texas and Oklahoma, often riding in parades in full regalia.

While exercising an influential leadership role and adopting various parts of white culture, Quanah Parker was also an important leader in the Native American Church movement. He also adopted Peyote religion after being gored by a bull and used Peyote during his recuperation. Later in his life, Parker traveled around the country teaching the Peyote religion and performing ceremonies. He was one of many roadmen who introduced the Native American Church to many tribal communities around the United States. The Native American Church was incorporated in 1918.

Quanah Parker died on February 23, 1911, and was buried in the Fort Sill Military Cemetery outside of Lawton, Oklahoma. His life illustrates the complex and contradictory choices that faced many native people during the late nineteenth and early twentieth centuries.

PROFILE: SARAH WINNEMUCCA—THOCMETONY—PAIUTE

Sarah Winnemucca was born in 1844 at Humboldt Sink in present-day Nevada. Her father, Winnemucca II, was a chief and an important leader among the Paiute. In her early life, she spent time in California, where she attended a convent school. After returning to Nevada, she lived with a white family where she took the name of Sarah Winnemucca.

In 1868, she served as translator for her people, working with officials on the Paiute Reservation and whites in the surrounding area. In the 1870s, she worked as a teacher at the Malheur Indian School and as a guide and translator for General Howard and the army during the Bannock War in 1878. After the war, when her people were forcibly removed to the Yakima Indian Reservation in Washington State, Winnemucca and her father traveled to Washington D.C. to protest the removal and request a return to their homeland in Nevada. They were unsuccessful, but Winnemucca became a passionate speaker on behalf of her people, testifying about their poor treatment by whites and the injustices that they faced.

In 1881, General Howard hired her to teach at a school at Fort Vancouver, Washington, where she met and married Lieutenant L. H. Hopkins. From 1883 to 1884, Winnemucca traveled the East Coast of the United States giving over 300 lectures about the history and plight of her people. It was during this time that she published *Life among the Piutes: Their Wrongs and Claims*, a passionate history of her people with autobiographical elements from her life. Her work was groundbreaking and was the first book published by a Native American woman.

After her husband's death in 1887, Sarah Winnemucca moved to Idaho where her sister operated a ranch. She died four years later in 1891. Winnemucca's life once again illustrates the depth of change and the difficult decisions that native people endured during this period. Her statue is on display in the rotunda of the U.S. Capitol Building.

PROFILE: SMOHALLA—WANAPUM

Smohalla was born between 1815 and 1820 near Wallula along the Columbia River in Washington State. A member of the Wanapum tribe, his name at birth was Wak-wei but was later changed to Smohalla, which means dreamer in Sahaptin, after his rise to prominence as a spiritual leader.

Smohalla was a warrior, but by 1850 he was recognized as a spiritual leader on the Columbia Plateau. Like many holy men and prophets among Native American tribes, Smohalla was reported to have died and then embarked on a spiritual journey, returning with teachings for the people. Central to Smohalla's teachings was the belief that Indian people should not till the earth or farm. Doing so would anger the Creator, and people could face divine retribution. In addition, Smohalla rejected white culture and taught that the Creator would renew the world, making whites disappear and dead loved ones' return to their families. This would occur if tribal communities performed the Washat or Prophet Dance.

By the late 1860s, Smohalla's prominence and teachings created conflict with government officials and tribal leaders in the region. Two of his chief rivals in the region were Chief Moses, a chief of the Sinkiuse-Columbia tribe, and Homily, a Walla Walla holy man. These disputes led Smohalla to relocate with his followers to the village of P'na near Priest Rapids on the Columbia River. Despite his rivalry with local chiefs, Smohalla's greatest adversaries were government officials and Indian agents in the region. Since he steadfastly refused to remove to a reservation and preached that Indians should not adopt farming and should reject white cultural influences, many Indian agents and reformers fought vigorously against him. Despite this resistance, Smohalla's teachings had a profound impact throughout the region, as many holy men and teachers from neighboring tribes followed the tenets of the Washat. His teachings inspired Chief Joseph and other non-treaty Nez Perce in their resistance to the U.S. government.

Smohalla continued to live at P'na near Priest Rapids until his death in 1895. Before his death he appointed his son as his successor. The Dreamer faith is still alive today on the Columbia Plateau where many Plateau tribes practice the Seven Drums or Longhouse religion that can trace its roots back to Smohalla and his teachings.

REFERENCES AND FURTHER READING

Adams, David Wallace. *Education for Extinction: American Indians and the Boarding School Experience, 1875–1928.* Lawrence: University of Kansas Press, 1995.

Edmunds, R. David, Frederick E. Hoxie, and Neal Salisbury. *The People: A History of Native America*. Boston: Houghton Mifflin Company, 2007.

Hoxie, Frederick E. *The Final Promise: The Campaign to Assimilate the Indians, 1888–1920*. Lincoln: University of Nebraska Press, 1984.

Keller, Robert H., Jr. *American Protestantism and United States Indian Policy, 1869–1882*. Lincoln: University of Nebraska Press, 1983.

Lomawaima, K. Tsianina. *They Called It Prairie Light: The Story of Chilocco Indian School*. Lincoln: University of Nebraska Press, 1994.

Smith, Sherry L. *Reimagining Indians: Native Americans through Anglo Eyes, 1880–1940*. New York: Oxford University Press, 2000.

Trafzer, Clifford E. *As Long as the Grass Shall Grow and Rivers Flow: A History of Native Americans*. Fort Worth, TX: Harcourt College Publishers, 2000.

Trafzer, Clifford E., Jean A. Keller, and Lorene Sisquouc, eds. *Boarding School Blues: Revisiting American Indian Educational Experiences*. Lincoln: University of Nebraska Press, 2006.

Chapter 12

Last Men, Wild West Shows, and Survival, 1890–1924

HISTORICAL AND ETHNOGRAPHIC DREAMS

The push to assimilate tribal communities involved many different avenues of pressure. While native people faced the loss of land, poor health conditions, and confinement to reservations, white academics, especially anthropologists and historians, also joined the effort to shape how Americans viewed Indians and their history. Throughout the history of Indian-white relations, European and American culture viewed Indians as primitive and inferior, fated to disappear as Euro-Americans took possession of their land. In the late nineteenth century, the disciplines of history and anthropology coalesced into "scientific" enterprises that attempted to understand human beings and their history.

It was during this period that anthropologists and historians, like Lewis Henry Morgan, Alice Fletcher, Frederick Jackson Turner, and many others, began to create frameworks for understanding American Indians and their place in history. Their focus on the dichotomy of civilization and primitiveness and the social evolutionary theories they embraced influenced the nature of academic research, the writing of history, government policy, and the day-to-day life of native people. The notion of the disappearing Indian or the "vanishing red race" came out of work completed by academics throughout the late nineteenth century and into the twentieth century. Vestiges of these ideas continue today, animating popular culture and views of Native Americans that are detrimental and racist.

During this period, anthropologists and archaeologists believed that Indian cultures would disappear either through their eventual population nadir or through the mixing of race, diluting "blood" to the point where there would no longer be Indians. All of these ideas and theories contributed to white Americans believing in the inevitable demise of Indian tribes and cultures. Since Indian communities were disappearing, it was imperative to document their cultures as soon as possible and collect their material culture for display in museums and public institutions in order to teach citizens of the United States about the progressive nature of civilization. For example, Franz Boas, one of the most significant anthropologists of this period, collected extensively in the Pacific Northwest Coast region, sending items back to museums like the Peabody Museum of Natural History at Yale University. These objects often held significant cultural and spiritual significance requiring special care, prayers, and songs for their use. The display of these objects fundamentally violated this significance and starkly demonstrated the power dynamics at play in Indian-white relations. In addition to collecting material culture, army officers, ethnographers, anthropologists, archaeologists, and private citizens searched for and collected the skeletal remains of Indian people throughout the United States. The collection of remains violated the sanctity of burials and added further distress and grief to Indian families already suffering through confinement to the reservation and coercive assimilation practices.

Material culture and human remains were not the only things collected by white Americans. The very words of native people were collected by researchers and private individuals. These stories and oral histories were published, profiting white authors and editors without compensating native informants and storytellers. White authors and academics also created narratives that reshaped the history of tribal communities and effectively silenced their voices. Historians like Frederick Jackson Turner, Edmund Meany, and Hubert Howe Bancroft wrote histories that recognized the role of Indians in American history but relegated them to a brief introductory chapter that set the stage for their eventual defeat and disappearance. For example, Turner's work would have a profound impact on the discipline of history, shaping how historians developed their craft and interpreted the broad scope of U.S. history. His focus on the importance of the frontier experience in the shaping of democracy in the United States would animate historical research for decades. The work of numerous academics, museum professionals, government bureaucrats, and private individuals manufactured an edifice of white cultural superiority and the belief in the eventual demise of Indian people.

One of the most disturbing yet fascinating cases of academics studying what they believed to be disappearing native cultures is the case of Ishi. Ishi was the last member of his tribe, and his name meant "man" in the dialect of the Yahi people. During the Gold Rush, as tens of thousands of outsiders streamed into California, native communities experienced brutality and violence unknown to them prior to this time. Ishi and his family were Yahi people who were part of a larger tribal group called the Yana. In 1865, his people were attacked by whites, and forty members of his community were killed. Shortly after this, half of the survivors were killed in an attack. Ishi and his family fled the area and hid for nearly forty-four years.

In August 1911, whites near Oroville, California, captured Ishi while he was foraging for food near their town. Ishi was around fifty years old at this point. His appearance and capture fascinated the public, eventually leading faculty at the University of California to ask for custody of Ishi. Ishi lived the rest of his life at the university, studied by anthropologists and eventually helping as a research assistant. Constantly ill because of his isolation from white populations, Ishi died from tuberculosis in 1916, about five years after he emerged from the wilderness. Ishi embodied the idea of the vanishing Indian for white Americans in the first decades of the twentieth century. He was proclaimed the last "wild Indian" in America and represented, for academics, a chance to study an Indian who had not been influenced by white culture.

INDIANS AND POPULAR CULTURE

While touting the inevitable demise of Indian cultures, whites also recognized the cultural value of native people and their role in the history of the United States. Popular culture used native people, their images, dress, history, and culture in diverse ways. These expressions do not have their roots in the late nineteenth century but were an extension and intensification of trends already present in U.S. society. For example, captivity stories from the colonial period and American literary works, like James Fenimore Cooper's *The Last of the Mohicans*, were popular cultural expressions using Indians and their culture earlier in U.S. history. Also, nearly everyone was familiar with wooden statues of Indians, used as advertisements and placed in front of stores selling tobacco. The use of Native American images, iconography, and culture by white culture was long-lived and extensive.

As printing and photography evolved in the late nineteenth century, images of native people were used more extensively for advertisements and in popular art like lithographs distributed by businesses to customers. Photographers also began to document Indian culture, frequently shaping the visual culture for white Americans and their perception of Indian people. Edward S. Curtis was undoubtedly the most famous of them. In 1906, Curtis was sponsored by J. P. Morgan to produce a photographic series of Native Americans. The resulting work created 22 volumes of 1,500 photographs that have influenced the perception of native people into the present. In 1912, Curtis also experimented with film and produced the first film to use an all Native American cast, called *In the Land of the Head Hunters*.

The film features the Kwakiutl tribes of British Columbia and depicted Native American life on the Pacific Northwest Coast.

Another influential portrayal of Indian culture and history was Buffalo Bill's Wild West show. Throughout his life, William Frederick Cody herded cattle, killed buffalo for railroad companies, and acted as a civilian scout for the U.S. Army during many campaigns against tribal communities. In 1883, Cody organized a show that highlighted the history he had experienced in the American West. The show featured acts about the Pony Express, buffalo hunting, and confrontations between settlers, soldiers, and Indians. The show's finale often featured an Indian attack on a white settlement that was subsequently rescued by Cody and his cowboys. The show was very successful, and in 1887, they performed before Queen Victoria in England. Cody and the Wild West show traveled to Europe several times during its existence. In 1890, after the murder of Sitting Bull and the massacre at Wounded Knee, Cody negotiated with the government to use one hundred Indians in his show, including survivors from Wounded Knee. The government hoped that participating in the Wild West show would help "civilize" them. An indicator of the show's success was their performance at the 1893 Chicago World's Fair where 18,000 people viewed the spectacle.

A poster for Buffalo Bill's Wild West Show from 1899. The Wild West Show began in 1883 and ran until 1913, when it closed due to competition from motion pictures. Shows employed Indians and created stirring and mythic depictions of the American West that often reinforced stereotypes held by white audiences. (Library of Congress)

Cody's Wild West show mythologized the frontier and the American West for tens of thousands of people in the United States and Europe, and it ran until 1913. The formula and events featured in the show would shape film and television portrayals of Indians and the American West. In addition, the show also equated Plains Indians with all native people, shaping the way white culture perceived tribal communities and their history (Edmunds, Hoxie, and Salisbury, 340–342).

While Wild West shows, photography, and academic research shaped the white histories and imaginings of Indians, the medium that exerted the greatest mass and popular influence was undoubtedly film. From the beginning, movies featured stories about the West, using cowboys, settlers, and Indians as prominent iconographic parts of their narrative. Until the 1970s, Hollywood and movie makers generally portrayed native people as wild-eyed savages bent on killing settlers and capturing young white women. One of the earliest depictions of this stereotype was D. W. Griffith's *The Battle of Elderbush Gulch* (1914). Native American men were almost always portrayed as warriors, and Indian women were either princesses, just like Disney's Pocahontas was part of their stable of princesses, or were depicted as dutiful and plain wives at the beck and call of their husbands. Quite frequently, prominent white actors played the role of the main Indian characters, donning wigs and using makeup to make them look more like an Indian. Interestingly, most of the other Indian characters were played by Navajo Indians. A colony of Navajo (Diné) lived in Malibu, and when needed, the studio picked them up for the film. Invariably this created opportunities for humor, as Navajo men were handed customs and props that were almost always derived from Plains culture and material culture. Often the Indian language spoken in early films was Navajo.

This form of popular entertainment appropriated earlier forms of popular culture and wove powerful myths about tribal communities and their history in the United States. The familiar story line of settlers or cowboys confronting and defeating "primitive and savage Indians" populated the imagination and cultural memory of whites throughout the twentieth century and into the present.

SURVIVAL IN THE EARLY DECADES
OF THE TWENTIETH CENTURY

From the 1890s to the late 1920s, tribal communities struggled against the colonization of their land, culture, and history. These assaults not only came from the world of academia and popular culture but also intensified as government bureaucrats and reformers sought to accelerate the assimilation of Indians through boarding schools, allotment, Christianization, and government policy. This colonization was not only a literal one that was fought out on Indian land and bodies but was also an attempted colonization of the mind, seeking to forever extinguish native cultures from the United States.

This colonization was most starkly demonstrated in the 1890 census. Before the arrival of Europeans, estimates of native population in North America ranged from 2 to 10 million. The 1890 census reported the total population of Indians in the United States as 237,196 (Judith Nies, 300). After centuries of warfare, land loss, disease, removal, and confinement to reservations, native populations in the United States reached their lowest level. While tribal communities continued to face enormous challenges to their lives and the continuation of their cultures, population numbers stabilized in the early twentieth century and would eventually begin a slow but steady increase. At present, there are nearly 2 million Indian people in the United States.

Through the first two decades of the twentieth century, allotment and the massive land loss associated with this policy continued. By this point, many reservations had undergone surveys, and Indians had received allotments. In 1898, Congress passed the Curtis Act, which extended allotment to Indian Territory and the Five Civilized Tribes and allowed, for the first time, allotment of mixed-bloods. The Act also extinguished tribal governments in the Territory in order to accelerate assimilation. Native leaders protested and resisted the Act, but the issue of allotment for mixed-bloods created political divisions that continue to this day. The Act eventually led to Oklahoma statehood in 1907 after the process of allotment and dismantling of tribal governments was complete.

In 1892, before the Curtis Act, Congress sent commissioners, known as the Jerome Commission, to Indian Territory to negotiate with the Kiowa concerning allotment since they were not part of the Five Civilized Tribes excluded from the original Dawes Act. The Medicine Lodge Treaty required that at least 75 percent of the Kiowa male population consent to any land cessation. The tribe, led by Lone Wolf, their chief, resisted the government, and the commissioners threatened the tribe with assertions that the government could simply take the land without compensation. After the negotiations stalled, government officials misled some male members of the tribe into signing allotment papers and then claimed that they had the required number of signatures to proceed with the allotment and sale of surplus land. Lone Wolf and other Kiowa leaders asserted that the government had acted deceptively and did not have the requisite number of signatures to move ahead with the allotment. Most male members of the tribe signed a petition requesting that Congress stop the allotment process, which was ignored. Lone Wolf filed a complaint with the federal courts, stating that Congress had violated the Constitution and the Medicine Lodge

Treaty by its actions. He was assisted by the Indian Rights Association, and the tribe's case eventually was heard by the U.S. Supreme Court.

The Court determined it would not accept any cases concerning allotment and that Congress had the right, since tribes had a special dependent relationship with the federal government, to allot land without the consent of the tribe or individual native persons. In addition, the ruling stated that Congress, in its exercise of plenary powers, could revoke treaties and treaty rights unilaterally, as long as these actions were for the care and protection of Indians. *Lone Wolf v. Hitchcock* had a devastating effect on tribal sovereignty and on Indian landholdings. In essence, the Court determined that Congress had absolute power to regulate Indian affairs as it saw fit, and it could do so without the consent of tribes.

Acting in accordance with the recent Supreme Court decision in *Lone Wolf v. Hitchcock*, Congress passed a new amendment to the Dawes Act that allowed the secretary of the interior to unilaterally remove allotments from government trust and issue fee patents, legal title to the land, to Indians who were deemed competent. Competency generally meant that an individual could manage their affairs but often was a measure of how assimilated an individual tribal member was or how desirable their land was to whites in the region. In addition to receiving title to their land, Indians, under the Burke Act, would also become citizens, the final signifier of their acculturation and assimilation into American culture. The important thing to note about the Burke Act is that granting fee patent meant that the land could be sold, have liens placed against it, and could be taxed like another piece of property owned by American citizens. In 1907, Congress amended the Burke Act, granting the Indian commissioner the power to sell the allotments of "noncompetent" Indians. Further amendments in the following year allowed the commissioner to arrange long-term leases for allottees.

The categories of competence and noncompetence often relied on the idea of blood quantum or determining who was Indian and who was not. Government officials made arbitrary determinations based on racial science that contended that people of mixed-blood heritage were intrinsically more "civilized" and therefore more competent to manage their own affairs. Using blood quantum to determine whether a person was an Indian had enormous implications for tribes and individual native people. Blood quantum frequently determined what happened to allotted land, how long a native person's land was held in trust, and when someone might be granted fee patent to his or her land and granted citizenship. The issue of blood quantum also divided tribes, pitting people of varying blood quantum levels against one another on reservations.

From the end of the Civil War through the 1920s, the issues of citizenship, the special status of Indian tribes vis-à-vis the federal government, and the power of Congress to regulate Indian affairs were continually litigated in the federal courts. This litigation not only demonstrates the desire by federal officials to accelerate the assimilation of native people, but it also shows how tribal communities resisted this effort and sought to assert their sovereignty.

Most of these cases centered on whether the newly added Fourteenth Amendment applied to Indians, particularly the citizenship clause. One of the most foundational cases to be heard was *Standing Bear v. Crook* decided in 1879. Standing Bear, one of the leaders of the Ponca, and about thirty members of his tribe left Indian Territory in 1878 to bury his son and visit relatives in Nebraska. Secretary of Interior Carl Shurz ordered General Crook to arrest the Ponca and return them to Indian Territory. Standing Bear, with help from white attorneys, sued for a writ of habeas corpus in a U.S. district court. The court ruled that Indians were considered persons and therefore entitled to all the rights, privileges, and protections afforded to persons under the Constitution.

While the courts recognized the legal personhood of Indians, the question of citizenship was far from clear. In 1884, the Supreme Court, in *Elk v. Wilkins*, declared that Indians, because they were part of distinct political communities regulated by treaties and Acts of Congress, were not citizens of the United States and were subject to the law passed by Congress regulating, among other things, sale of alcohol on reservations and to individual Indians. Alcohol had been a problem in Indian-white relations for centuries. As Indians confronted enormous problems during this period, many people turned to alcohol as a way to deal with the psychological devastation occurring to their families and communities.

An important follow-up case was *United States v. Kagama* in 1886 that challenged Congress's Major Crimes Act that gave the U.S. government jurisdiction over certain crimes committed on reservations. The Supreme Court held that Congress can exercise these powers under provisions of the Constitution and could charge and try Indians in federal courts. This case was the first in a series of cases that outlined the powers of Congress in regulating Indian affairs in the United States.

The Dawes Act of 1887 stipulated that Indians who had received allotments also were to be granted citizenship. Congress also wanted to regulate the importation and sale of alcohol on reservation during this period. Both of these actions led to further litigation in the courts. As noted earlier, *Lone Wolf v. Hitchcock* permitted Congress to unilaterally abrogate treaties and reinforced the doctrine of Congress using its plenary powers to legislate for the benefit and care of Indians. In 1913, the Supreme Court issued a ruling on *United States v. Sandoval*, a case centering on the status of the New Mexico Pueblos and whether Congress had the power to regulate them, especially in regard to regulating the sale of alcohol. The Court decided that the Pueblos were under the jurisdiction of Congress and repudiated an earlier decision, stating that Pueblos were not Indians.

As individual Indians were deemed competent, issued fee patent to their land, and given citizenship, the question was whether granting citizenship changed the nature of the guardianship Congress held over Indians. In 1897, the Dawes Act was amended, stating that the extension of citizenship to Indians allotted under the Act could not occur until the twenty-five-year trust period expired. Even with this amendment, some native people became citizens, some contending that the granting of citizenship ended the guardian relationship with the United States and made them citizens of their states, meaning that they were not subject to the authority of Congress to regulate Indian affairs. In 1916, the Supreme Court, in *United States v. Nice*, held that Congress continued to exercise plenary power over Indians, whether they were citizens or not. The case focused on the enforcement of laws forbidding the sale of alcohol to Indians and once again reinforced the arbitrary and absolute power of Congress to regulate the lives, land, and culture of American Indians.

ORGANIZING AND RESISTING

In the face of these consistent threats to their land, culture, and communities, native people and tribal communities found numerous ways to protest and resist the efforts of the federal government to assimilate them into white society. Some individuals and tribes used the courts to attempt to thwart government efforts. Some people tried to delay the allotment process or refused to select land during the process. Young native people, who were educated either at boarding schools or in local schools, helped their elders to negotiate the complexities of language and often capably helped their families and tribes to resist government policies. A large number of people continued to value their tribal identity and culture, frustrating Indian agents, missionaries, and government officials in their efforts to solve what they called the Indian problem.

Another way to resist these policies and actions was the creation of regional and national organizations that sought to organize Indians across the United States. The first of these organizations was the Society of American Indians. The Society of American Indians was formed by a generation of Indians that were known as the Red Progressives. They were often highly educated men and women like Charles Eastman and Carlos Montezuma who often supported the goal of assimilation and acculturation. The society was established in 1911, working for nearly twelve years on the most important issues of this period. Many contentious debates occurred among its members who argued about the role of the Bureau of Indian

A photograph of the fifth annual meeting of the Society of American Indians at Haskell Institute in Lawrence, Kansas, on October 1, 1915. The Society was the first Indian rights organization run by Native Americans. The Society sought to establish full citizenship for American Indians, and was the forerunner of other organizations like the National Congress of Indians. (*Quarterly Journal of the Society of American Indians* 3, no. 4 (October–December 1915), Plate 14)

Affairs in Indian Country, the use of peyote among tribes, and how to address the effects of federal Indian policy on tribal communities across the United States. The society advocated for establishing an American Indian Day, fought for the extension of citizenship to native people, backed the establishment of a claims commission to address Indian complaints, and was instrumental in the adoption of the 1924 Indian Citizenship Act. The society was significant since it was the first national Indian rights organization and played a crucial role in developing the idea of Pan-Indianism in the United States, which meant they sought to unify native people regardless of their tribal origin or affiliation. Many of its members would go on to play important roles in other national organizations seeking to advocate for Indian rights.

On a regional level, a number of tribes in the Puget Sound region of the Pacific Northwest formed the Northwest Federation of American Indians in 1913. The federation was organized by tribes who did not remove themselves to reservations after the 1855 Treaty of Point Elliott. Members sought to resolve their status as tribes with the U.S. government and stress their treaty rights in relation to surrounding white communities. The Northwest Federation of American Indians was one of a number of local and regional organizations seeking to advocate for Indian rights in the United States.

WORLD WAR I

Many tribal communities, despite their removal and confinement to reservations, maintained warrior societies and traditions during this period. In 1917, when the United States declared war on Germany, many Indians responded by volunteering for the armed forces. While the U.S. government reinstated the draft for the conflict, most Native Americans were not eligible for the draft because they were not considered citizens. Nearly 12,000 Indian men entered military service. Nearly 1,000 volunteers came from the former Indian Territory, joining the 36th Division in France. During operations in 1918, Choctaw soldiers became the first code talkers when they both spoke their language and used code words to frustrate German abilities to decode their communications. In 1919, Congress passed a law granting citizenship to all Indians who served in the military during World War I.

On the home front, Indians across the United States bought war bonds and sought to participate in patriotic duties like giving to the Red Cross and sending packages to soldiers overseas. Unfortunately, this patriotism was not rewarded, since it was during the war when the loss of Indian land under the Dawes Act accelerated. The government issued more fee patents during the war years than it had in the previous ten years. In addition, ranchers, farmers, and corporations lobbied the government to grant them long-term leases to Indian land since it was a war emergency. These leases were often granted without the approval of tribes or individual allottees. Despite the patriotism and sacrifice of Native Americans across the country, the project of assimilating and acculturating native people continued unabated.

THE SPECIAL STATUS OF ALASKA NATIVES

Russia had interests in the Alaska region since 1725 when Peter the Great sent Vitus Bering to explore the region. Lacking the resources to effectively colonize Alaska, Russia found itself in greater competition with Americans as the nineteenth century progressed. In 1859, Russia offered to sell Alaska to the United States, but a treaty was not signed until 1867. The United States paid little attention to Alaska until 1896 when gold was discovered in Yukon, and the region became the gateway to the gold fields. Within three years, nearly 100,000 people were in the region prospecting for gold.

Alaska's indigenous people are generally divided into five groups: the Aleuts, who lived on the Alaska Peninsula and Aleutian Islands, the Inupiat, the Yuit, and the Southeast Coastal Indians that include the Tlingit and Haida. Most of these communities did not have much contact with Europeans or Americans until the gold rushes of the late nineteenth and early twentieth centuries. Up to this point the U.S. government did not conclude any treaties or establish reservations with or for native people in Alaska, since there were very few nonnatives in the region. In addition, Alaska's native peoples were not allotted land under the Dawes Act. After the gold rush, Congress passed the Alaska Native Allotment Act of 1906, which permitted Native Alaskans to procure title up to 160 acres in a manner similar to how allotment worked for other Indians in the United States.

In light of the gold rushes and allotment, a small group of Alaska native men, who were former students of boarding schools in Alaska and the United States, started the Alaska Native Brotherhood in 1912. The Brotherhood was similar to the Society of American Indians in that it advocated for citizenship and education for Native Alaskans. By the early 1920s, nearly every native village in Alaska had a chapter of the Brotherhood or its counterpart for women, the Alaska Native Sisterhood. The fight to protect native people in Alaska would continue into the twentieth century, culminating in the 1970s with the Alaska Native Claims Settlement Act.

CONCLUSION

The period between 1890 and the early years of the 1920s witnessed some of the most profound challenges to tribal communities since the arrival of Europeans in the Americas. Facing wretched conditions on reservations, the loss of land, pressure to convert to Christianity, and a white culture determined to destroy their culture while at the same time appropriating their images and history for their purposes, native people and communities throughout the United States consistently resisted efforts to make them disappear. Whether through protesting allotment, organizing regional and national organizations, or finding ways to pass on their culture and language, Indians persisted in their tribal identities, refusing and frustrating government policies and actions to "kill the Indian to save the man." These efforts would begin to bear fruit in the 1920s and 1930s, as tribal communities sought to reassert their sovereignty.

PROFILE: CHARLES EASTMAN—OHIYESA—SANTEE SIOUX

Charles Eastman was born in 1858 in Minnesota to Many Lightnings (Tawakanhdeota) and Mary Eastman, the daughter of Seth Eastman, a well-known army officer and artist. At first he was named Hakadah, which means the pitiful last, since he was the last of five children. Later in his youth he earned the name Ohiyesa, the Winner.

Raised by his grandmother, he learned traditional ways in his early years. During the Sioux Uprising, his family fled to Canada where he remained until he was fifteen years old. During his exile in Canada, Ohiyesa believed his father was executed in the mass hanging of Santee Sioux. He was wrong and in 1873 his father returned, taking Ohiyesa back to the United States.

During his captivity, Many Lightnings converted to Christianity and took the name Jacob Eastman. He called his son Charles Eastman and sent him to mission day school. After his early education, Eastman was accepted at Beloit College in Wisconsin. He eventually graduated from Dartmouth College in 1887. He then enrolled in Boston University as a medical student, graduating in 1890 with a medical degree.

His first position was at the Pine Ridge Reservation, as the agency physician. His time at Pine Ridge coincided with the Ghost Dance and the Wounded Knee Massacre, where he cared for the wounded. During his tenure at Pine Ridge, he met Elaine Goodale who worked at the agency and spoke Sioux. Shortly after his marriage, Eastman was forced out of his position at Pine Ridge, leaving to establish a medical practice in Saint Paul, Minnesota.

Charles Eastman worked tirelessly as a physician and as an advocate for assimilation and progressive ideals. For three years, he traveled across the United States and Canada as a field secretary for the Young Men's Christian Association (YMCA), attempting to start new YMCAs in areas with Indian tribes. In 1897, he became a legal representative for the Sioux in Washington D.C. and from 1899 to 1902 once again accepted the position of agency physician at the Crow Creek Agency in South Dakota.

Charles Eastman was also an author, writing eleven books. He was a tireless advocate for assimilation and believed deeply in educating native children in white culture. Eastman also supported allotment and other acculturation practices of the time. He was part of a group of assimilated Indians that was called the "Red Progressives" and was a member of progressive organizations, including being a founding member of the Society of Americans Indians.

While Eastman worked for the assimilation and acculturation of American Indians, he also believed that aspects of Indian culture could coexist with white culture. In 1921, he separated from his wife and in 1928 purchased land along the shore of Lake Huron in Canada. There he lived in a primitive cabin until his death on January 8, 1939. Ohiyesa/Charles Eastman's life reflects the profound struggle that many native people experienced during this period, whether to assimilate or remain Indian. While he adopted white culture, religion, and became a symbol for assimilating Indians in the United States, Eastman demonstrated that this process was not an all or nothing proposition.

PROFILE: MOURNING DOVE—HUMISHUMA—CHRISTINE QUINTASKET—COLVILLE/OKANOGAN

Humishuma was born in 1885 during a canoe trip across the Kootenay River to Lucy and Joseph Quintasket. Her mother was Colville and her father Lower Okanogan. During her childhood and early adult years, Mourning Dove was raised by her grandmother for a short while and then attended various schools throughout northeast Washington, gaining about three years of formal education. Humishuma was constantly moving, often working itinerant jobs and attending local schools or colleges to improve her English. She was married twice. Her first marriage to Hector McLeod (Flathead) was short-lived. In 1919, she married Fred Galler (Wenatchi). Between these two marriages Mourning Dove lived in Portland, Oregon, where she decided to become a writer. Eventually she met Lucullus V. McWhorter, who was a well-known rancher and advocate for tribal communities on the Columbia Plateau, and he encouraged her to write down traditional stories and agreed to edit her novel *Cogewea*. There is some controversy over McWhorter's role in the writing and publishing of the novel, with some scholars contending that he extensively modified Mourning Dove's manuscript. After great delay, *Cogewea* was published in 1927. The book is the fictionalized account of a mixed-blood woman in Montana and is one of the first novels written by a Native American woman.

Mourning Dove continued to write and published *Coyote Stories* in 1933. Once again working with a nonnative editor, many of the traditional stories were altered to appeal to nonnative audiences. In 1935, she was elected to the Colville Tribal Council and often spoke in the region on native and women's issues. She died in 1936 at the state hospital in Medical Lake, Washington.

PROFILE: CARLOS MONTEZUMA—WASSAJA— YAVAPAI/APACHE

Wassaja was born in 1866 in what is now central Arizona. His people are Yavapai, and he was given the name Wassaja, which means signaling or beckoning. During the 1871 campaign by General Crook, Wassaja was captured and sold to Carlo Gentile, a photographer who accompanied the army during its campaign, for thirty silver dollars. Gentile adopted the boy and renamed him Carlos Montezuma. Wassaja accompanied Gentile on many photographic and ethnographic expeditions. Living off and on in Chicago, Illinois, Montezuma attended school and eventually was placed in the care of a Baptist minister from Urbana, Illinois, after Gentile lost all his possessions in a fire. Montezuma excelled at school and graduated from high school in 1879 and enrolled at the University of Illinois in 1880. After undergraduate work, Montezuma enrolled in Chicago Medical School, graduating in 1889. Wassaja was the first Indian man to receive a medical degree in the United States.

After medical school, he worked as a physician for the Office of Indian Affairs, working at Fort Stevenson, the Western Shoshone Agency, and briefly at the Colville Agency in Washington State. He also worked as a physician at the Carlisle Indian Industrial School where he also served as the football team's physician. The Carlisle team traveled extensively, and it was during one of those trips that he met his Yavapai relatives in Arizona. He resigned from this position in 1896 and started a private medical practice that he continued until 1922.

Montezuma traveled numerous times to Arizona to visit his relatives. After moving to Chicago, Montezuma frequently helped Indian people by showing hospitality, lecturing for Indian rights, and caring for people less fortunate in his community. Wassaja was also involved in the organization of national Indian rights organizations. He was instrumental in the founding of the National Indian Republican Association, the Indian Progressive Organization, and the Society of American Indians. Unlike Charles Eastman, Montezuma attacked the government and Bureau of Indian Affairs for injustices, corruption, and malfeasance that were endemic in the treatment of Indians across the country.

In 1922, Montezuma became very ill with tuberculosis. He decided to return to his people in Arizona and died on January 31, 1923.

REFERENCES AND FURTHER READING

Conn, Steven. *History's Shadow: Native Americans and Historical Consciousness in the Nineteenth Century.* Chicago: University of Chicago Press, 2004.

Deloria, Philip. *Indians in Unexpected Places.* Lawrence: University Press of Kansas, 2004.

Edmunds, R. David, Frederick E. Hoxie, and Neal Salisbury. *The People: A History of Native America.* Boston: Houghton Mifflin Company, 2007.

Holm, Tom. *The Great Confusion in Indians Affairs: Native Americans and Whites in the Progressive Era.* Austin: University of Texas Press, 2005.

Maddox, Lucy. *Citizen Indians: Native American Intellectuals, Race, and Reform.* Ithaca, NY: Cornell University Press, 2005.

Moses, L. G. *Wild West Shows and the Images of American Indians, 1883–1933.* Albuquerque: University of New Mexico Press, 1996.

Nie, Judith. *Native American History: A Chronology of a Culture's Vast Achievements and Their Links to World Events.* New York: Ballantine Books, 1996.

Trachtenberg, Alan. *Shades of Hiawatha: Staging Indians, Making Americans, 1880–1930.* New York: Hill and Wang, 2004.

Chapter 13

The Indian New Deal and World War II, 1924–1945

REFORMING INDIAN COUNTRY

Life for most tribal communities in the United States during the first two decades of the twentieth century was punctuated by loss of land, assaults on their culture, and increasing pressure to assimilate. Despite these pressures, Indian people resisted land loss, organized local, regional, and national organizations to advocate for their rights, and sought to continue their cultural and spiritual life the best way they could. In the 1920s, the decade-long effects of allotment, boarding schools, and poor health conditions on reservations began to gain public attention.

Throughout the western United States, tribal communities coped with the exploitation of their natural resources and their land. On reservations that had been allotted, Indian landholdings were interspersed with nonnative land, and many people lost their land to bad business deals, inability to pay taxes, or simply selling land to pay for expenses. Along with the loss of land, Indian communities dealt with the exploitation of natural resources, including water, oil and gas, timber, and other minerals. Miners trespassed on Indian land and placed mineral claims on tribal land. In Oklahoma, the secretary of the interior began issuing oil and gas leases and unleashed a cycle of exploitation that bilked enormous amounts of money out of tribes. On many reservations, the Bureau of Indian Affairs worked with local ranchers and farmers to take advantage of water and grazing rights on Indian land, often leaving these parcels unfit for cultivation. All of these abuses took place in the climate of legal and bureaucratic decisions that reinforced the ability of the federal government and its representatives to make decisions for Indians without their input or permission. The trust and guardianship relationship led to enormous corruption and abuse that would not be fully addressed by the federal government until the beginning of the twenty-first century.

In the light of these abuses, the Pueblo people of New Mexico faced threats from squatters, miners, and others out to exploit their land and resources. Law enforcement did not recognize Pueblo land rights and therefore failed to address these trespasses. In 1922, Congress proposed to let squatters keep their land, essentially negating Pueblo claims to the land. The bill, known as the Bursum Bill, required that the Pueblos had to prove their ownership of the land instead of making white settlers prove their claims, which was the usual way this was handled in court. In response, the Pueblos met to organize protests and resistance to the proposed legislation.

The Pueblos sought the help of outside organizations, such as the American Indian Defense Association led by John Collier, the future leader of the Bureau of Indian Affairs. The Pueblos and their allies successfully generated support among white reformers and numerous groups ranging from the General Federation of Women's Groups to the Indian Rights Association. Garnering increasing support and visibility, the Pueblos pressured Congress to pass new legislation that recognized Pueblo title to the land and created the Pueblo Land Board to investigate and resolve land issues. Native people and communities across the United States recognized the power of collaboration and cooperation, often using the tools of white society to their advantage as they created organizations that advocated for Indian rights and improved conditions for their people.

As the reform impulse strengthened, the secretary of the interior formed an advisory panel, commonly called the Committee of One Hundred, in 1923 to make recommendations on Indian policy. The committee's report would influence later efforts to investigate and reform Indian policy, but one of its most immediate effects was its recommendation for the immediate granting of citizenship to all Indians who had not received it through prior Acts of Congress or other means. In 1924, Congress passed the Indian Citizenship Act, following through on the recommendation. This was not necessarily something that Indians pressed for but was more an expression of reformers wanting Indians to assimilate. Congress saw granting citizenship as a means to achieve this end.

Indian and non-Indian pressure continued on the secretary of the interior and the federal government and, in 1926, Secretary of the Interior Hubert Work requested that the Board of Indian Commissioners investigate the condition of tribal communities across the United States. The board called for an investigation that was independent and composed of experts who could evaluate the status of Indian communities. The investigation was led by Lewis Meriam, a scholar and government researcher, and also received a substantial grant from John D. Rockefeller Jr. to complete the report.

After two years of exhaustive research in the field, Meriam and his team published their findings. The Meriam Report was one of the most influential investigations of the Bureau of Indian Affairs and of the condition of American Indians in the United States. The investigators concluded that Indian education, particularly boarding schools, allotment, and efforts to assimilate and acculturate were failures. In particular, the report outlined the meager incomes of most Indians and the lack of educational opportunity and achievement among Indian children. It urged Congress to make loans available to native people to start businesses, make changes in the curriculum for educating children, and take other measures to alleviate the poverty and lack of education among native people.

The most devastating part of the report focused on Indian health. The report outlined the abysmal health conditions on reservations and among Indian people. The panel criticized the Indian Health Service and was appalled at the lack of recordkeeping and statistics available for their research. Meriam and the other panel members noted the high mortality rate among American Indians and also highlighted the abnormally high infant mortality rate. The roots of poor Indian health were in the poverty, malnutrition, lack of sanitation, and poor living conditions on reservations. In addition, the report found that expenditures to improve health and living conditions were inadequate. Meriam discovered that the Bureau of Indian Affairs spent only 50 cents per year on medical care for each Indian child (Trafzer, 347).

Public outcry and tribal criticism of the government in the aftermath of the report forced the Hoover administration to act. In 1929, Hoover appointed Charles Rhoads as commissioner of Indian affairs. Rhoads was a former president of the Indian Rights Association and quickly began work to address the problems outlined in the Meriam Report. Unfortunately, these actions came on the eve of the Great Depression, and once the economic catastrophe hit, budgets were cut and tribal communities often were in worse condition than they were before the report. The situation grew so dire that the Bureau of Indian Affairs was forced to appeal to the American Red Cross and the U.S. Army to feed Indian people in the winter of 1931.

THE NEW DEAL AND INDIANS

The election of Franklin D. Roosevelt in 1932 promised to bring change to Indian Country. After his inauguration, Roosevelt appointed Harold Ickes as secretary of the interior and John Collier as commissioner of Indian affairs. Both men were members of the American Indian Defense Association and had been critical of how the Bureau of Indian Affairs and the U.S. government dealt with Indians. Educated at Columbia as a sociologist,

John Collier, Commissioner of Indian Affairs, with Blackfeet chiefs in 1934. The Meriam Report, issued in 1928, detailed the desperate living conditions of Indians on many reservations. During the Great Depression and the New Deal, President Franklin D. Roosevelt appointed Collier to reform the government's relationship with Indian tribes and improve conditions on reservations. (Library of Congress)

Collier had worked for the General Federation of Women's Clubs and helped found the American Indian Defense Association. He was a passionate and energetic advocate for Indian rights and a powerful critic of government policy toward Indians.

Collier and Ickes immediately started to change the way the government interacted with native people and tribal communities. For decades, the federal government implemented policies to destroy Indian culture and communities, whether through allotment, proselytization by missionaries, or prohibitions on speaking their languages, dancing, or religious practices. Shortly after his confirmation, Collier called for the end of restrictions on Native American religion and practices. Collier's policy on religious freedom for Indians opened up vociferous criticism from missionaries, Bureau of Indian Affairs officials, and some Indians who had assimilated. Collier also supported the use of medicine men and traditional medicine practiced by many tribes. The Indian Shaker Church and the Native American Church had been opposed by government officials through much of the 1920s, but a reassessment of these religious organizations occurred as government officials discovered that native people involved in these movements often helped their members remain sober due to their prohibition on the use of alcohol. Collier's order to practice religious tolerance and freedom led to a renewal of Indian medicine across the United States.

Collier also stopped the practice of destroying Native American languages. This was particularly important for children in boarding schools and reservation day schools where staff diligently worked to suppress Indian languages and teach English. Collier and Ickes also sought to increase the number of Indians working for the Bureau of Indian Affairs, actively recruiting young and talented Indians to help institute these programs and give native people more voice in how the bureau operated. One of the other important early moves made in 1933 was the end of the sale of allotments. Ickes, Collier, and other reformers were alarmed at the loss of Indian land, and this order was only the first of a number of attempts to stop and reverse this trend.

In January 1934, Collier asked the superintendents of the Indian agencies to hold meetings with tribal communities for input on establishing self-government and increasing the power of tribes to control their own affairs. Self-determination was a key principle of Collier's reform agenda. Before receiving input from the tribes, members of Congress introduced a massive reform package in both the House and the Senate. The bill was Collier's work and contained four key points: the creation of tribal governments, the employment of qualified Indians at the Bureau of Indian Affairs, the end of allotment, and the creation of a national court of Indian affairs that would hear cases concerning criminal and civil cases involving Indians (Edmunds, Hoxie, and Salisbury, 379). Powerful critics in Congress, among tribes and in the general public, forced Collier to compromise if he wanted the bill to pass. He negotiated with Senator Burton K. Wheeler of Montana, who chaired the Senate Committee on Indian Affairs, and a condensed version of the bill was passed by Congress and signed into law on June 18, 1934 (Edmunds, Hoxie, and Salisbury, 380). The Indian Reorganization Act (IRA) of 1934, also known as the Wheeler-Howard Act, impacted tribal communities in five fundamental ways. The IRA ended allotment, granted tribal communities the right to organize governments, increased appropriations to the Bureau of Indian Affairs to encourage tribal businesses and fund educational programs, encouraged Indian employment at the Bureau of Indian Affairs by exempting them from civil service regulations, and gave tribes the right to vote on participation in the IRA (Edmunds, Hoxie, and Salisbury, 380–381).

The passage of the IRA was followed by three additional laws that sought to address problems outlined in the Meriam Report. The Johnson-O'Malley

Act, passed in 1934, authorized the Bureau of Indian Affairs to increase its contracts with state and local authorities to provide education, medical care, and social services to Indians rather than relying on the bureau to provide these services. The Act accelerated a trend to educate native children in their communities rather than sending them off to boarding schools or reservation day schools. In 1935, Congress also passed the Indian Arts and Crafts Act, which created a board to establish standards of authenticity and helped in the promotion of Indian art. In that same year, Congress also passed the Oklahoma Welfare Act, which extended the right to create tribal governments to all Indian communities in the state. In 1936, the IRA was extended to include Native Alaskan communities, many of whom organized tribal governments and took advantage of money to create tribal businesses and enterprises.

INDIAN REACTIONS TO THE IRA

There were varied responses to the IRA. Some communities saw the IRA as a way to reassert tribal authority and attempt to reestablish a land base for their community. This was especially true for smaller communities that had lost most of their lands due to allotment. Other communities were suspicious of the new provisions of the Act and did not approve of the process of establishing tribal governments because they felt that these were only new means of controlling their communities and did not allow for true self-determination. On many reservations, political organizing around voting to approve the IRA split communities and led to bitter divisions that persist to the present.

The most notable debate and rejection of the IRA occurred on the Navajo Reservation. A number of reasons led to the eventual rejection of the IRA among the Navajo. Many people were suspicious of the government and its programs, since this was not the first attempt to "reform" Indian affairs. In addition, many elders had been children when the United States forced them onto the Bosque Redondo Reservation and remembered the many broken promises offered by government officials during that time. The greatest hindrance to Navajo acceptance of the IRA was the presence of John Collier himself.

Due to increased population and the size of their goat and sheep herds, Collier, in the first year as commissioner, had ordered agency employees to reduce the size of the herds. He eventually ordered Navajo stock owners to sell 10 percent of their herds. Collier and Bureau of Indian Affairs staff believed that the only way to increase incomes among the Navajo, save grazing land, and stop soil erosion was to decrease the number of animals in Navajo herds. The methods and actions of Collier and bureau employees angered and alienated many Navajo. According to tradition, herds were owned by women in the matrilineal system of the Navajo, and they were not consulted prior to the reduction of herds. The assault on their livelihoods and the paternalistic nature of the stock reduction program caused enormous resentment and opposition on the reservation. For these reasons, the tribe rejected inclusion in the IRA by a slim margin. In the years following the vote, the Navajo reformed their tribal government and charted their own course outside of the IRA.

In the end, 181 communities voted to accept the IRA, and 78 rejected the program. Of the 181 affirmative votes, 135 tribes wrote new constitutions and set up tribal governments. Collier and his allies in the Roosevelt administration also extended many New Deal programs into Indian Country. For example, the Civilian Conservation Corps created an Indian Division that hired many Indian men to work. Relief money was directed to reservations, and infrastructure projects built new buildings and created other infrastructure on reservations.

EVALUATION OF THE IRA

As with many reform movements seeking to change the lives of native people, the IRA and the New Deal had both positive and negative effects on Indian people. Probably the biggest change was that the federal government was finally listening somewhat to tribal leaders and communities. While Collier and government officials could still be paternalistic, arrogant, and controlling, the IRA did give tribal communities some measure of self-determination. One of the major problems with this self-determination was that it was a top-down measure that reflected the values and experience of Collier and white reformers rather than those of the people it was designed to serve. Historians and other critics note that the IRA only gave the illusion of democracy for tribes, forcing them to start and practice self-determination as outlined by the Bureau of Indian Affairs and its officials. The votes for the IRA were a problem, since the base rolls for allotment were used to determine who was eligible to vote, and it was blood quantum that had been used to create the rolls in the first place. Certain people were excluded from tribal membership. In addition, critics assert that the governments formed under the IRA were subordinate to the Bureau of Indian Affairs and could not truly exercise authority and power on their reservation since the Bureau of Indian Affairs still had the final say.

Despite these handicaps, the IRA, New Deal legislation, and Collier's policies did have positive impacts on native communities. The end of religious and language restrictions would usher in a revitalization of culture led by Indians themselves. Ending allotment was certainly a positive event, and by the end of Collier's tenure as commissioner, tribes added nearly 4 million acres to their landholdings through purchase and government programs. While problems occurred with voting and Bureau of Indian Affairs oversight, tribes organized governments and tribal business enterprises that served as platforms to advocate for rights and economic change for Indian people. Indian education began a long process of improvement, especially since children were educated in their communities and not in boarding schools. One of Collier's first actions as commissioner was to close six boarding schools and begin to reform others. This mixed legacy of the Indian New Deal would impact tribes throughout the twentieth century, with lingering positive and negative results from Collier's reform efforts.

WORLD WAR II AND NATIVE AMERICANS

The Great Depression continued into the early 1940s and did not fully end until the United States's entry into World War II. On December 7, 1941, the Japanese attacked Pearl Harbor, the home base for America's Pacific Fleet. During the attack, the first Indian casualty of the war occurred – Henry Nolatubby, a young Choctaw man on the Arizona (Edmunds, Hoxie, and Salisbury, 390). Native Americans were patriotic Americans and responded in the same ways as the white population to the attack. During World War I, 10,000 Indians served in the U.S. military, and the response to the declaration of war after Pearl Harbor followed this earlier example. Why did native people react in this way, given their long history of abuse and maltreatment by the U.S. government? There are a number of reasons for this response. Many tribal communities continued a warrior tradition, and many elders remembered either their service as scouts with the U.S. Army or fighting against U.S. forces. Also many younger Indian people had attended boarding schools and reservation day schools where they learned patriotism and even military skills like marching.

During the war, 25,000 Native Americans served in the armed forces. Nearly 22,000 men served in the Army with the remainder joining the navy, the Marine Corps, and the Coast Guard (Trafzer, 374). Unlike African American troops, Indian soldiers were not segregated into separate units with white officers. While experiencing harassment and name calling, Native American soldiers served with distinction in all theaters of the war. Due to recruitment before the war started, Indian soldiers were present during the defense of the Philippines. The survivors of the battle were forced on the Bataan Death March. In the European theater, the 45th Army Infantry Division, comprised of whites and Indians from Oklahoma and Texas, won distinction, fighting in nearly every major action of U.S. forces in Europe (Edmunds, Hoxie, and Salisbury, 392).

Henry Bake and George Kirk, Navajo Code Talkers for the Marines, in December, 1943. During World War II, the code talkers encrypted military communications using the Navajo language as a code. Their service is one example of the important role that American Indians played in the war, both overseas and on the home front. (National Archives)

Native Americans in the Marine Corps stirred the imagination of the American public both during and after the war. Ira Hayes, a young Pima soldier, saw action in the Guadalcanal Campaign and the Bougainville Campaign before taking part in the assault on Iwo Jima. Hayes was part of the second flag raising on Mount Suribachi that was immortalized through a war correspondent's photograph. After Iwo Jima, he and his surviving flag raisers toured the United States as part of the war bond effort.

Probably the most famous Native American contribution to the war effort was the Navajo code talkers. Early in 1942, Philip Johnston, the son of a missionary who learned Diné Bizaad (Navajo) on the reservation, convinced a reluctant Marine Corps general to allow him and a group of Navajo to demonstrate the value of communicating in a Navajo code. Convinced of the code's value and searching for ways to keep communications secret, the Marine Corps authorized the creation of a unit to train Navajo men in the code. The code talkers did not form a distinct unit; instead the Marine Corps distributed the code talkers to units throughout the Pacific theater. The Japanese military never broke the code, and nearly 400 Navajo men participated in the code talker program. The code and information about the program remained classified information until 1969. Since then the code talkers formed their own association, and their actions have been portrayed in books and film (Trafzer, 382–383).

NATIVE AMERICANS ON THE HOME FRONT

While the contributions of Native American soldiers are most often remembered in popular culture, the impact of tribal communities on the war effort at home was just as important. Nearly 46,000 Indians worked in war industries and other important war-related activities. Some people stayed at home and worked at facilities and factories close to the reservation, but most people left the reservation and moved to cities where they procured jobs building ships or aircraft or manufacturing munitions for the war effort. Reservation life was also changed because so many men left to either join the armed forces or work elsewhere, contributing to lower unemployment rates. In addition to fostering economic growth, the U.S. government also used reservations as places to build internment camps for Japanese Americans during the war. The most famous of these was the Poston War Relocation Center built on the Colorado River Indian Reservation.

The greatest change for tribal communities came from the movement of Indian people to work in the war industry. Many of these jobs were in urban areas like Los Angeles, San Francisco, Seattle, and other cities across the United States. In 1941, 24,000 native people lived in urban areas. By 1950, that number had risen to 56,000 (Trafzer, 384). The movement of so many native people to urban areas had a profound impact, both positive and negative, on their communities and reservations. While escaping the poverty of the reservation, many urban Indians found it difficult to maintain family and cultural ties with their communities on the reservation. The diversity of Indian communities led many native people to highlight common threads of Indian experience in the United States and would foster the creation of organizations that sought to address the challenges of being Indian in an urban environment.

CONCLUSION

When the war ended, Native American veterans returned home, often to a hero's welcome. The sacrifices and contributions of native people to the war effort made it easier for tribal governments and individuals to protest injustices on their reservations or in urban environments. Native American soldiers broke down stereotypes and impressed their white counterparts with their bravery and patriotism. The experience transformed veterans, helping them to become leaders in their communities and giving them confidence and a platform for pushing for reforms and fighting for the rights of their communities in the decades after the war.

While some of the barriers of discrimination had been broken down during the war, Indian communities still faced daunting challenges after the war. Many politicians continued to question the government's relationship with tribes, some arguing for an end to the Bureau of Indian Affairs and forcing native communities to fully integrate into white society. Understanding these forces, Indian leaders like D'Arcy McNickle, who had worked at the Bureau of Indian Affairs under Collier and helped implement the IRA, and Archie Phinney, a Nez Perce scholar who worked for the Bureau of Indian Affairs as superintendent of the Northern Idaho Indian Agency, joined other Indian activists in founding the National Congress of American Indians, an organization of Native Americans that sought to offer a united voice for Indians in the coming decades.

Despite their sacrifices and contributions, tribal communities would face another assault on their communities and way of life after the war that would have profound implications for all Indians in the United States.

PROFILE: D'ARCY McNICKLE—(MÉTIS)

D'Arcy McNickle was born in St. Ignatius, Montana, on January 14, 1904. The son of Philomena Parteneau, a Métis from Canada who had been formally adopted by the Flathead tribe, and William McNickle, a local rancher, who was an enrolled member of the Salish and Kootenai tribes. In his early years, he was educated at the St. Ignatius Catholic School and was later sent to Chemawa Indian School in Oregon, over his mother's protests. After finishing his studies at Chemawa, he attended the University of Montana and studied literature and languages. Professors at the university encouraged him to attend Oxford University in England, and McNickle sold his allotment to finance the trip. After spending nearly three years in Europe, he returned to New York City in 1928, where he worked as an editor for various publications. While in New York, McNickle wrote his first novel, *The Surrounded*, in 1936.

In the midst of the Great Depression, McNickle moved to Washington DC to work for the Federal Writers' Project. Soon he found a job at the Bureau of Indian Affairs working with John Collier to implement the IRA. While working at the Bureau of Indian Affairs, McNickle sought to address the issues of land loss and tribal government. His experience at the bureau led him to political activism, and in 1944, he was the one of the founders of National Congress of American Indians, a national organization that sought to advocate for increased control and preservation of Indian land and sovereignty.

McNickle left the Bureau of Indian Affairs in the 1950s, frustrated about the effects of Indian termination and relocation. He worked for the American Indian Development Corporation and sat on the U.S. Commission on Civil Rights. In 1966, he received an honorary doctorate from the University of Colorado and was hired by the University of Saskatchewan to establish their department of anthropology. During all of this activity and work, McNickle wrote a number of influential works that included *They Came Here First: The Epic of the American Indian* (1949) and *The Indian Tribes of the United States: Ethnic and Cultural Survival* (1962).

In 1971, McNickle retired from the University of Saskatchewan, and a year later, he was instrumental in founding the Center for the History of the American Indian at the Newberry Library in Chicago, Illinois. The Newberry Library is an independent research library with extensive holdings in the humanities. After retiring to Albuquerque, he died of a heart attack in 1977.

PROFILE: YELLOW WOLF—HEMENEME MOXMOX—NEZ PERCE

Yellow Wolf was born around 1855 and was a cousin of Chief Joseph. He was a warrior and accompanied the nontreaty Nez Perce on their flight from the U.S. Army. After the surrender of the survivors in Montana, he fled to Canada. On his return to the United States, he was arrested and sent to Indian Territory where the Nez Perce survivors of the war had been moved.

Yellow Wolf returned to the Pacific Northwest, eventually settling on the Colville Reservation with a portion of the nontreaty Nez Perce who were not allowed to return to the Nez Perce Reservation. In 1907, while returning to the Colville Reservation after picking hops in Yakima, Washington, Yellow Wolf met Lucullus Virgil McWhorter, a local rancher and Indian rights activist. During their long friendship, Yellow Wolf told his story to McWhorter, who would eventually write down his story and have it published in 1940. *Yellow Wolf: His Own Story* was an important corrective to white versions of the 1877 Nez Perce War. His motivation to tell his story was laid out at the end of the book: "The story will be for people who come after us. For them to see, to know what was done here. Reasons for the war, never before told. Nobody to help us tell our side—the whites told only one side. Told it to please themselves. Told much that is not true" (McWhorter, 291). Yellow Wolf's succinct analysis of how native history has been told by white historians was on the mark, and it would take three or four decades before historical narratives began to reflect the views of native people.

Yellow Wolf was married twice and had nine children. By the time of his death, only one son had survived, highlighting the precarious nature of life on the reservation. Yellow Wolf lived on the Colville Reservation until his death in 1935 and was buried near Chief Joseph in Nespelem, Washington.

PROFILE: IRA HAMILTON HAYES—PIMA

Born in Sacaton, Arizona, in the Gila River Indian Community on January 23, 1923, Ira Hamilton Hayes was the son of Nancy Hamilton and Joseph Hayes. Members of his family remember him as a shy and sensitive child who learned English quickly and was an avid reader. He and his five siblings attended school in Sacaton and later went to Phoenix Indian School in Phoenix, Arizona.

After the Pearl Harbor attack, Hayes wanted to join the Marine Corps and on August 26, 1942, he enlisted in the corps. He was trained as a paratrooper, receiving his silver jump wings and a promotion after successful completion of the school. After training, Hayes was deployed to the Pacific theater where he served in Guadalcanal and the Bougainville Campaigns. In 1944, he returned to the United States and was assigned to the 5th Marine Division, which was training to invade the island of Iwo Jima.

The landing on Iwo Jima occurred on February 19, 1945. Hayes and his company captured Mount Suribachi on February 23. At first a small American flag was raised to signify the surrender, but this flag was replaced with a larger one in a second flag raising. It was the second flag raising that was captured in the famous photograph by Joe Rosenthal, becoming one of the most recognized photos of the war. Hayes and the other flag raisers became national heroes, and he and two of the surviving flag raisers helped to sell war bonds in the United States. Hayes was honorably discharged from the Marine Corps on December 1, 1945.

Haunted by his war experiences, Hayes was unable to hold down any jobs. In 1949, he portrayed himself in the John Wayne film *The Sands of Iwo Jima*, and his story has been related in book and film form many times, the latest being the 2006 film *Flags of Our Fathers*, directed by Clint Eastwood. Until his death in 1955, Hayes struggled with alcoholism and was arrested numerous times for public intoxication.

On January 24, 1955, Ira Hayes was found dead outside an abandoned building near his home in Sacaton, Arizona. There are uncertainties surrounding his death, since it was not investigated by the police nor was any autopsy performed. The official cause of death was listed as exposure and alcohol poisoning, but Hayes's brother contends that his death was the result of an argument he had with a Pima named Henry Setoyant. Despite his difficulties after the war, Ira Hayes proudly talked of his service in the Marine Corps and was able to attend the dedication of the Marine Corps War Memorial in 1954 where he met President Eisenhower.

REFERENCES AND FURTHER READING

Biolsi, Thomas. *Organizing the Lakota: The Political Economy of the New Deal on the Pine Ridge and Rosebud Reservations*. Tucson: University of Arizona Press, 1992.

Carroll, Al. *Medicine Bags and Dog Tags: American Indian Veterans from Colonial Times to the Second Iraq War*. Lincoln: University of Nebraska Press, 2008.

Edmunds, R. David, Frederick E. Hoxie, and Neal Salisbury. *The People: A History of Native America*. Boston: Houghton Mifflin Company, 2007.

McWhorter, Lucullus V. *Yellow Wolf: His Own Story*. Caldwell, ID: Caxton, 1940.

Rosier, Paul C. *Serving Their Country: American Indian Politics and Patriotism in the Twentieth Century*. Cambridge, MA: Harvard University Press, 2009.

Taylor, Graham D. *The New Deal and American Indian Tribalism*. Lincoln: University of Nebraska Press, 1980.

Townsend, Kenneth William. *World War II and the American Indian*. Albuquerque: University of New Mexico Press, 2000.

Trafzer, Clifford E. *As Long as the Grass Shall Grow and Rivers Flow: A History of Native Americans*. Fort Worth, TX: Harcourt College Publishers, 2000.

Weisiger, Marsha. *Dreaming of Sheep in Navajo Country*. Seattle: University of Washington Press, 2009.

Chapter 14

Relocation, Termination, and Self-Determination

The Indian New Deal and World War II transformed the landscape of Indian Country and set the stage for profound change after the war. As native men and women returned to their homes after the war, they found that reservation life had changed with many of their friends and relatives now living in urban areas around the country. They also found that it was increasingly difficult to make a living through farming, ranching, or resource extraction, employment that had been the bedrock of economic activity on reservations since the late nineteenth century. Tribal communities also experienced increasing pressure from government officials and Congress to sever their ties with the United States and become fully assimilated into white society. The old visions of destroying native culture and tribal life experienced new life after the war despite the sacrifices and contributions of Indians to the war effort.

John Collier was Indian commissioner until 1945, and after his departure, Congress began to move forward with terminating the federal government's relationship with some tribes in the United States. A confluence of events and beliefs led to termination. After World War II, many politicians and whites believed that Indians were ready to be fully integrated into society, referencing the stories and experiences of Native American soldiers during the war. Another powerful impetus for termination was the desire by many to access the wealth contained on reservations and native landholdings. Corporations, ranchers, farmers, and businessmen pressured Congress to end the tax-exempt status of Indian land and open up land for exploitation.

In addition, New Deal policies and programs came under assault after the war, and a powerful group of senators and representatives in Congress thought that tribal communities and their culture should be fully assimilated into American society. Critics of the Indian New Deal pointed out that the

Indian Reorganization Act (IRA) and the New Deal had not changed conditions on reservations or solved problems facing Indians. In addition, they also pointed out that New Deal programs smacked of communism and allowed tribal communities to continue communal practices and hold land in common, which they argued was un-American. The Cold War and the fear of communism were powerful forces that were effectively used by politicians on the Right to assault the New Deal and its policies. Chief among these critics were Senators Elmer Thomas of Oklahoma, Joseph O'Malley of Wyoming, and Arthur V. Watkins of Utah. Watkins played the leading role in introducing termination as a policy.

One of the first steps in the termination process was the establishment of the Indian Claims Commission in 1946. The authorizing legislation allowed Indians to file claims against the United States for failing to fulfill treaty rights. The Indian Claims Commission was limited in scope because it only applied to land purchased by the U.S. government, excluding tribal lands that had been seized without payment like much of the land east of the Mississippi River. In addition to these restrictions, tribal communities and individuals had only five years to file claims with all awards paid in cash. No transfer of land was allowed under the law. An obscure portion of the law allowed the commission to deduct money from the award for expenses incurred by the U.S. government to care for claimants. Many tribes and individuals received awards, which were then reduced to a pittance due to these expenses. The Indian Claims Commission continued to work until 1970. It heard 850 cases, of which 366 were dismissed, and 484 were decided. The commission awarded a total of $657 million, which was approximately $1,000 per Indian in the United States (Edmunds, Hoxie, and Salisbury, 407–408).

Eight years after the war, in August 1953, Congress passed Concurrent Resolution 108, a nonbinding resolution that laid out the desire of Congress to abolish the status of Indians as wards of the United States and make Indians subject to the nation's laws. During this time, the Bureau of Indian Affairs was led by two men, Dillon S. Myer and Glen Emmons, who actively worked with Congress to establish termination and end the cultural revitalization programs started under the IRA. Two weeks after passage of the resolution, Congress passed Public Law 280 (PL 280), which placed Indian land in California, Wisconsin, Oregon, Nebraska, and Minnesota under the civil and criminal jurisdiction of the states. Contrary to practice under the Indian New Deal, tribes were not consulted regarding the law and were surprised to learn of the measure.

Opposition to termination was hastily organized by Indian organizations and the tribes themselves. The most concerted protest and organizing came from the National Congress of American Indians (NCAI). While previous leaders of the organization supported some of the efforts at termination, activists like D'Arcy McNickle and others helped select new leadership in 1953 that opposed termination. In 1954, the NCAI selected Joseph Garry, a Coeur d'Alene man and veteran, as president of the organization. Garry, along with Helen Peterson, an Oglala Sioux and director of the Denver Commission on Community Relations, traveled the United States organizing opposition to termination. In the midst of this change of leadership, Congress passed the Klamath Termination Act in 1954. The Act ended the federal government's relationship with the various tribal communities on the Klamath Reservation. Individual Indians were given a choice: either stay with the tribe or end their tribal membership and receive a portion of tribal assets. In 1958, over 75 percent of the Klamath voted to terminate their membership, and the Bureau of Indian Affairs sold off hundreds of thousands of acres of land to pay for the one-time payment. This left less than 150,000 acres of land for 23 percent of the tribe members who voted to remain with the tribe (Trafzer, 595).

Termination meant that children born to Klamath parents who ended their tribal membership were not enrolled in the tribe. Many people who received the cash payment quickly spent the money, and many others ended up leaving the area to look for work in cities like Portland, Oregon, or San Francisco, California. In addition, alcoholism and domestic violence increased dramatically as well.

The Menominee also experienced termination first hand. In 1961, Congress passed the Menominee Termination Act. While a handful of Menominee people voted for termination, the majority did not vote. Termination was a disaster for this tribal community. Since the tribe had few resources due to termination, healthcare services declined, leading to a dramatic increase in tuberculosis and an infant mortality rate nearly 200 percent higher than the national average (Trafzer, 394). Many people sold their property around lakes and rivers to whites, and they were now under the jurisdiction of Minnesota law. Menominee were often arrested for hunting and fishing without a license or out of season.

Congress passed legislation to terminate 109 tribes, about 3 percent of tribes recognized by the U.S. government. The California Rancheria Termination Act affected forty-one reservations in California alone, and while these tribes tended to be smaller, these actions still affected thousands of people (Trafzer, 392). Termination also occurred to native people in Kansas, Oklahoma, Iowa, and New York. Many of the terminated tribes eventually requested to return to their status as federally recognized tribes. In 1975, the Klamath tribe reformed their tribal government and lobbied Congress to restore their federal status, and in 1978, they were successful. For the Menominee, it was similar story. Activists in the tribe, led by Ada Deer, formed Determination of Rights and Unity for Menominee Shareholders (DRUMS) in 1970 and gained control of Menominee Enterprises, Inc., the corporation that controlled tribal assets after termination. Through tireless advocacy and lobbying, DRUMS successfully petitioned Congress to pass the Menominee Restoration Act in 1973, reversing termination and receiving federal status. Many terminated tribes petitioned the federal government for recognition and regained their status as federally recognized tribes. This process continues today, as the Pamunkey tribe in Virginia recently gained federal recognition in February 2016 despite challenges from groups opposed to extending federal recognition to additional tribes in the United States. Termination was the de facto Indian policy of the United States from the early 1950s through the early 1960s. Both Presidents Johnson and Nixon opposed termination, supporting self-determination instead.

POSTWAR CHANGES IN NATIVE AMERICAN LIFE

In addition to termination, the U.S. government, acting through the Bureau of Indian Affairs, also instituted the practice of relocation for Indian people in the post–World War II period. Worried about the financial condition of returning Indian veterans and interested in severing tribal ties and accelerating assimilation, the Bureau of Indian Affairs worked with other federal agencies to help find employment and housing for Native Americans, particularly veterans, in urban areas. In 1951, Congress passed a bill to fund this program, and in the years to follow, the Bureau of Indian Affairs would open field relocation offices in many major American cities, including Denver, Phoenix, Los Angeles, Chicago, New York, and Seattle.

Relocation was ostensibly a voluntary program, but there were incentives and also coercive tactics used to persuade Native Americans to move to urban areas. Slick advertisements were developed with colorful and well-designed pamphlets and posters. Funds were provided for the move, housing, and to get people started in their new homes. Coercion could also occur as superintendents and Bureau of Indian Affairs officials controlled subsidies, scholarship, and other incentives. Even with help, many relocated Native Americans found urban life difficult. The routines and stresses were very different from life on the reservation, and many people faced discrimination in their jobs and neighborhoods. Around 100,000 native people moved to urban areas between 1945 and 1960, and of those only about a third participated in the relocation programs of the Bureau of Indian Affairs (Trafzer, 397). Many people also returned to the reservation, the number depending on proximity to the reservation, connections with family and relatives, and other factors.

Moving to cities changed the lives of Indian people in many different ways. The postwar period was a time of great mobility across all groups in the United States. Urban areas were growing rapidly, and native people were part of this growth. As people searched for work and new homes, they encountered Indians from across the country who were going through the same experience. Many people formed friendships, and these new communities began to organize themselves to provide social activities and services to help one another. Community centers, powwows, and other centers of social activity were created to help with the transition to urban life. In urban areas, Native Americans were involved mainly in wage labor, which often differed from the work they did on reservations. Indians in urban areas earned more than those who remained on the reservation, and this explains some of the draw of moving to cities. Native people did face discrimination and harassment, either when seeking jobs or while on the job. Moving to urban areas was a national trend not only for Native Americans but also for African-Americans, Latino/as, and other minorities. They all competed for jobs and housing in American cities, often taking the least skilled jobs and worst housing.

The postwar years brought other changes as well. One of the biggest changes was the dramatic increase in population that occurred over a twenty-year period from 1950 to 1970. In 1950, the U.S. census reported a population of 357,000 Indians, while twenty years later the population rose to 793,000 (Edmunds, Hoxie, and Salisbury, 398). This population increase was mainly due to improvements in health care for American Indians. In 1955, the Public Health Service took over management of health services for Indians, replacing the inefficient and underfunded services provided by the Bureau of Indian Affairs. As native people moved to cities, they also received better health care since it was more widely available. Rates of infectious disease declined, with the most significant decline coming with the rate of tuberculosis. With better health care people lived longer, infant mortality decreased, and life expectancies rose.

Changes occurred on reservations as well. Since most reservations were in rural areas, the reliance on farming and ranching hurt tribal communities as farm commodity prices fell after the war. These economic activities were also affected by the departure of so many young people to urban areas. If they had allotments, they were either leased or a family member used them. The push for termination also coincided with both whites and Native Americans pushing for greater freedom to use their land as they saw fit. The decline in farming led many native people to look for alternative income with the use of their land. For example, tribes and individual allottees sometimes turned to resource extraction like mining or to logging to exploit resources and generate income. Outsiders sometimes placed pressure on tribal communities to open up their land for exploitation. On the Navajo Reservation, uranium mining boomed after the war due to restriction on importation of foreign sources of the ore. Mining occurred on the reservation, and thousands of Navajo worked in these operations. The health and environmental consequences of this mining continue to confront the Navajo. Abandoned mines and their waste products pose a danger to reservation communities, and the legacy of cancer and radiation-related diseases continues to this day.

Reservations were also impacted by the enormous flow of federal dollars into the western United States. Whether it was new interstate freeways, military bases, or hydroelectric dams, this infrastructure often had an adverse impact on tribal communities. For example, the building of dams on the Columbia, Snake, and Colorado Rivers inundated sacred sites and tribal land throughout the West. Often tribes were forced to sell land to the federal government to make way for the reservoirs of dams or right-of-ways for federal highways and freeways.

Indian communities, both on and off the reservation, also experienced important religious and social changes after the war. After World War II, the rate of intermarriage with other ethnic groups increased dramatically. "In 1940, 88 percent of Indian men and 85 percent of Indian women were married to other Indians; by 1970, those figures had dropped to 65 percent and 60 percent respectively. In 1970 at least a third of Indians were marrying outside their group and producing offspring of mixed ancestry" (Edmunds, Hoxie, and Salisbury, 399). These changes had important consequences for tribal membership and would result in much debate within tribal communities about who should be enrolled in the tribe.

Important religious changes also occurred during this period. After the war, both fundamentalist Protestant and Latter Day Saints missionaries sought Indian converts in greater number and increased their activities on reservations and in urban Indian communities. The Native American Church continued to expand during the postwar years and won important legal protections for the use of peyote in its religious rites. The Native American Church has many different branches and differing ceremonies, but the use of peyote is central to them all. Adherents believe that the use of peyote helps believers to commune with God and the spirits, thereby receiving power and healing. Opposition to the use of peyote came from both native and nonnative communities. For example, a bitter debate on the Navajo Reservation led to a ban on the use of peyote in the 1940s, which was not ended until 1967. Whites also attacked the use of peyote, particularly in urban areas, and took the church to court. In 1964, the California State Supreme Court issued a decision in *People v. Woody*, contending that the possession and use of peyote by Native Americans was protected under the First Amendment as an expression of personal religious worship (Edmunds, Hoxie, and Salisbury, 405).

Navajo Indians take part in a peyote ceremony in a hogan near Pinon, Arizona, 1954. Peyote, a plant with psychoactive properties, is used in the Native American Church for spiritual purposes. The use of peyote was controversial, and the federal government banned it in the 1940s. The ban was lifted in 1976, following a long-fought battle by Native Americans for religious freedom. (Carl Iwasaki/Time Life Pictures/Getty Images)

Native Americans also struggled to enhance and broaden their rights during this period. After World War II, veterans and political activists fought to end Congress's ban on the sale of alcohol on reservations. They argued that their communities knew best how to deal with alcohol and did not need the federal government to dictate this for all Indians. After ending the ban in 1953, Congress also repealed the prohibition on the sale of firearms and ammunition on reservations. This was a leftover of nineteenth-century fears about Indian uprisings and war. Indian activists also worked to end restrictions and discrimination related to Indian voting. Many native people experienced discrimination when they tried to vote, either outright denial of their franchise or facing hurdles in the way that Indians cast a ballot. While most states removed bans or restrictions by the early 1960s, all of these restrictions were made illegal by the Voting Rights Act of 1965.

FIGHTING FOR RIGHTS DURING THE JOHNSON AND NIXON YEARS

The fight for rights and self-determination continued through the 1960s and 1970s. While an in-depth discussion of Indian activism and protest will occur in Chapter 15, it is important to set the stage for these broader efforts at self-determination and sovereignty in this chapter. During the Kennedy and Johnson administrations, Native Americans took advantage of the New Frontier and Great Society initiatives promoted by these administrations. Most of these initiatives focused on promoting economic development in depressed areas and attempting to grapple with the issue of poverty in the United States.

After Kennedy's assassination, Lyndon Johnson included tribal communities in the War on Poverty. The Economic Opportunity Act, passed in 1964, created the Office of Economic Opportunity (OEO). The OEO had an Indian Division, which dealt specifically with issues of poverty and economic opportunity on reservations across the country. Tribal governments sought and received government grants to increase opportunities, create jobs, and fight poverty in their communities. While these programs had limited impact on the problems faced by tribal communities, they differed from other government programs in that they relied on communities to decide what to do with funds and how to organize efforts to address these problems. The reliance on native communities to build organizations and programs to address poverty and economic opportunity provided a rich opening for native people to exercise self-determination and learn how to deal with the federal government. In addition to including native people in the War on Poverty, Johnson appointed Robert Bennett to the post of Indian commissioner in 1966. Bennett, an Oneida, was the first Native American to hold the post of Indian commissioner since Ely Parker in the 1870s.

Richard Nixon surprised many people with his strong support of self-determination and sovereignty. Under his administration, efforts to reverse termination bore fruit, and many tribes began to seek recognition by the federal government. Termination ended shortly after the resignation of Nixon with the passage of the Indian Self-Determination and Education Assistance Act in 1975. Clifford Trafzer notes that after the Nixon administration, the fight to address Indian grievances and legal problems shifted to the courts (Trafzer, 404).

CONCLUSION

The post–World War II era brought profound change to many tribal communities, as they struggled to defend their homelands and people from renewed efforts to force their assimilation into white society. Native Americans developed effective organizations and tactics to counter the federal government's efforts to end its relationship with tribes. Instead of ending tribal communities and cultures, termination and relocation strengthened the determination of native people to protect their communities and way of life.

During the 1960s and 1970s, a determined and aggressive activism grew out of the experiences of native people in the United States. The actions and protests of Indians would change the very nature of how Indians were viewed in the United States and force the federal government and white society to deal with the issues of self-determination and sovereignty.

PROFILE: JOSEPH GARRY—SPOKANE/KALISPEL

Joseph Richard Garry was born on the Coeur d'Alene Reservation in 1910. His father, Ignace, was Spokane, and his mother, Suzette, was from the Kalispel tribe. Since the Coeur d'Alene Reservation was at the end of its allotment period, Ignace enrolled Joseph with the Kalispel tribe. Joseph was related to Chief Spokane Garry, who was educated by the Hudson's Bay Company and returned to the region to educate and Christianize his people.

Garry attended the De Smet Mission School and in 1926 enrolled in Gonzaga High School, a Jesuit Catholic school, in Spokane, Washington. He graduated in 1930 and then enrolled at Haskell Institute in Lawrence, Kansas. After two years, he graduated from Haskell and briefly attended Butler University in Indianapolis, Indiana. Returning to the Pacific Northwest, Garry worked for the Northern Idaho Agency for four years, and he took a job in Washington DC with the U.S. Navy. After a year he returned to Idaho to his family. While there he married a young woman, but the marriage did not work out.

In 1942 Joseph Garry was drafted into the Army, fought bravely in Europe, and was honorably discharged in 1945. After the war, Garry became involved in tribal politics and was elected as the Coeur d'Alene tribe's first chairman when the new tribal council was formed in 1948. The creation of a constitution and tribal government were part of tribe's reorganization under the IRA of 1934. Even though Garry was selected chairman in the new tribal government, his father, Ignace Garry, was selected as the last traditional chief in 1949 and served in that position until his death in 1965.

Joseph Garry began his leadership role during a period of great transition for American Indians. In 1953, Garry helped found the Affiliated Tribes of Northwest Indians in response to the termination policy pushed by the federal government. In November 1953, Garry was elected president of the NCAI and remained president until 1960. During his tenure, Garry helped to organize opposition to termination bills and the policy proposed by Congress. Garry and others in the NCAI proved instrumental in challenging termination by traveling across the country to educate tribes on this policy and organizing effective resistance to the paternalistic actions of Congress.

In 1956, he was elected to the Idaho State Legislature and served as its first Native American legislator, and in 1966, he was elected to the Idaho State Senate.

Joseph Garry served on the Coeur d'Alene Indian Tribal Council for twenty-five years, thirteen as chairman. Garry died in 1975 after a life devoted to working for his people.

PROFILE: N. SCOTT MOMADAY—KIOWA

The acclaimed poet and author N. Scott Momaday was born on February 27, 1934, in Lawton, Oklahoma. His parents were Alfred and Natachee Scott Momaday. Early in his life he was given the name Tsoai-talee, which means "Rock-Tree Boy," which is a reference to Devil's Tower, a sacred place for the Kiowa and other native people.

In 1936, his family moved to the Navajo Reservation, spending seven years there, and later the family moved to the Jemez Pueblo in New Mexico where his parents accepted positions to teach at a day school. Momaday's experience in these places informed his writing later in life and gave him a broader Pan-Indian perspective.

Momaday enrolled in the University of New Mexico, where he graduated with a B.A. in Political Science in 1958. He briefly worked as a teacher on the Jicarilla Apache Reservation but in 1959 won the Wallace Stegner Creative Writing Scholarship from Stanford University. He attended Stanford University, receiving his M.A. in 1960 and his Ph.D. in 1963. After graduation he was offered a teaching position at the University of California, Santa Barbara.

In 1968, Momaday published *House Made of Dawn* and was awarded the Pulitzer Prize for it in 1969. The book tells the story of a Jemez man named Abel, who through the course of the story experiences many of the profound changes affecting Native Americans during the twentieth century. He wrote during a fertile period for American Indian authors. Other well-known authors of this period are Leslie Silko, Gerald Vizenor, James Welch, and Louise Erdrich. Each of these authors explored the contemporary struggles of native people in the United States.

Momaday continued to write throughout his career, publishing novels, poetry, plays, and children's books. He has also taught at a number of universities across the country, including Stanford, the University of Arizona, Columbia, Princeton, and the University of California, Berkeley. Most recently he was a visiting professor at the University of New Mexico. During his career, he received the first Lifetime Achievement Award from Native Writer's Circle of the Americas, was awarded the National Medal of Arts in 2007, and accepted an honorary doctorate from the University of Illinois in 2010.

PROFILE: ADA DEER—MENOMINEE

Ada Deer was born in Keshena, Wisconsin, in 1935. Her parents were Constance Stockton Deer and Joseph Deer. During her childhood, her family lived in a log cabin with no electricity or running water. She attended public school and then enrolled at the University of Wisconsin-Madison, graduating in 1957 with a B.A. in Social Work. She was the first Menominee to graduate from the university. She continued her education at Columbia University where she became the first native person to receive a M.A. in Social Work.

After graduating from Columbia, Deer worked for public schools in New York and Minnesota. She also served in the Peace Corps. Between 1964 and 1967, she worked for the Bureau of Indian Affairs as a community service coordinator in Minnesota. She was attending law school when she returned to her community during the struggle over termination.

The disastrous results of termination for the Menominee led Ada Deer and many others in the community to start DRUMS. With the assistance of other national Indian rights organizations, DRUMS fought to regain federal recognition for the tribe. Their efforts won national attention, and in 1973, President Nixon signed the Menominee Restoration Act, reinstating the Menominee's federal recognition.

Deer was elected tribal chair from 1974 to 1976 and became involved in state and national politics, working for the Native American Rights Fund and serving as a delegate at the Democratic National Convention. She was appointed undersecretary of the interior in charge of the Bureau of Indian Affairs from 1993 to 1997 during the Clinton administration where she sought to reorganize the bureau to support Indian self-determination.

After her work in the bureau, Deer held varied positions in academia and continued her activist work. In 2009, she retired as director of the University of Wisconsin-Madison's American Indian Studies Program.

REFERENCES AND FURTHER READING

Cobb, Daniel M. *Native Activism in Cold War America: The Struggle for Sovereignty*. Lawrence: University of Kansas Press, 2008.

Cowger, Thomas W. *The National Congress of American Indians: The Founding Years*. Lincoln: University of Nebraska Press, 1999.

Edmunds, R. David, Frederick E. Hoxie, and Neal Salisbury. *The People: A History of Native America*. Boston: Houghton Mifflin Company, 2007.

Fixico, Donald L. *Termination and Relocation: Federal Indian Policy, 1945–1960*. Albuquerque: University of New Mexico Press, 1986.

Fixico, Donald L. *The Urban Indian Experience in America*. Albuquerque: University of New Mexico Press, 2000.

O'Neill, Colleen M. *Working the Navajo Way: Labor and Culture in the Twentieth Century*. Lawrence: University of Kansas, 2005.

Trafzer, Clifford E. *As Long as the Grass Shall Grow and Rivers Flow: A History of Native Americans*. Fort Worth, TX: Harcourt College Publishers, 2000.

Ulrich, Roberta. *American Indian Nations from Termination to Restoration, 1953–2006*. Lincoln: University of Nebraska Press, 2010.

Chapter 15

Red Power, Resistance, and Self-Determination, 1960–1980

The post–World War II era transformed the lives and conditions of Indians across the United States. With more people living in cities, greater opportunities for employment and education, and a growing desire to protest and fight for sovereignty and self-determination, Indian people were pushing the agenda of change on their reservations and in cities across the United States. Many of the old problems remained: poverty, poor health care, discrimination, lack of education, and the vestiges of trying to extinguish native spiritual and cultural life. New challenges also emerged: how to deal with living in cities, how to stay connected to family and friends on the reservation, and how to maintain language and cultural practices in new settings. During the 1960s, 1970s, and 1980s, tribal communities, both on the reservation and in cities, found new ways to meet these challenges.

FISH-INS

Fishing is a central part of many Indian cultures in the United States. In the Pacific Northwest, tribes had reserved the right, during the 1854 and 1855 treaty negotiations, to fish, hunt, and gather food at places where they had done this since time immemorial. When the treaties were negotiated, whites were not using fish, animal, and plant resources in ways that they would later in the nineteenth and twentieth centuries. As states like Washington began to regulate hunting and fishing, state officials began insisting that Indians should purchase licenses and hunt during seasons determined by state governments. Game wardens and police often arrested Indians who exercised their treaty rights and impounded game, fish, and equipment that were essential to the livelihood of Indian people. During the late nineteenth and early twentieth centuries, a number of federal court cases were heard on the issue of treaty rights and fishing in the Pacific Northwest. In *United States v. Winans*, the Supreme Court in 1905 held that Indians had reserved fishing rights in the treaties and could not be barred from crossing private land to fish at traditional locations. In 1914, in *Seufert Bros. Co. v. United States*, the Supreme Court upheld the right of Yakama Indians to fish at Celilo Falls on the Columbia River, even if non-Indians owned the land on the river. Once again in 1939, the Supreme Court ruled in *Tulee v. Washington* that the state of Washington had no power to charge Indians a fee for fishing.

In 1954, the police arrested Robert Satiacum for fishing out of season. Satiacum was of Yakama and Puyallup heritage, but the state did not recognize his treaty rights and tried and convicted him. He appealed his conviction and the Washington State Supreme Court did not resolve the issue. State officials maintained that Native Americans used gill nets and would damage the fish runs and spawning areas. Native people argued that if whites were concerned about fish, they should do something about the dams, pollution, and overfishing, which were truly impacting fish populations. In addition, they contended that they had fished this way and in these places for thousands of years and had not damaged fish populations the way that whites had in less than a century of fishing (Trafzer, 420).

As termination became the official policy of the U.S. government, state officials and law enforcement ramped up their arrest of Indians fishing and hunting without licenses and out of season. During the 1950s and 1960s, the National Congress of American Indians (NCAI) and the National Indian Youth Council (NIYC) worked on the issue of treaty rights and advocated for the hunting and fishing rights as spelled out in treaties. These issues were not limited to the Pacific Northwest. Many tribes, like those in the Great Lakes region, were also protesting and working on the issue. This renewed political activism often led to splits between older and younger leaders in the Indian rights movement. Younger leaders accused older leaders of being timid and conservative, calling them Uncle Tomahawks or Apples—red on the outside but white on the inside (Trafzer, 420).

In 1963, the Washington State Supreme Court ruled in *Washington v. McCoy* that the state possessed the right to regulate Indian fishing because of the state's interest in conservation (Trafzer, 420). In response to the decision, the Makah Tribe partnered with NIYC to organize protests. After consulting with tribal elders, the idea of fish-ins emerged as a viable tactic to challenge the state. The inspiration for this came from tactics used during the civil rights and student protest movement, which had successfully used this tactic to protest discrimination, issues of free speech, and for other rights during the 1950s and 1960s. A year after the *McCoy* decision, a massive fish-in occurred where state authorities once again arrested Robert Satiacum and hundreds of other protesters, including nonnative supporters.

A series of Supreme Court cases involving the Puyallup Tribe and the Washington State Department of Game upheld the right of Indians to exercise their fishing rights but did not clarify the issue of regulation by the state. Oregon and Washington continued to arrest and prosecute Indians for fishing without a license and out of season. Litigation continued and in 1974, Judge George H. Boldt of the Ninth District Court issued a ruling that was one of the major decisions in Indian law and treaty rights. He ruled in favor of treaty fishing rights and declared that the state could only regulate Indian fishing to ensure that fish runs continued. The state had to show that it could not achieve this first by regulating non-Indian fishing. In addition, Boldt determined that the treaties mandated that the fish harvest be shared and that Native Americans were entitled to 50 percent of the catch. The decision was appealed by the state and the Supreme Court upheld Boldt's decision.

RED POWER

The fish-ins and legal battle over fishing rights were important steps in the fight for self-determination and rights. The Civil Rights Movement inspired many people in other communities to fight for their civil, political, and economic rights during this period. The Kennedy, Johnson, and Nixon administrations responded in varying ways to these movements, but they were generally predisposed to support the efforts of tribes at self-determination. By Nixon's administration, the government was squarely behind the end of termination and sought to encourage tribes to exercise self-determination and self-government.

In 1961, Indian leaders and activists met in Chicago to discuss common issues and determine ways to address these problems. The American Indian Chicago Conference was a springboard for organizing around the issue of self-determination. One of the first organizations to emerge out of the conference was the NIYC. NIYC was comprised of mainly young, educated Native Americans who often were unhappy with older leadership. The organization worked to support and protect treaties rights, including fishing and hunting rights. They were instrumental in organizing fish-ins in the Pacific Northwest and would be powerful advocates and members of the Red Power and American Indian Movements.

In 1968, the American Indian Movement (AIM) was born in Minneapolis, Minnesota. AIM was founded by Dennis Banks, George Mitchell, and Clyde and Vernon Bellecourt as a means to monitor police mistreatment of native people in the city. The organization quickly expanded across the country, with chapters in most major American cities. AIM leaders and organizers rejected the tactics of earlier Indian organizations, instead focusing on direct action as a way to garner attention and success. After 1968, many younger civil rights and student protesters began to question the tactics of nonviolence and gradual change and instead focused on more direct methods for accelerating change.

The Red Power movement came into its own during the 1969 occupation of Alcatraz Island. Once a federal prison, the island had been occupied earlier in the 1960s by Indians from the San Francisco Bay area. Impetus for the occupation came from the example of Mohawk activists who blocked the Cornwall International Bridge between the United States and Canada to protest Canada's failure to live up to treaty obligations to First Nations. On November 20, 1969, eighty-nine activists from tribes all over the United States calling themselves Indians of All Tribes claimed the island as a reservation. They set up a Bureau of Caucasian Affairs and offered to buy the island for $24 and some beads, the same price paid for Manhattan Island. The occupation lasted for nineteen months, ending on June 11, 1971, when law enforcement arrested fifteen people on the island (Trafzer, 425). This was a watershed event for Indian activists, as they confronted the

Max Bear, Chief Eagle Feather, and Dennis Banks at the Alcatraz Island protest in 1978. Native people occupied the former federal prison, demanding recognition of treaty rights. (AP Photo/Paul Sakuma)

federal government over Indian policy and racism. It also inspired other occupations like the Fort Lawton occupation in Seattle, Washington, by United Indians of All Tribes, a Seattle-based Indian rights organization.

AIM continued to organize protests and occupations throughout the early 1970s. On Thanksgiving Day, 1970, AIM leaders, including Russell Means, demonstrated at Plymouth, Massachusetts, and occupied the *Mayflower II*. In 1971, the organization staged a protest at Mount Rushmore that garnered widespread praise and attention. One of the most important protests occurred in Gordon, Nebraska, in 1972. In January 1972, Raymond Yellow Thunder, an Oglala Sioux, was tortured and murdered by two residents of the community. Local authorities did not respond to the family's pleas to investigate the crime, so they turned to AIM for help. With AIM's help, over a thousand Indians arrived in Gordon to demand action by local authorities and threatened to take action if they did not. The Hare brothers were arrested and convicted of the murder, the first whites in Nebraska history to be convicted and imprisoned for killing an Indian (Johansen and Pritzker, 639).

AIM's confrontational politics drew many young Indian activists into the organization. In 1972, activists on the Pine Ridge Reservation, who had gathered for a Sun Dance, and activists who were attending the funeral of Richard Oakes, the leader of the Alcatraz occupation who had been killed by a security guard in Northern California, both came up with the idea of caravanning across the country and converging on Washington DC. The cross-country trip was meant to highlight the condition of Indian people across the country and protest the racism and injustices faced by them in contemporary society and was called the "Trail of Broken Treaties." Joining forces, both groups converged on Washington DC. in November 1972. During the trip, a list of "Twenty Points" was drawn up, and activists planned to submit these demands to government officials. As activists were attempting to negotiate with Bureau of Indian Affairs officials, the police arrived and attempted to remove people from the building. The protestors seized the building, renaming the Bureau of Indian Affairs headquarters "Native American Embassy." They held the building for six days, only ending the occupation after the Nixon administration gave the occupiers money to return home and promised to look into the Twenty Points list. Activists left with truckloads of Bureau of Indian Affairs documents, and damage was done to the building. Government officials and the press painted an ugly picture of the protests, and the Nixon administration launched a campaign to discredit AIM and other Indian activists.

Shortly after the occupation of the Bureau of Indian Affairs building in Washington DC, AIM leaders and activists converged on Custer, South Dakota, to intervene in the trial of a white man who had murdered Wesley Bad Heart Bull, a Sioux man from Pine Ridge Reservation. Negotiations at first went well but then broke down into a battle between protesters and the police. People on both sides were hurt, the courthouse was set on fire, and scores of activists were arrested. AIM had been deeply involved in the Pine Ridge Reservation and its politics. The newly elected tribal government, led by Dick Wilson, used money from the Bureau of Indian Affairs to fund a paramilitary organization, the Guardians of the Oglala Nation (GOONs), that intimidated political opponents of Wilson and his faction. An impeachment effort was launched by the Oglala Sioux Civil Rights Organization. When the impeachment vote occurred, there were accusations of corruption and voter fraud, and the Bureau of Indian Affairs sent in sixty U.S. Marshals to maintain order. Wilson was retained as chairman and immediately banned all political meetings and organizing on the reservation. Elders from the traditionalist camp on the reservation appealed to AIM for assistance.

To protest these moves, AIM activists organized a press conference in Wounded Knee, close to the site of the 1890 Wounded Knee Massacre on February 28, 1973. One hundred and fifty AIM activists spent the night in the town and woke up the next morning surrounded by GOONs, federal

American Indian Movement (AIM) activists stand guard during the occupation of Wounded Knee, South Dakota, March 7, 1973. The occupation was a protest of abuses by Richard (Dick) Wilson, leader of the elected tribal government. The standoff lasted 70 days and was one of AIM's most significant protests. (Bettmann/Getty Images)

marshals, and the Federal Bureau of Investigation (FBI). Using the media, the protesters asked for supporters to help them. For two months, Indians in Wounded Knee faced off with increasing numbers of federal law enforcement, GOONs, local vigilantes, and Bureau of Indian Affairs police. Nearly 1,200 persons were arrested trying to break the siege, and by the end of it, 350 Indians had joined those in Wounded Knee. Daily gun battles occurred between both sides, with a federal marshal seriously wounded and two Indian men, Buddy LaMonte and Frank Clearwater, killed. The standoff was very difficult to end and brought to light the conditions on the Pine Ridge Reservation and the political corruption that young activists had pointed out on many reservations. On May 8, an agreement was reached. The government agreed to investigate the tribal government and conditions on Pine Ridge, and the protesters agreed to leave Wounded Knee (Edmunds, Hoxie, and Salisbury, 430).

Wounded Knee marked the high point of AIM's confrontational tactics. While further militant action occurred like the "Longest Walk," which was a walk from Alcatraz to Washington DC in 1978, the government moved to quell the movement through the prosecution of its leaders in court. The subsequent legal bills nearly bankrupted AIM, and many of its leaders, including Russell Means and Dennis Banks, served prison time. The most famous of these trials occurred in 1975. In June 1975, two FBI agents were shot and killed at Pine Ridge. Three AIM members were arrested and tried for their murder. Two were acquitted, but Leonard Peltier, an Ojibwe man, was convicted of the crimes on flimsy testimony and evidence. He is serving two life sentences. Despite these setbacks, Indians across the United States continued to work for self-determination and advocated for their treaty rights. New organizations took up this work. For example, in 1974, women activists started Women of All Red Nations (WARN) to work on issues affecting native women. Scholarly journals were started, and many tribal communities started newspapers as a way of communicating news and protesting actions of the federal government.

Scholars and native people disagree on the impact of AIM and the Red Power Movement. Some believe that the organization was a flash in the pan, principally concerned about media coverage and publicity, and did not substantively change the condition of tribal communities. The other viewpoint is that the movement was transformative and set the groundwork for further developments such as new organizations, tribal colleges, and Indian studies programs at universities, raising awareness of issues across the country (Calloway, 552). The AIM, regardless of the perspective one takes, underscored issues of self-determination and signaled to non-Indians that tribal communities were acting on their desires for self-determination and sovereignty.

LEGISLATIVE CHANGE

During this period of militant action by Indian activists, other streams of change were converging in the legal and legislative realms. The federal courts have long been one of the major arenas of struggle for self-determination since the beginning of the United States. The struggle over Cherokee removal was one of the first cases to deal with self-determination, land rights, and sovereignty. In the post–World War II era, court decisions and legislative action by Congress substantially changed the nature of the relationship between tribal communities and the U.S. government.

In the 1970s, significant legislation was passed by Congress, addressing land claims, treaty rights, and self-determination. One of the first dealt with Alaska Natives. In Alaska, native communities organized early to press for land claims. In the Organic Act of 1884 and the law granting statehood to Alaska, land claims by Alaska Natives were not dealt with. In 1965, native communities across Alaska established the Alaska Federation of Natives (AFN) to press for a resolution to their claims. With the discovery of oil and other natural resources, renewed attention was brought to their claims. In 1971, Congress passed the Alaska Native Claims Settlement Act (ANCSA), which gave nearly $1 billion and 44 million acres to Alaska Natives to extinguish land claims to most of Alaska. The money and land were placed in the Alaska Native Fund, and thirteen regional corporations were created to manage economic development and pay dividends to Alaska Natives who owned the corporations (Calloway, 553).

In 1972, Congress passed the Indian Education Act, providing funding for Indian children who attended public school. Three years later, Congress passed the Indian Self-Determination and Educational Assistance Act, which mandated that tribes, not the federal government, had the right to administer federal programs. This law was a major victory for self-determination and allowed Indians and their governments to make decisions about how to best use money from federal programs. It was during the early 1970s that Congress also began moves to reverse termination. In 1973, after tireless lobbying by Ada Deer and many others, the Menominee Restoration Act was passed by Congress. Other tribes followed suit and recognition cases and legislation continue at this time.

In 1974, Choctaw physician Connie Pinkerton-Uri discovered that the Indian Health Service (IHS) had been sterilizing Indian women in their facility at Claremore, Oklahoma. Congress ordered an investigation and found that numerous IHS sites had sterilized women, often through coercion and threats. It is estimated that IHS sterilized at least 25 percent and maybe as much as 50 percent of women in their service areas between 1970 and 1976 (Calloway, 555). The sterilization of Native American women had a profound impact both personally and on their communities. The press and public reaction led Congress to pass legislation to tightly control these practices. In 1976, Congress also passed the Indian Health Care Improvement Act that allowed tribes to manage IHS programs, helping to curb these types of abuses.

Not only were Native women mistreated and abused, but Indian children continued to be taken from their families and communities. They were not sent to boarding schools but instead were placed in the state child welfare systems and then adopted by nonnative adults. Up to a quarter of Indian children were adopted into nonnative families. In 1978, Congress passed the Indian Child Welfare Act, which mandated that courts use native values when placing children and stopped the practice of removing children from families and tribes without notice. In that same year, Congress passed the American Indian Religious Freedom Act that stated Congress's desire to protect freedom of religion for native people. Unfortunately, the law did not have enforcement provisions in the text, and Indian people continued their long fight to practice their religions (Calloway, 556).

SELF-DETERMINATION AND THE COURTS

Indian rights and self-determination were high on the agenda of the federal courts as well during this period. As noted earlier in the chapter, fishing and hunting rights often came before the court during this period in an ongoing effort to exercise and strengthen treaty rights. In addition to fishing and hunting rights, tribes also brought suit to protect water rights. In 1976, in *Colorado River Water Conservation District v. U.S.*, the Supreme Court dealt a blow to tribal sovereignty when it recognized the right of states to regulate water that flowed through reservations. This was consistent with the rulings on hunting and fishing rights that gave states the right to regulate or limit those treaty rights in the interest of conservation.

During the 1960s, the Office of Economic Opportunity funded legal services for poor and disadvantaged people throughout the United States. Through these efforts, government officials and lawyers recognized the unique problems facing Indian clients in the legal system. With funding from the Ford Foundation, California Indian Legal Services started a program to extend legal services to Indians across the country. The program was called the Native American Rights Fund (NARF). Shortly thereafter, NARF separated from California Indian Legal Services and became an independent nonprofit organization with an all-Indian board of directors. NARF played a key role in many of the legal battles that occurred from the early 1970s to today.

One of the most important cases of this period was decided in 1978. The case revolved around whether the tribal government of the Santa Clara Pueblo, which had passed a law denying membership to children of Pueblo women who married outside the tribe, could deny tribal membership to the children of Julia Martinez, since her husband was Navajo. In *Santa Clara Pueblo v. Martinez*, the Supreme Court ruled that the Santa Clara Pueblo had the right to determine its own membership because of its status as a political community and can pass laws governing internal matters. This was an important decision establishing self-determination for tribes as an important legal construct.

The Supreme Court has often created conflicting trends in its legal findings, and its ruling on Indian issues is no exception. While it upheld sovereignty and self-determination in the *Martinez* case, in the same year it dealt a blow to tribes in *Oliphant v. Suquamish*. This case centered on the arrest of a white man for assault and battery on the Suquamish Reservation. The Supreme Court decided that tribal governments and courts do not have jurisdiction over crimes committed on reservations by non-Indians. This decision effectively forced Indians to seek redress in federal courts for crimes committed on the reservation. In 1990, the Court went further and expanded the ruling and decided that tribes did not have criminal jurisdiction over Indians from other tribes on the reservation.

The trend of extending and protecting self-determination on the one hand and limiting it on the other has been a constant feature of the federal and Supreme Court's handling of cases brought by tribes or the U.S. government on behalf of tribes. In addition, as Congress passed legislation aimed at expanding tribal self-determination, the courts become involved because tribal communities are independent political communities that make laws and decisions to regulate their internal affairs. Often these laws affect non-Indians and Indians in ways that lead to litigation. Cases on land claims, treaty rights, religious rights, and self-determination continue into the present.

CONCLUSION

The post–World War II period brought enormous change to Indian communities. With the government's termination policy and continued efforts to assimilate Indians, Indian activists sought to address threats to their communities and cultures through many different avenues. Some chose to start regional and national organizations designed to fight for treaty rights and land, like the Alaska Native Federation of Natives. Others chose to join AIM and through militancy hoped to change how Native Americans were viewed and treated in the United States. Individuals and organizations pursued legal remedies for their grievances, while others sought to influence Congress and the legislative process. Whichever path that Indian people chose, the decades following World War II to the 1980s brought enormous change, most frequently brought up and controlled by Indians themselves. The spirit of fighting for self-determination continues into the present and remains a central aspect of Indian communities in the twenty-first century.

PROFILE: RUSSELL MEANS—OGLALA SIOUX

Russell Means was born on November 10, 1939, to Theodora Louise Feather and Walter "Hank" Means. Moving from the Pine Ridge Reservation in South Dakota to Vallejo, California, in 1942, the Means family was one of many to take advantage of wartime jobs and left the reservation in hopes of a better life. His father worked as a welder at the Mare Island shipyard, but his alcoholism disrupted the family and contributed to troubled years as a teen for Means. He graduated from high school in 1958 and attended a number of colleges without graduating.

In 1964, Means accompanied his father during a brief takeover of Alcatraz Island by a small group of Indian activists. After the takeover, he worked at a number of different jobs around the United States. Eventually he ended up at Cleveland, Ohio, where he met Clyde Bellecourt and Dennis Banks in 1969. Together they worked to establish the AIM. During 1969, he participated in the 1969 occupation of Alcatraz Island.

On Thanksgiving Day, 1970, Means, Banks, and other AIM activists protested at Plymouth, Massachusetts, leading to the occupation of the *Mayflower II*, a replica of the original *Mayflower*. This protest garnered Means and AIM national attention. In 1970, Means was appointed as the first national director of the organization.

AIM used occupations as one of its principal tactics. In June 1971, they occupied Mount Rushmore, once again bringing attention to the group and its goals. Late in 1972, Means and AIM helped organize, with eight other organizations, the Trail of Broken Treaties Caravan, which was a cross-country protest that reached Washington DC in early November. After President Nixon declined to meet the protestors, many of the participants occupied the Bureau of Indian Affairs building. After a week, the occupation ended with concessions to the protesters.

In its most well-known protest and action, AIM and its supporters occupied the town of Wounded Knee, South Dakota. The occupation was the result of failed attempts to impeach the tribal president of Pine Ridge Indian Reservation, Richard Wilson. Activists occupied the town for 71 days while surrounded by local law enforcement, the FBI, and the U.S. Marshals. Shootings occurred frequently, with two activists killed and one federal marshal wounded. The goal of the occupation was to highlight the corruption and abuse of power on the reservation and the federal government's failure to fulfill its treaty obligations.

After the end of the occupation, Means and Banks were charged with various charges, which were eventually dismissed. In 1974, Means resigned from AIM to run for the presidency of the Oglala Sioux Tribe. He was defeated, but this was the beginning of Means's political career. In 1983, he supported Larry Flynt in his failed presidential bid and in 1983 traveled to Nicaragua to support the Miskito Indians in their fight against the Sandinistas. During the 1988 presidential primaries, Means sought the Libertarian Party's nomination, losing to Congressman Ron Paul. He also ran for New Mexico governor and for the presidency of the Oglala Tribe but lost. Means also had a career in film and the arts. He acted in numerous films, including *The Last of the Mohicans*, and performed voice work for Disney's *Pocahontas*. In addition to acting, Means also was a painter and a musician.

Over the course of his long life, Means was married five times. He had five children and adopted three more and was the grandfather of twenty-two grandchildren. In 2011, he was diagnosed with esophageal cancer, underwent chemotherapy, and died on October 22, 2012.

PROFILE: VINE DELORIA JR.—HUNKPAPA SIOUX

Vine Deloria Jr. was born on March 26, 1933, in Martin, South Dakota, on the Pine Ridge Reservation. Deloria's parents were Barbara Sloat and Vine Victor Deloria Sr., who was an Episcopal missionary on the Standing Rock Indian Reservation. He went to school on the reservation and later graduated from high school in Minnesota. After graduation, he served three years in the Marine Corps and then attended Iowa State University, graduating in 1958. He later earned a theology degree from the Lutheran School of Theology in Illinois in 1963.

In 1965 he was selected as the executive director of the NCAI. By 1967, he was back in school and earned a law degree from the University of Colorado in 1970. During his time at law school, Deloria wrote *Custer Died for Your Sins*, the influential book published in 1969 that masterfully critiqued white anthropology and history and called for Native Americans to free themselves from the narratives and words created by these academics. Deloria's writings spurred the development of American Indian Studies.

Deloria taught at a number of universities from 1970 to 1990: Western Washington University, the University of California, Los Angeles, and the University of Arizona. While at the University of Arizona, Deloria established the first master's program in American Indian Studies in the United States. From 1990 to 2000, he was a professor at the University of Colorado, Boulder. After retiring he returned to Arizona where he taught at the University of Arizona's law school, James E. Rogers College of Law. Deloria died on November 13, 2005.

Vine Deloria Jr. was a prolific author and wrote numerous books and over 200 articles. Some of his most well-known works are *God Is Red* (1973), *Behind the Trail of Broken Treaties* (1974), *American Indian Policy in the Twentieth Century* (1985), and *Red Earth, White Lies* (1995). Deloria's work critiqued the Western tradition of rationality and science and defended native knowledge and ideas as better alternatives to white culture. He also scathingly wrote about the relationship between tribal communities and the United States, combining a scholarly and native perspective to the debate over Native American history.

PROFILE: WALTER ECHO-HAWK—PAWNEE

Walter Echo-Hawk was born in rural Oklahoma on the Pawnee Indian Reservation. His father was an air force officer, and his family moved frequently. Echo-Hawk graduated from the U.S. Defense Department's High School in Puerto Rico. After graduation, he attended Oklahoma State University where he received a B.A. in Political Science in 1970. He enrolled in the University of New Mexico School of Law and obtained his Juris Doctor in 1973.

He began his law career with the NARF in Boulder, Colorado, where he worked for the organization as a staff attorney for thirty-five years. During his years at NARF, Echo-Hawk has been involved in many of the most important legal cases and legislation in recent memory. He worked on cases dealing with fishing and water rights along with religious and treaty rights for tribes across the United States.

Echo-Hawk worked on the American Indian Religious Freedom Act of 1978, which mandated that the federal government protect the free exercise of Native American religion and give them unfettered access to sacred sites. He was also one of four attorneys who negotiated the National Museum of the American Indian Act of 1989, which established the museum as part of the Smithsonian Institution and was the precursor to the Native American Graves Protection and Repatriation Act (NAGPRA) of 1990. The Museum Act required that the Smithsonian Institution prepare an inventory of all Native American and Native Hawaiian human remains and funerary objects held in its collections. The passage of NAGPRA in 1990 was an important victory for tribal communities seeking to have their relatives returned to them for proper burial. NAGPRA provides a process where federal agencies and museums are required to inventory and return human remains, funerary objects, and items of cultural patrimony to individuals and tribes.

In addition to his legal work, Echo-Hawk has taught at various universities and written scholarly works. He has taught at the University of Tulsa, Oklahoma State University, and Lewis and Clark Law School in Portland,

Oregon. He has written three books, including *In the Courts of the Conqueror: The 10 Worst Indian Law Cases Ever Decided* (2010). After retiring from NARF, Echo-Hawk was appointed to the Supreme Court of the Kickapoo Tribe and serves as its chief justice. He also works as an attorney for Crowe and Dunlevy Attorneys and Counselors at Law in Oklahoma.

REFERENCES AND FURTHER READING

Calloway, Colin G. *First Peoples: A Documentary Survey of American Indian History*. 4th ed. Boston: Bedford St. Martin's, 2012.

Deloria, Vine, Jr., and Clifford Lytle. *The Nations Within: The Past and Future of American Indian Sovereignty*. New York: Pantheon, 1984.

Duthu, N. Bruce. *American Indians and the Law*. New York: Viking Penguin, 2008.

Echo-Hawk, Walter R. *In the Courts of the Conqueror: The 10 Worst Indian Law Cases Ever Decided*. Golden, CO: Fulcrum, 2010.

Edmunds, R. David, Frederick E. Hoxie, and Neal Salisbury. *The People: A History of Native America*. Boston: Houghton Mifflin Company, 2007.

Hosmer, Brian, and Colleen O'Neill, eds. *Native Pathways: American Indian Culture and Economic Development in the Twentieth Century*. Boulder: University Press of Colorado, 2004.

Johansen, Bruce E., and Barry M. Pritzker, eds. *Encyclopedia of American Indian History*. 4 vols. Santa Barbara, CA: ABC-CLIO, 2008.

Trafzer, Clifford E. *As Long as the Grass Shall Grow and Rivers Flow: A History of Native Americans*. Fort Worth, TX: Harcourt College Publishers, 2000.

Williams, Robert A., Jr. *Like a Loaded Weapon: The Rehnquist Court, Indian Rights, and the Legal History of Racism in America*. Minneapolis: University of Minnesota Press, 2005.

_____ *Chapter 16* _____

Looking to the Future

The unprecedented era of Indian activism changed the relationship between the U.S. government and tribal communities across the country. The fight for recognition has continued with many tribes reestablishing their relationship with the federal government. Litigation over Indian rights persists into the present, and recent cases have seen substantive victories for native people and some losses. In addition, tribal communities and organizations have continued to press Congress to address their concerns and treaty rights. Many tribes are still dealing with issues of natural resource use and access as well as trying to provide economic development and security for their people. Since 1990, Native Americans have continued the long tradition of fighting for their people and culture. In this chapter, a few of the important recent developments in Indian Country will be highlighted.

FIGHTING FOR CULTURAL PATRIMONY AND LAND RIGHTS

Since the arrival of Europeans in the Americas, collecting Native American material culture has been a common practice. Museums, archives, and cultural institutions in Europe and the United States hold enormous collections of Native American objects, even preserving funerary materials and human remains. In the late nineteenth century, the U.S. Army routinely sent human remains to the Smithsonian Institution for study, and many private collectors robbed graves for grave goods and bones. Archaeology in the past 150 years has also participated in this. The 1906 Antiquities Act and the Archaeological Resources Protection Act mandated that any Indian remains or material culture found on federal land was the property of the U.S. government. It is estimated that "between 600,000 and two million skeletal remains were housed in museums, laboratories, historical societies, and universities across the country" (Calloway, 559).

From the 1970s to the present, Indian activists and communities have raised the holding of human remains by cultural institutions in the United States as an affront to their ancestors and their culture. During the 1970s and 1980s, tribes confronted cultural institutions, private collectors, and state and federal governments over their holding of Indian material culture and human remains. For example, the Pawnee tribe fought a protracted battle with the Nebraska State Historical Society for the return of Pawnee remains, while the Zuni tribe has frequently protested the collection of carved wooden war gods by museums and archives (Calloway, 560). Most recently in 2015, the Hopi tried, unsuccessfully, to stop the Paris auction of sacred masks and statues to private collectors.

Congress passed a bill in 1989, responding to pressure from Native American activists, tribes, and Native American Rights Fund (NARF), requiring the Smithsonian Institution to repatriate human remains and grave goods to the appropriate tribal communities. In 1990, the Native American Graves Protection and Repatriation Act (NAGPRA) was signed into law. The law required that any institution receiving federal funding must inventory their collections, inform tribes of relevant materials for repatriation, and then comply with tribes' requests for return of the items or human remains. While some protests occurred, NAGPRA has successfully created a process for returning sacred items and human remains to native communities. After return of the objects or skeletal remains, tribal communities determine what should be done with them, with many communities opting to rebury their ancestors.

One of the greatest challenges to NAGPRA and the process of repatriation was the case of Kennewick Man. In July 1996, the skeletal remains of an approximately 8,500-year-old man were discovered along the banks of the Columbia River in Washington State. For twenty years, scholars and Native Americans in the region have been locked in litigation over the disposition of "The Ancient One," as Indians call Kennewick Man. At issue was whether the remains were of Native American origin and whether scientific analysis should be conducted on the remains. In 2004, the federal courts ruled that testing could occur and that since a genetic link between contemporary Indians and Kennewick Man could not be established, the U.S. Army Corps of Engineers (USACE) should retain custody of the remains. Until recently, Kennewick Man has been housed at the Burke Museum in Seattle. In 2015, genetic testing determined that the remains were Native American and that Kennewick Man is related to Native Americans on the Columbia Plateau. The Confederated Tribes of the Umatilla have called for the remains to be returned to them for appropriate ceremony and reburial. Recent federal legislation has paved the way for Kennewick Man to be repatriated to tribes on the Columbia Plateau for reburial.

1n 1996, shortly after the passage of NAGPRA, one of the most important legal cases regarding Indian land, the trust system of the U.S. government, and compensation for Native Americans was filed in federal court. The class-action suit was brought by Elouise Cobell, a Blackfeet woman, who as treasurer for the tribe noticed that there were massive discrepancies regarding how the United States held trust assets for Native Americans. These trust assets were lease payments, use payments, and other fees that the United States had collected on behalf of Indian people, since the government held their land in trust through much of the twentieth century.

After fifteen years of litigation, the U.S. government, during the Obama administration, settled the case for $3.4 billion, 1 billion to go to the plaintiffs and over 2 billion into a fund to repurchase land and return it to tribal ownership.

In one of the most important cases on tribal sovereignty since *Oliphant v. Suquamish Indian Tribe*, which denied tribal courts the right to prosecute non-Indians for crimes committed on tribal land, the Supreme Court recently issued a ruling in *Dollar General v. Mississippi Band of Choctaw Indians*. The case was about whether tribal courts had civil jurisdiction to hear a case against the retailer Dollar General who operated a store on tribal land. The suit concerned alleged sexual assault by an employee against two tribal members.

One of the victims' families filed a civil suit in Choctaw tribal court claiming that Dollar General did not properly vet or train the person accused of sexual assault. The Choctaw tribe had a contract with Dollar General stating that the corporation was under the jurisdiction of the tribal court. The two lower federal courts who heard the case ruled for the Choctaw tribe and upheld the viability of tribal sovereignty and courts in this situation. The Supreme Court was deadlocked on their ruling, which meant that the lower courts' rulings remain in effect, thereby allowing the suit to continue in Choctaw tribal court. Tribal sovereignty is a difficult issue and is still being litigated in federal courts.

NATURAL RESOURCES

Tribal landholdings were most often established during the second half of the nineteenth century. Since the creation of reservations through treaty or executive order, the federal government and surrounding white communities have violated treaties and sought mineral resources, agricultural land, timber, and water resources from tribes. For example, the U.S. government seized the sacred Black Hills when gold was discovered there, violating the treaty signed with the Sioux. During World War II, reservation land was often requisitioned by the federal government for military installations, training grounds, or internment camps. Some of this land was returned to tribes, while substantial portions were retained by the federal government.

In the late twentieth century to the present, tribal communities have continued to feel enormous pressure to allow outsiders to utilize the natural resources present on tribal land. The exploration and exploitation of oil, coal, natural gas, and uranium have accelerated in the western United States, including around and on Indian reservations. Often touted as economic boons for tribes, the extraction of these resources has created unexpected economic, environmental, and health consequences. On the Navajo Reservation, uranium mining after World War II produced mine waste and sickened workers, many of them Navajo. In the late 1960s, the Navajo and Hopi nations signed contracts to allow strip mining for coal on their reservations. These projects rarely brought economic prosperity and did not help with poverty on the reservations (Calloway, 561–562). In the 1980s and 1990s, both the Navajo and the Hopi renegotiated their contracts with mining companies for better environmental protections and greater profits for the tribes.

Oil drilling, the mining of tar sands, and the construction of pipelines have increased across the West in the past two decades. In Canada, the Athabasca oil sands in northeast Alberta have become major sources of oil and revenue. Mining for tar sand happens on the land regulated by treaty with First Nations people. Some tribes have organized companies to take advantage of the oil boom, while others have protested the environmental devastation of the mining, pipelines, and waste created by the industry. Native Americans in the United States have worked in conjunction with Canadian First Nations to protest and take action. For example, Nez Perce tribal council and tribal members were arrested in 2013, as they blocked U.S. Highway 12 near Lewiston, Idaho, to prevent passage of mega-load equipment headed to the Alberta tar sands.

In addition to protesting oil and gas extraction, tribal communities have also taken on oil and coal rail shipments. Since 1992, Pacific International Terminals and SSA Marine of Seattle have been fighting to construct a pier on Puget Sound to ship coal and other products to international markets. The Gateway Pacific Terminal project was to be the largest coal port in North America. From the start, the Lummi tribe, which had retained fishing rights to the area in the 1855 Point Elliott Treaty, opposed the project, arguing that it would infringe on their rights to fish. On May 9, 2016, the USACE sided with the tribe and rejected permits for the terminal, ruling that it would infringe on the Lummi's fishing rights.

Native Americans protesting the Dakota Access oil pipeline in North Dakota, December 1, 2016. Native people from around the world joined the Standing Rock Sioux to protest the threat to water and sacred sites posed by the construction of an oil pipeline under the Missouri River. (AP Photo/David Goldman)

Tribal communities exercise their sovereignty when they control the natural resources within the boundaries of their reservations. Despite pressure from corporations and the federal governments of the United States and Canada, tribal government and Indian activists have significantly impacted how these resources have been extracted, gaining greater control over the environmental and human impacts on their communities. They have also acted to protect their tribal lands and environment, going to court when needed or standing in protest to prevent destructive machinery from crossing their homelands.

GAMING

While taking greater control of their natural resources, tribes have also sought to find ways to develop the economic base of their communities. Some have established tribal businesses or contracted with outside companies and corporations to bring economic development to their reservations. The federal government has also sought to aid Indian communities by extending grants and economic development monies through various government agencies. Since the passage of the Indian Self-Determination and Educational Assistance Act, tribes have administered these funds more than the federal government.

One of the ways that Indian communities tried to address economic development was through introduction of gaming on reservations. Gambling and gaming have been part of many Native American groups in North America. The first tribe to introduce gaming on their reservation was the Seminole tribe of Florida in 1979 when they began high stakes bingo. The tribe maintained that since they exercised sovereignty over their reservation and had a relationship with the U.S. government, the state law of Florida did not apply to their gaming operation. Seeing the success of Seminole gaming, many other tribes introduced gaming onto their reservations in hope of using the proceeds to benefit the tribe economically.

In the early 1980s, a number of Southern California tribes introduced bingo parlors. Sheriffs raided Indian bingo parlors in the San Diego area and the parlors operated by the Cabazon and Morongo bands of Mission Indians, maintaining that the games violated California state regulations regarding gaming. The Cabazon tribe filed suit, and the Supreme Court eventually made a ruling on the case. The Court held that California permitted many forms of gambling, including a state lottery, and that since it was not a criminal activity, the state could not regulate Indian gaming on tribal lands. As Indian gaming proliferated, state officials complained about the lack of regulation and were also resentful that they could not control the tribes or gain access to gaming proceeds (Trafzer, 441). In response, Congress passed the Indian Gaming Regulatory Act (IGRA) in 1988, laying out a framework of guidelines and compelling tribes to negotiate with state governments.

Gaming has helped tribes that have successfully set up gaming operations, although it has not been a smooth process in all cases. For example, in the 1990s, the California state government refused to negotiate with tribes about gaming and gaming operations. The tribes and their supporters eventually placed a proposition on the ballot, which California voters approved, supporting Indian gaming in the state. Sometimes the problems come from the proximity of tribal lands to cities or other tribes with gaming operations. Since 2006, the Spokane Tribe in Washington State has proposed developing some of its tribal land into a gaming facility near the city of Spokane. Located near Fairchild Air Force Base and the Northern Quest Casino, operated by the Kalispel Tribe, the proposal had significant critics. In June 2015, the Department of Interior approved construction of the casino, and a year later, Governor Jay Inslee approved the project for the tribe.

CONCLUSION

The history of Native Americans in the United States is a living testament to the resilience of Indian cultures. Faced with choices to acculturate or perish, Native people forged their own ways of dealing with the dominant culture. Indian people like Geronimo, Chief Joseph, Tenskwatawa, Chief Pontiac, Joe Garry, M. Scott Momaday, Elouise Cobell, Mourning Dove, and many others made decisions that preserved the identity of their people while adapting to and communicating with outsiders who often sought to extinguish their identities as Indians. While tribal communities continue to face challenges in areas as varied as economic development, resource conservation, language preservation, and education, their experiences in the last century have prepared them for any challenges that they may meet in the future. In 1989, Congress passed Public Law 101-185, the legislation establishing the National Museum of the American Indian (NMAI) as part of the Smithsonian Institution. By 2004, a new museum stood on the National Mall, telling the story of native people in the United States and beyond. The exhibits showcased contemporary native art, history, and the contributions of contemporary Indian communities. As Native Americans tell their narrative in this century, they will tell the story of struggles to maintain their sovereignty, protect their culture, and expand understanding of their values and ways of life. The future will attest to the fact that Indian people are still here and continue to contribute to the stories and identity of our nation.

PROFILE: WINONA LADUKE—ANISHINAABEKWE (OJIBWE)

Winona LaDuke was born on August 18, 1959, in Los Angeles to Vincent and Betty LaDuke. She is enrolled at White Earth Reservation in Minnesota. She grew up in Ashland, Oregon, where she graduated from public high school. LaDuke attended Harvard University and graduated in 1982 with a degree in rural economic development. She was influenced by her father's activism on treaty rights and tribal issues.

After graduating from Harvard, LaDuke worked as a high school principal on the White Earth Reservation. She did not speak Ojibwe and knew few people and had difficulty, at first, being accepted by people on the reservation. During her tenure as principal, she graduated with an M.A. in Community Economic Development at Antioch University.

While working on the reservation, LaDuke began her career as an activist, addressing environmental issues and the recovery of Native American land. In 1985, she helped found the Indigenous Women's Network, and in 1989, she founded the White Earth Land Recovery Project (WELRP) with $20,000 she received from being awarded the first Reebok Human Rights Award. WELRP worked to recover the land base of the White Earth Reservation, of which 93 percent was owned by nonnatives. In addition to recovering land, WELRP has worked to create jobs on the reservation, reforest land, and revive the cultivation of traditional foods.

In addition to these efforts on White Earth Reservation, LaDuke has protested and wrote about uranium mines on the Navajo Reservation, toxic waste sites on Native Alaskan and Canadian First Nations land, and other pressing environmental challenges in Indian Country. In 1993, she cofounded Honor the Earth with the Indigo Girls, an environmental nonprofit that seeks to develop financial and political resources for sustainable native communities. LaDuke was asked to run as the vice president candidate for the Green Party in 1996 and 2000, and she was on the ticket with Ralph Nader. LaDuke remained the executive director of WELRP and Honor the Earth until 2014.

PROFILE: ELOUISE PEPION COBELL—NIITSITAPI (BLACKFOOT CONFEDERACY)

Elouise Pepion Cobell was born on November 5, 1945, and grew up on her parents' cattle ranch on the Blackfeet Reservation in Montana. She had eight brothers and sisters and was the granddaughter of Mountain Chief, an important leader among the Blackfeet. She attended public school and after graduating from high school attended Great Falls Business College and Montana State University before leaving to take care of her mother who was dying of cancer.

Elouise Pepion moved to Seattle after her mother's death, where she met Alvin Cobell, a Blackfeet. They were married and had one child, a son named Turk. After returning to the Blackfeet Reservation, Cobell helped with father's ranch and became treasurer for the Blackfeet Nation. As treasurer she helped found the Blackfeet National Bank, which was the first national bank located on a reservation and owned by a tribe. Cobell won the MacArthur Genius Award for her work on the bank. Other tribes have joined the bank, and it is now known as the Native American Bank. She served as the cochair of the Native American Bank and was the executive director of the Native American Community Development Corporation.

During her tenure as treasurer for the Blackfeet Nation, Cobell noticed that there were substantial irregularities in the financial dealings of the tribe with the U.S. government. Specifically, the government had collected funds from fees generated by leases for Indian trust lands. Cobell attempted to present her findings to the government but was not successful. In the mid-1990s, she approached the NARF and two other banking lawyers to bring a class-action suit against the government to seek redress for the financial malfeasance she had discovered.

The class-action suit was filed in June 1996 and is known as *Cobell v. Salazar*, who was the secretary of the interior at the time. By 2010, the Obama administration negotiated a $3.4 billion settlement of the suit.

Congress passed a bill approving the settlement, and most awardees will receive about $1,800.

Cobell worked with her husband on their Montana ranch throughout her life. She was active in local environmental issues and founded the first land trust on the Blackfeet Reservation. She was also a trustee for the Nature Conservancy in Montana. Elouise Cobell died on October 16, 2011, after a brief battle with cancer.

PROFILE: WILMA MANKILLER—CHEROKEE

Wilma Pearl Mankiller was born on November 18, 1945, in Tahlequah, Oklahoma. Her father was Charley Mankiller and her mother was Clara Irene Sitton. Her family was very poor and lived on her father's allotment. During World War II, the U.S. Army used eminent domain to take their land. In 1956, Mankiller's family moved to San Francisco, California, as part of the Bureau of Indian Affairs's relocation program. They later settled in Daly City, close to San Francisco.

Mankiller was married in 1963 to Hugo Olaya, and they had two children together. She was hired as director of the American Indian Youth Center in East Oakland, California, and raised money to support the occupiers of Alcatraz Prison in 1969. She also worked as the coordinator of Indian programs for the Oakland Public Schools. She was divorced from Olaya in 1977 and returned to Oklahoma to raise her two daughters. She attended Skyline College, San Francisco State University, and Flaming Rainbow University where she received her B.A. in Social Sciences.

She was hired as the economic stimulus coordinator for the Cherokee Nation, and in 1981, she founded the community development department for the tribe. Because of the success of the department, Ross Swimmer, the tribe's principal chief, selected her as his running mate for deputy chief in 1983. After Swimmer's resignation to work at the Department of Interior, Mankiller took the job of principal chief and held that position for the next ten years.

During her tenure as principal chief, Mankiller focused on economic development and oversaw many new tribal enterprises. She also improved government-to-government relations with the United States and worked to increase self-determination for the tribe. As principal chief, Mankiller was involved in many conflicts with the United Keetoowah Band of Cherokee Indians, which was another federally recognized Cherokee tribe principally made up of descendants of Cherokee who moved to present-day Oklahoma and Arkansas before forced removal in the 1830s. Her administration also generated controversy when it excluded the membership of the Freedmen section of Cherokee Indians. The Cherokee Freedmen were African-American slaves that became citizens of the Cherokee Nation after the Civil War when the tribe renegotiated their treaty with the United States in 1866. This generated the Cherokee Freedmen controversy, which continues to be litigated in federal court up to the present.

Mankiller suffered numerous health problems during her life, but despite these problems she served the Cherokee Nation until 1995 as principal chief. In 1986, she married her second husband, Charlie Lee Soap. She won numerous honors and awards during her life: the Humanitarian Award from the Ford Foundation, induction into the National Women's Hall of Fame in 1993, and the Presidential Medal of Freedom, the country's highest civilian honor, in 1998. She also wrote an autobiography in 1993, *Mankiller: A Chief and Her People*, which was a national bestseller. Wilma Mankiller died from pancreatic cancer on April 6, 2010, at her home in Tahlequah, Oklahoma.

PROFILE: SHERMAN ALEXIE—SPOKANE/COEUR D'ALENE

Sherman Joseph Alexie Jr. was born on October 7, 1966, in Spokane, Washington. His father was Sherman Joseph Alexie, a member of the Coeur d'Alene tribe, and his mother was Lillian Agnes Cox. As an infant, Alexie was diagnosed with hydrocephalus, a condition where too much fluid is in the cranial cavity causing the skull to enlarge. He underwent surgery successfully but was teased in school because of his condition. He had a number of health problems as a child but decided to attend school in Reardan, Washington, off the reservation. He was the only Native American in the small high school. He excelled academically, played basketball, and was elected class president.

He won a scholarship to Gonzaga University but dropped out to enroll in Washington State University in 1987. Under the mentorship of Alex Kuo, a poet of Chinese American background, Alexie found his voice as an author, publishing his first collection of poems in 1992. He left Washington State University just three credits short of a bachelor's degree; however, in 1995, he was awarded his B.A. by Washington State University.

Sherman Alexie's career as a poet and writer has won him wide acclaim and readership around the world. He has written numerous collections of poetry and short stories, including *The Business of Fancy Dancing—Stories and Poems* (1992), *The Man Who Loves Salmon* (1998) and *Face* (2009). In 1993, Alexie published *The Lone Ranger and Tonto Fistfight in Heaven*, a collection of short stories that connected together through the main characters. In 2010, Alexie won the PEN/Faulkner Award for Fiction for *War Dances,* a collection of short stories and poems.

In addition to poems and short stories, Alexie has written a number of novels that have won critical acclaim. *Reservation Blues* (1995) was his first novel that continued the narrative of the central characters from his earlier short stories. In 2007, he wrote *The Absolutely True Diary of a Part-Time Indian*, which was a semiautobiographical novel that depicted the life of a fourteen-year-old Indian, named Arnold Spirit. Alexie has also been involved in films. In 1998, he created the first all-Indian movie, *Smoke Signals*. Based on characters from his short story, the film won critical acclaim and top honors at the Sundance Film Festival.

Sherman Alexie lives in Seattle with his family and was a founding member of Longhouse Media, a nonprofit company that teaches Native American youth film making and other means to create cultural change.

REFERENCES AND FURTHER READING

Austin, Raymond D. *Navajo Courts and Navajo Common Law: A Tradition of Tribal Self-Governance*. Minneapolis: University of Minnesota Press, 2009.

Braun, Sebastian Felix. *Buffalo Inc.: American Indians and Economic Development*. Norman: University of Oklahoma Press, 2008.

Calloway, Colin G. *First Peoples: A Documentary Survey of American Indian History*. 4th ed. Boston: Bedford St. Martin's, 2012.

Deloria, Philip J. *Playing Indian*. New Haven, CT: Yale University Press, 1998.

Fixico, Donald L. *American Indians in a Modern World*. Lanham, MD: AltaMira Press, 2008.

Light, Steven Andrew, and Kathryn R. L. Rand. *Indian Gaming and Tribal Sovereignty: The Casino Compromise*. Lawrence: University of Kansas Press, 2005.

Trafzer, Clifford E. *As Long as the Grass Shall Grow and Rivers Flow: A History of Native Americans*. Fort Worth, TX: Harcourt College Publishers, 2000.

Wilkins, David E., and K. Tsianina Lomawaima. *Uneven Ground: American Indian Sovereignty and Federal Law*. Norman: University of Oklahoma Press, 2002.

Bibliography

Ackerman, Lillian A. *A Necessary Balance: Gender and Power among Indians of the Columbia Plateau.* Norman: University of Oklahoma Press, 2003.

Adams, David Wallace. *Education for Extinction: American Indians and the Boarding School Experience, 1875–1928.* Lawrence: University of Kansas Press, 1995.

Albers, Patricia, and Beatrice Medicine, eds. *The Hidden Half: Studies of Plains Indian Women.* Lanham, MD: University Press of America, 1983.

Anderson, Gary Clayton. *The Conquest of Texas: Ethnic Cleansing in the Promised Land, 1820–1875.* Norman: University of Oklahoma Press, 2005.

Anderson, Gary Clayton. *The Indian Southwest, 1580–1830: Ethnogenesis and Reinvention.* Norman: University of Oklahoma Press, 1999.

Anderson, William L., ed. *Cherokee Removal: Before and After.* Athens: University of Georgia Press, 1991.

Banner, Stuart. *How the Indians Lost Their Land: Law and Power on the Frontier.* Cambridge, MA: Belknap Press of Harvard University Press, 2007.

Barr, Juliana. *Peace Came in the Form of a Woman: Indians and Spaniards in the Texas Borderlands.* Chapel Hill: University of North Carolina Press, 2007.

Basso, Keith H. *Wisdom Sits in Places: Landscape and Language among the Western Apache.* Albuquerque: University of New Mexico Press, 1996.

Beckham, Stephen Dow, ed. *Oregon Indians: Voices from Two Centuries.* Corvallis: Oregon State University Press, 2006.

Beckham, Stephen Dow. *Requiem for a People: The Rogue Indians and the Frontiersmen.* Northwest Reprint ed. Corvallis: Oregon State University Press, 1996.

Binnema, Theodore. *Common and Contested Ground: A Human and Environmental History of the Northwestern Plains.* Norman: University of Oklahoma Press, 2001.

Biolsi, Thomas. *Deadliest Enemies: Law and the Making of Race Relations on and off Rosebud Reservation.* Berkeley: University of California Press, 2001.

Biolsi, Thomas. *Organizing the Lakota: The Political Economy of the New Deal on the Pine Ridge and Rosebud Reservations.* Tucson: University of Arizona Press, 1992.

Bird, S. Elizabeth, ed. *Dressing in Feathers: The Construction of the Indian in American Popular Culture.* Boulder, CO: Westview Press, 1996.

Black Hawk. *Life of Black Hawk, or Ma-ka-tai-me-she-kia-kiak.* Edited by J. Gerald Kennedy. New York: Penguin, 2008.

Blackhawk, Ned. *Violence over the Land: Indians and Empires in the Early American West.* Cambridge, MA: Harvard University Press, 2006.

Blee, Lisa. *Framing Chief Leschi: Narratives and the Politics of Historical Justice.* Chapel Hill: University of North Carolina Press, 2014.

Bowes, John P. *Exiles and Pioneers: Eastern Indians in the Trans-Mississippi West.* New York: Cambridge University Press, 2007.

Bowes, John P. *Land Too Good for Indians: Northern Indian Removal.* Norman: University of Oklahoma Press, 2016.

Boyd, Colleen E., and Coll Thrush, eds. *Phantom Past, Indigenous Presence: Native Ghosts in North American Culture and History.* Lincoln: University of Nebraska Press, 2011.

Boyd, Robert. *The Coming of the Spirit of Pestilence: Introduced Infectious Diseases and Population Decline among Northwest Coast Indians, 1774–1874.* Seattle: University of Washington Press, 1999.

Bragdon, Kathleen J. *Native People of Southern New England, 1650–1775.* Norman: University of Oklahoma Press, 2009.

Braund, Kathryn E. Holland. *Deerskins and Duffels: The Creek Indian Trade with Anglo-America, 1685–1815.* 2nd ed. Lincoln: University of Nebraska Press, 2008.

Brink, Jack W. *Imagining Head-Smashed-In: Aboriginal Buffalo Hunting on the Northern Plains.* Athabasca, AB: AU Press, 2008.

Brooks, James F. *Captives and Cousins: Slavery, Kinship, and Community in the Southwest Borderlands.* Chapel Hill: University of North Carolina Press, 2002.

Bross, Kristina. *Dry Bones and Indian Sermons: Praying Indians in Colonial America.* Ithaca, NY: Cornell University Press, 2004.

Calloway, Colin G. *First Peoples: A Documentary Survey of American Indian History.* 4th ed. Boston: Bedford St. Martin's, 2012.

Calloway, Colin G. *The Victory with No Name: The Native American Defeat of the First American Army.* New York: Oxford University Press, 2014.

Calloway, Colin G. *White People, Indians, and Highlanders: Tribal Peoples and Colonial Encounters in Scotland and America.* New York: Oxford University Press, 2008.

Carroll, Al. *Medicine Bags and Dog Tags: American Indian Veterans from Colonial Times to the Second Iraq War.* Lincoln: University of Nebraska Press, 2008.

Carter, William. *Indian Alliances and the Spanish in the Southwest, 750–1750.* Norman: University of Oklahoma Press, 2009.

Castile, George Pierre. *Taking Charge: Native American Self-Determination and Federal Indian Policy, 1975–1993*. Tucson: University of Arizona Press, 2006.

Castile, George Pierre. *To Show Heart: Native American Self-Determination and Federal Indian Policy, 1960–1975*. Tucson: University of Arizona Press, 1999.

Cave, Alfred A. *Prophets of the Great Spirit: Native American Revitalization Movements in Eastern North America*. Lincoln: University of Nebraska Press, 2006.

Cebula, Larry. *Plateau Indians and the Quest for Spiritual Power, 1700–1850*. Lincoln: University of Nebraska Press, 2003.

Child, Brenda J. *Boarding School Seasons: American Indian Families, 1900–1940*. Lincoln: University of Nebraska Press, 1998.

Child, Brenda J. *My Grandfather's Knocking Sticks: Ojibwe Family Life and Labor on the Reservation, 1900–1940*. St. Paul: Minnesota Historical Society Press, 2014.

Clark, Laverne Harrell. *They Sang for Horses: The Impact of the Horse on Navajo and Apache Folklore*. Tucson: University of Arizona Press, 1983.

Cobb, Daniel M. *Native Activism in Cold War America: The Struggle for Sovereignty*. Lawrence: University of Kansas Press, 2008.

Cobb, Daniel M., and Loretta Fowler, eds. *Beyond Red Power: American Indian Politics and Activism since 1900*. Santa Fe, NM: School for Advanced Research, 2007.

Confer, Clarissa W. *The Cherokee Nation in the Civil War*. Norman: University of Oklahoma Press, 2007.

Conn, Steven. *History's Shadow: Native Americans and Historical Consciousness in the Nineteenth Century*. Chicago: University of Chicago Press, 2004.

Corntassel, Jeff, and Richard C. Witmer III. *Forced Federalism: Contemporary Challenges to Indigenous Nationhood*. Norman: University of Oklahoma Press, 2008.

Cothran, Boyd. *Remembering the Modoc War: Redemptive Violence and the Making of American Innocence*. Chapel Hill: University of North Carolina Press, 2014.

Coward, John M. *The Newspaper Indian: Native American Identity in the Press, 1820–90*. Urbana: University of Illinois Press, 1999.

Cowger, Thomas W. *The National Congress of American Indians: The Founding Years*. Lincoln: University of Nebraska Press, 1999.

Cronon, William. *Changes in the Land: Indians, Colonists, and the Ecology of New England*. Twentieth Anniversary ed. New York: Hill and Wang, 2003.

Crum, Steven J. *The Road on Which We Came: A History of the Western Shoshone*. Salt Lake City: University of Utah Press, 1994.

Delage, Denys. *Bitter Feast: Amerindians and Europeans in Northeastern North America, 1600–64*. Vancouver: University of British Columbia Press, 1993.

Delcourt, Paul A., and Hazel R. Delcourt. *Prehistoric Native Americans and Ecological Change: Human Ecosystems in Eastern North America since the Pleistocene*. New York: Cambridge University Press, 2008.

Deloria, Philip J. *Indians in Unexpected Places*. Lawrence: University Press of Kansas, 2004.

Deloria, Philip J. *Playing Indian*. New Haven, CT: Yale University Press, 1998.

Deloria, Vine, Jr. *Custer Died for Your Sins: An Indian Manifesto*. Norman: University of Oklahoma Press, 1969.

Deloria, Vine, Jr. *Evolution, Creationism, and Other Modern Myths: A Critical Inquiry*. Golden, CO: Fulcrum, 2002.

Deloria, Vine, Jr., and Raymond J. DeMallie, eds. *Documents of American Indian Diplomacy: Treaties, Agreements, and Conventions, 1775–1979*. 2 vols. Norman: University of Oklahoma Press, 1999.

Den Ouden, Amy, and Jean O'Brien, eds. *Recognition, Sovereignty Struggles, and Indigenous Rights in the United States: A Sourcebook*. Chapel Hill: University of North Carolina Press, 2013.

Dennis, Matthew. *Seneca Possessed: Indians, Witchcraft, and Power in the Early American Republic*. Philadelphia: University of Pennsylvania Press, 2010.

Dippie, Brian W. *The Vanishing American: White Attitudes and U.S. Indian Policy*. Lawrence: University Press of Kansas, 1991.

Douthit, Nathan. *Uncertain Encounters: Indians and Whites at Peace and War in Southern Oregon, 1820s–1860s*. Corvallis: Oregon State University Press, 2002.

Dowd, Gregory Evans. *A Spirited Resistance: The North American Indian Struggle for Unity, 1745–1815*. Baltimore: Johns Hopkins University Press, 1992.

Dowd, Gregory Evans. *War under Heaven: Pontiac, the Indian Nations, and the British Empire*. Baltimore: Johns Hopkins University Press, 2002.

Dunbar-Ortiz, Roxanne. *An Indigenous Peoples' History of the United States*. Boston: Beacon Press, 2015.

Duthu, Bruce. *Shadow Nations: Tribal Sovereignty and the Limits of Legal Pluralism*. New York: Oxford University Press, 2013.

DuVal, Kathleen. *The Native Ground: Indians and Colonists in the Heart of the Continent*. Philadelphia: University of Pennsylvania Press, 2007.

Echo-Hawk, Walter R. *In the Courts of the Conqueror: The 10 Worst Indian Law Cases Ever Decided*. Golden, CO: Fulcrum, 2010.

Edmunds, R. David, Frederick E. Hoxie, and Neal Salisbury. *The People: A History of Native America*. Boston: Houghton Mifflin Company, 2007.

Elliott, Michael A. *Custerology: The Enduring Legacy of the Indian Wars and George Armstrong Custer*. Chicago: University of Chicago Press, 2007.

Ethridge, Robbie. *Creek Country: The Creek Indians and Their World, 1796–1816*. Chapel Hill: University of North Carolina Press, 2003.

Ethridge, Robbie. *From Chicaza to Chickasaw: The European Invasion and the Transformation of the Mississippian World, 1540–1715*. Chapel Hill: University of North Carolina Press, 2010.

Ethridge, Robbie, and Sheri M. Shuck-Hall, eds. *Mapping the Mississippian Shatter Zone: The Colonial Indian Slave Trade and Regional Instability in the American South*. Lincoln: University of Nebraska Press, 2009.

Fagan, Brian M. *The First North Americans: An Archaeological Journey*. New York: Thames & Hudson, 2011.

Fahey, John. *Saving the Reservation: Joe Garry and the Battle to Be Indian*. Seattle: University of Washington Press, 2001.

Fenn, Elizabeth A. "Biological Warfare in Eighteenth-Century North America: Beyond Jeffery Amherst." *Journal of American History* 86, no. 4 (2000): 1552–1580.

Fenn, Elizabeth A. *Encounters at the Heart of the World: A History of the Mandan People*. New York: Hill and Wang, 2014.

Fisher, Andrew H. *Shadow Tribe: The Making of Columbia River Indian Identity*. Seattle: University of Washington Press, 2010.

Fixico, Donald L. *American Indians in a Modern World*. Lanham, MD: AltaMira Press, 2008.

Fixico, Donald L. *Indian Resilience and Rebuilding: Indigenous Nations in the Modern American West*. Tucson: University of Arizona Press, 2013.

Fixico, Donald L. *Termination and Relocation: Federal Indian Policy, 1945–1960*. Albuquerque: University of New Mexico Press, 1986.

Fixico, Donald L. *The Invasion of Indian Country in the Twentieth Century American Capitalism and Tribal Natural Resources*. Niwot: University Press of Colorado, 1998.

Fixico, Donald L. *The Urban Indian Experience in America*. Albuquerque: University of New Mexico Press, 2000.

Fletcher, Matthew L. *American Indian Education: Counternarratives in Racism, Struggle, and the Law*. New York: Routledge, 2008.

Flores, Dan. "Bison Ecology and Bison Diplomacy: The Southern Plains from 1800 to 1850." *Journal of American History* 78, no. 2 (1991): 465–485.

Forbes, Jack D. *Apache, Navajo, and Spaniard*. 2nd ed. Norman: University of Oklahoma Press, 1994.

Franks, Kenny A. *Stand Watie and the Agony of the Cherokee Nation*. Memphis, TN: Memphis State University Press, 1979.

Furtwangler, Albert. *Bringing Indians to the Book*. Seattle: University of Washington Press, 2005.

Gallay, Alan. *Indian Slavery in Colonial America*. Lincoln: University of Nebraska Press, 2009.

Gallay, Alan. *The Indian Slave Trade: The Rise of the English Empire in the American South, 1670–1717*. New Haven, CT: Yale University Press, 2002.

Galloway, Patricia. *Choctaw Genesis, 1500–1700*. Lincoln: University of Nebraska Press, 1995.

Gamble, Lynn H. *The Chumash World at European Contact: Power, Trade, and Feasting among Complex Hunter-Gatherers*. Berkeley: University of California Press, 2008.

Garrison, Tim Alan. *The Legal Ideology of Removal: The Southern Judiciary and the Sovereignty of Native American Nations*. Athens: University of Georgia Press, 2002.

Getches, David H., Charles F. Wilkinson, and Robert A. Williams Jr., eds. *Cases and Materials on Federal Indian Law*. 4th ed. St. Paul: West Group, 1998.

Gibbon, Gay. *The Sioux: The Dakota and the Lakota Nations*. Malden, MA: Blackwell, 2003.

Green, Michael D. *The Politics of Indian Removal: Creek Government and Society in Crisis*. Lincoln: University of Nebraska Press, 1985.

Greenwald, Emily. *Reconfiguring the Reservation: The Nez Perces, Jicarilla Apaches, and the Dawes Act*. Albuquerque: University of New Mexico Press, 2002.

Greer, Alan. *Mohawk Saint: Catherine Tekakwitha and the Jesuits*. New York: Oxford University Press, 2004.

Haas, Lisbeth. *Saints and Citizens: Indigenous Histories of Colonial Missions and Mexican California*. Berkeley: University of California Press, 2013.

Hackel, Steven W. *Children of Coyote, Missionaries of Saint Francis: Indian-Spanish Relations in Colonial California, 1769–1850*. Chapel Hill: University of North Carolina Press, 2005.

Hall, Joseph M., Jr. *Zamumo's Gifts: Indian-European Exchange in the Colonial Southeast*. Philadelphia: University of Pennsylvania Press, 2009.

Hämäläinen, Pekka. *The Comanche Empire*. New Haven, CT: Yale University Press, 2008.

Harmon, Alexandra. *Indians in the Making: Ethnic Relations and Indian Identities around Puget Sound*. Berkeley: University of California Press, 1998.

Harmon, Alexandra, ed. *The Power of Promises: Rethinking Indian Treaties in the Pacific Northwest*. Seattle: University of Washington Press, 2008.

Harris, Cole. *Making Native Space: Colonialism, Resistance, and Reserves in British Columbia*. Vancouver: University of British Columbia Press, 2002.

Hauptman, Laurence M. *The Tonawanda Senecas' Heroic Battle against Removal: Conservative Activist Indians*. Albany, NY: Excelsior Editions, 2011.

Hinderaker, Eric. *The Two Hendricks: Unraveling a Mohawk Mystery*. Cambridge, MA: Harvard University Press, 2011.

Hittman, Michael. *Great Basin Indians: An Encyclopedic History*. Reno: University of Nevada Press, 2013.

Holder, Preston. *The Hoe and the Horse on the Plains: A Study of Cultural Development among North American Indians*. Lincoln: University of Nebraska Press, 1970.

Holm, Tom. *The Great Confusion in Indians Affairs: Native Americans and Whites in the Progressive Era*. Austin: University of Texas Press, 2005.

Hosmer, Brian C, and Colleen O'Neill, eds. *Native Pathways: American Indian Culture and Economic Development in the Twentieth Century*. Boulder: University Press of Colorado, 2004.

Hoxie, Frederick E. *The Final Promise: The Campaign to Assimilate the Indians, 1888–1920*. Lincoln: University of Nebraska Press, 1984.

Hudson, Angela Pulley. *Creek Paths and Federal Roads: Indians, Settlers, and Slaves and the Making of the American South*. Chapel Hill: University of North Carolina Press, 2010.

Hull, Kathleen L. *Pestilence and Persistence: Yosemite Indian Demography and Culture in Colonial California*. Berkeley: University of California Press, 2009.

Hunn, Eugene S., with James Selam and Family. *Nch'i-Wana "The Big River": Mid-Columbia Indians and Their Land*. Seattle: University of Washington Press, 1990.

Hurt, R. Douglas. *Indian Agriculture in America: Prehistory to the Present.* Lawrence: University Press of Kansas, 1996.

Hurtado, Albert L. *Indian Survival on the California Frontier.* New Haven, CT: Yale University Press, 1988.

Hutchinson, Elizabeth. *The Indian Craze: Primitivism, Modernism, and Transculturation in American Art, 1890–1915.* Durham: Duke University Press, 2009.

Isenberg, Andrew C. *The Destruction of the Bison: An Environmental History, 1750–1920.* New York: Cambridge University Press, 2000.

Iverson, Peter. *When Indians Became Cowboys: Native Peoples and Cattle Ranching in the American West.* Norman: University of Oklahoma Press, 1994.

Jackson, Robert H., and Edward Castillo. *Indians, Franciscans, and Spanish Colonization: The Impact of the Mission System on the California Indians.* Albuquerque: University of New Mexico Press, 1995.

Jacobs, Margaret D. *White Mother to a Dark Race: Settler Colonialism, Maternalism, and the Removal of Indigenous Children in the American West and Australia, 1880–1940.* Lincoln: University of Nebraska Press, 2009.

Jacoby, Karl. *Shadows at Dawn: A Borderlands Massacre and the Violence of History.* New York: Penguin Press, 2008.

Jetté, Melinda Marie. *At the Hearth of the Crossed Races: A French-Indian Community in Nineteenth-Century Oregon, 1812–1859.* Corvallis: Oregon State University Press, 2015.

Johansen, Bruce E., and Barry M. Pritzker, eds. *Encyclopedia of American Indian History.* 4 vols. Santa Barbara, CA: ABC-CLIO, 2008.

John, Elizabeth A. H. *Storms Brewed in Other Men's Worlds: The Confrontation of Indians, Spanish, and French in the Southwest, 1540–1795.* 2nd ed. Norman: University of Oklahoma Press, 1996.

Josephy, Alvin M., Jr. *The Civil War in the American West.* New York: Knopf, 1992.

Josephy, Alvin M., Jr. *The Nez Perce Indians and the Opening of the Northwest.* Lincoln: University of Nebraska Press, 1965.

Karson, Jennifer. *As Days Go By: Our History, Our Land, and Our People the Cayuse, Umatilla, and Walla Walla.* Seattle: University of Washington Press for Tamástslikt Cultural Institute, 2006.

Keller, Robert H., Jr. *American Protestantism and United States Indian Policy, 1869–1882.* Lincoln: University of Nebraska Press, 1983.

Kelton, Paul. *Cherokee Medicine, Colonial Germs: An Indigenous Nation's Fight against Smallpox, 1518–1824.* Norman: University of Oklahoma Press, 2015.

Kelton, Paul. *Epidemics and Enslavement: Biological Catastrophe in the Native Southeast, 1492–1715.* Lincoln: University of Nebraska Press, 2007.

Kenny, Kevin. *Peaceable Kingdom Lost: The Paxton Boys and the Destruction of William Penn's Holy Experiment.* New York: Oxford University Press, 2009.

Kilpatrick, Jacquelyn. *Celluloid Indians: Native Americans and Film.* Lincoln: University of Nebraska Press, 1999.

Klein, Kerwin Lee. *Frontiers of Historical Imagination: Narrating the European Conquest of Native America, 1890–1990.* Berkeley: University of California Press, 1997.

Knaut, Andrew L. *The Pueblo Revolt of 1680: Conquest and Resistance in Seventeenth-Century New Mexico*. Norman: University of Oklahoma Press, 1995.

Krouse, Susan Applegate. *North American Indians in the Great War*. Lincoln: University of Nebraska Press, 2007.

Leavelle, Tracy Neal. *The Catholic Calumet: Colonial Conversions in French and Indian North America*. Philadelphia: University of Pennsylvania Press, 2014.

Lepore, Jill. *The Name of War: King Philip's War and the Origins of American Identity*. New York: Alfred A. Knopf, 1998.

Lewis, David Rich. *Neither Wolf Nor Dog: American Indians, Environment, and Agrarian Change*. New York: Oxford University Press, 1997.

Liberty, Margot. "Hell Came with Horses: Plains Women in the Equestrian Era." *Montana: The Magazine of Western History* 32, no. 3 (1982): 10–19.

Lightfoot, Kent G., and Otis Parrish. *California Indians and Their Environment: An Introduction*. Berkeley: University of California Press, 2009.

Lindsay, Brendan C. *Murder State: California's Native American Genocide, 1846–1873*. Lincoln: University of Nebraska Press, 2012.

Lipman, Andrew. *The Saltwater Frontier: Indians and the Contest for the American Coast*. New Haven, CT: Yale University Press, 2015.

Lomawaima, K. Tsianina. *They Called It Prairie Light: The Story of Chilocco Indian School*. Lincoln: University of Nebraska Press, 1994.

Maddox, Lucy. *Citizen Indians: Native American Intellectuals, Race, and Reform*. Ithaca, NY: Cornell University Press, 2005.

Madley, Benjamin. *An American Genocide: The United States and the California Indian Catastrophe, 1846–1873*. New Haven, CT: Yale University Press, 2016.

Makley, Matthew S., and Michael J. Makley. *Cave Rock: Climbers, Courts, and a Washoe Indian Sacred Place*. Reno: University of Nevada Press, 2010.

Mandell, Daniel R. *Tribe, Race, History: Native Americans in Southern New England, 1780–1880*. Updated ed. Baltimore: Johns Hopkins University Press, 2007.

Mann, Charles C. *1491: New Revelations of the Americas before Columbus*. New York: Knopf, 2005.

Margolin, Malcolm. *The Ohlone Way: Indian Life in the San Francisco—Monterey Bay Area*. Berkeley, CA: Heyday Books, 1978.

Mayfield, Thomas Jefferson. *Indian Summer: Traditional Life among the Choinumne Indians of California's San Joaquin Valley*. Edited by Malcolm Margolin. Berkeley, CA: Heyday Books, 1993.

McCool, Daniel C. *Native Waters: Contemporary Indian Water Settlements and the Second Treaty Era*. Tucson: University of Arizona Press, 2006.

McCoy, Robert R. *Chief Joseph, Yellow Wolf, and the Creation of Nez Perce History in the Pacific Northwest*. New York: Routledge, 2004.

McDonnell, Michael. *Masters of Empire: Great Lakes Indians and the Making of America*. New York: Hill and Wang, 2015.

McGinnis, Anthony. *Counting Coup and Cutting Horses: Intertribal Warfare on the Northern Plains, 1738–1889*. Reprint ed. Lincoln: University of Nebraska Press, 2010.

McMillen, Christian W. *Making Indian Law: The Hualapai Land Case and the Birth of Ethnohistory*. New Haven, CT: Yale University Press, 2007.

McWhorter, Lucullus V. *Yellow Wolf: His Own Story*. Caldwell, ID: Caxton, 1940.

Meltzer, David J. *First Peoples in a New World: Colonizing Ice Age America*. Berkeley: University of California Press, 2009.

Merrell, James H. *Into the American Woods: Negotiators on the Pennsylvania Frontier*. New York: W. W. Norton, 1999.

Merrell, James H. *The Indians' New World: Catawbas and Their Neighbors from European Contact through the Era of Removal*. Chapel Hill: University of North Carolina Press, 1989.

Merritt, Jane T. *At the Crossroads: Indians and Empires on a Mid-Atlantic Frontier, 1700–1763*. Chapel Hill: University of North Carolina Press, 2003.

Milanich, Jerald T. *Florida Indians and the Invasion from Europe*. Tallahassee: University Press of Florida, 1995.

Milanich, Jerald T. *Laboring in the Fields of the Lord: Spanish Missions and Southeastern Indians*. Gainesville: University Press of Florida, 2006.

Miller, Robert J. *Native America, Discovered and Conquered: Thomas Jefferson, Lewis and Clark, and Manifest Destiny*. Westport, CT: Praeger, 2006.

Miller, Susan A. *Coacoochee's Bones: A Seminole Saga*. Lawrence: University Press of Kansas, 2003.

Moses, L. G. *Wild West Shows and the Images of American Indians, 1883–1933*. Albuquerque: University of New Mexico Press, 1996.

Nichols, Roger L. *Indians in the United States and Canada: A Comparative History*. Lincoln: University of Nebraska Press, 1998.

Nies, Judith. *Native American History: A Chronology of a Culture's Vast Achievements and Their Links to World Events*. New York: Ballantine Books, 1996.

O'Brien, Jean M. *Dispossession by Degrees: Indian Land and Identity in Natick, Massachusetts, 1650–1790*. Lincoln: University of Nebraska Press, 2003.

O'Brien, Jean M. *Firsting and Lasting: Writing Indians out of Existence in New England*. Minneapolis: University of Minnesota Press, 2010.

O'Neill, Colleen M. *Working the Navajo Way: Labor and Culture in the Twentieth Century*. Lawrence: University Press of Kansas, 2005.

Ostler, Jeffrey. *The Lakotas and the Black Hills: The Struggle for Sacred Ground*. New York: Viking Penguin, 2010.

Ostler, Jeffrey. *The Plains Sioux and U.S. Colonialism from Lewis and Clark to Wounded Knee*. New York: Cambridge University Press, 2004.

Otto, Paul. *The Dutch-Munsee Encounter in America: The Struggle for Sovereignty in the Hudson Valley*. New York: Berghahn Books, 2006.

Owens, Louis. *Other Destinies: Understanding the American Indian Novel*. Norman: University of Oklahoma Press, 1992.

Pasternak, Judy. *Yellow Dirt: An American Story of a Poisoned Land and a People Betrayed*. New York: Free Press, 2010.

Pauketat, Timothy R., and Susan M. Alt, eds. *Medieval Mississippians: The Cahokian World*. Santa Fe, NM: School for Advanced Research Press, 2014.

Pearson, J. Diane. *The Nez Perces in the Indian Territory: Nimiipuu Survival*. Norman: University of Oklahoma, 2008.

Peck, Trevor R. *Light from Ancient Campfires: Archaeological Evidence of Native Lifeways on the Northern Plains.* Vancouver: UBC Press, 2011.

Perdue, Theda, and Michael D. Green. *The Cherokee Nation and the Trail of Tears.* New ed. New York: Viking, 2007.

Peterson, Jacqueline. *Sacred Encounters: Father DeSmet and the Indians of the Rocky Mountain West.* Norman: University of Oklahoma Press, 1993.

Phillips, George Harwood. *Indians and Intruders in Central California, 1769–1849.* Norman: University of Oklahoma Press, 1993.

Pinkham, Allen V., and Steven R. Evans. *Lewis and Clark among the Nez Perce: Strangers in the Land of the Nimiipuu.* Washburn, ND: Dakota Institute Press, 2015.

Plane, Ann Marie. *Colonial Intimacies: Indian Marriage in Early New England.* Ithaca, NY: Cornell University Press, 2002.

Pommersheim, Frank. *Broken Landscape: Indians, Indian Tribes, and Constitution.* New York: Oxford University Press, 2009.

Powell, Joseph F. *The First Americans: Race, Evolution, and the Origin of Native Americans.* New York: Cambridge University Press, 2005.

Prucha, Francis Paul. *American Indian Treaties: The History of a Political Anomaly.* Berkeley: University of California Press, 1997.

Prucha, Francis Paul. *The Great Father: The United States Government and the American Indians.* Abridged ed. Lincoln: University of Nebraska Press, 1986.

Raibmon, Paige. *Authentic Indians: Episodes of Encounter from the Late Nineteenth-Century Northwest Coast.* Durham, NC: Duke University Press, 2005.

Reid, Joshua L. *The Sea Is My Country: The Maritime World of the Makahs.* New Haven, CT: Yale University Press, 2015.

Reséndez, Andrés. *A Land So Strange: The Epic Journey of Cabeza de Vaca.* New York: Basic Books, 2007.

Reséndez, Andrés. *The Other Slavery: The Uncovered Story of Indian Enslavement in America.* Boston: Houghton Mifflin Harcourt, 2016.

Rice, James D. *Tales from a Revolution: Bacon's Rebellion and the Transformation of Early America.* New York: Oxford University Press, 2012.

Richter, Daniel. *Facing East from Indian Country: A Native History of Early America.* Cambridge, MA: Harvard University Press, 2001.

Riley, Carroll L. *Rio Del Norte: People of Upper Rio Grande from Earliest Times to Pueblo Revolt.* Salt Lake City: University of Utah Press, 2007.

Robertson, Lindsay G. *Conquest by Law: How the Discovery of America Dispossessed Indigenous Peoples of Their Lands.* New York: Oxford University Press, 2005.

Rockwell, Stephen J. *Indian Affairs and the Administrative State in the Nineteenth Century.* New York: Cambridge University Press, 2010.

Rosier, Paul C. *Serving Their Country: American Indian Politics and Patriotism in the Twentieth Century.* Cambridge, MA: Harvard University Press, 2009.

Ruby, Robert H., and John A. Brown. *Dreamer-Prophets of the Columbia Plateau: Smohalla and Skolaskin.* Norman: University of Oklahoma Press, 2002.

Ruppel, Kristin T. *Unearthing Indian Land: Living with the Legacies of Allotment.* Tucson: University of Arizona Press, 2008.

Rushforth, Brett. *Bonds of Alliance: Indigenous and Atlantic Slaveries in New France.* Chapel Hill: University of North Carolina Press, 2012.

Salisbury, Neal. *Manitou and Providence: Indians, Europeans, and the Making of New England, 1500–1643.* New York: Oxford University Press, 1984.

Sando, Joe S., and Herman Agoyo, eds. *Po'pay: Leader of the First American Revolution.* Santa Fe, NM: Clear Light, 2005.

Sandos, James A. *Converting California: Indians and Franciscans in the Missions.* New Haven, CT: Yale University Press, 2004.

Saunt, Claudio. *Black, White, and Indian: Race and the Unmaking of an American Family.* New York: Oxford University Press, 2006.

Schmidt, Ethan A. *Native Americans in the American Revolution: How the War Divided, Devastated, and Transformed the Early American Indian World.* Santa Barbara, CA: Praeger, 2014.

Schutt, Amy C. *Peoples of the River Valleys: The Odyssey of the Delaware Indians.* Philadelphia: University of Pennsylvania Press, 2007.

Shannon, Timothy. *Iroquois Diplomacy on the Early American Frontier.* New York: Viking, 2008.

Shefveland, Kristalyn. *Anglo-Native Virginia: Trade, Conversion, and Indian Slavery in the Old Dominion, 1646–1722.* Athens: University of Georgia Press, 2016.

Shoemaker, Nancy. *A Strange Likeness: Becoming Red and White in Eighteenth-Century North America.* New York: Oxford University Press, 2006.

Shoemaker, Nancy. *Native American Whalemen and the World: Indigenous Encounters and the Contingency of Race.* Chapel Hill: The University of North Carolina Press, 2015.

Sider, Gerald. *Living Indian Histories: The Lumbee and Tuscarora People in North Carolina.* Chapel Hill: University of North Carolina Press, 2003.

Silverman, David J. *Red Brethren: The Brothertown and Stockbridge Indians and the Problem of Race in Early America.* Ithaca, NY: Cornell University Press, 2010.

Silverman, David J. *Thundersticks: Firearms and the Violent Transformation of Native America.* Cambridge, MA: Belknap Press of Harvard University Press, 2016.

Smith, F. Todd. *From Dominance to Disappearance: The Indians of Texas and the Near Southwest, 1786–1859.* Lincoln: University of Nebraska Press, 2008.

Smith, Paul Chaat, and Robert Allen Warrior. *Like a Hurricane: The Indian Movement from Alcartraz to Wounded Knee.* New York: New Press, 1996.

Smith, Sherry L. *Reimagining Indians: Native Americans through Anglo Eyes, 1880–1940.* New York: Oxford University Press, 2000.

Smithers, Gregory D. *The Cherokee Diaspora: An Indigenous History of Migration, Resettlement, and Identity.* New Haven, CT: Yale University Press, 2015.

Smoak, Gregory. *Ghost Dances and Identity: Prophetic Religion and American Indian Ethnogenesis in the Nineteenth Century.* Berkeley: University of California Press, 2006.

Snyder, Christina. *Slavery in Indian Country: The Changing Face of Captivity in Early America*. Cambridge, MA: Harvard University Press, 2010.

Spence, Mark David. *Dispossessing the Wilderness: Indian Removal and the Making of the National Parks*. New York: Oxford University Press, 1999.

Spruce, Duane Blue, and Tanya Thrasher, eds. *The Land Has Memory: Indigenous Knowledge, Native Landscapes, and the National Museum of the American Indian*. Chapel Hill: University of North Carolina Press, 2008.

Spruill, Marjorie Julian, Joan Marie Johnson, and Valinda W. Littlefield. *South Carolina Women: Their Lives and Times*. Athens: University of Georgia Press, 2009.

Steward, Julian H. "Some Western Shoshoni Myths." In *Bureau of American Ethnology Bulletin*, Vol. 136, 249–299. Washington, DC: Smithsonian Institution, 1943.

Stewart, Omer C. *Forgotten Fires: Native Americans and the Transient Wilderness*. Edited by Henry T. Lewis and Kat Anderson. Norman: University of Oklahoma Press, 2009.

Stuart, David E. *Anasazi America: Seventeen Centuries on the Road from Center Place*. 2nd ed. Albuquerque: University of New Mexico Press, 2014.

Sweeney, Edwin R. *From Cochise to Geronimo: The Chiricahua Apaches, 1874–1886*. Norman: University of Oklahoma Press, 2010.

Taylor, Graham D. *The New Deal and American Indian Tribalism*. Lincoln: University of Nebraska Press, 1980.

Thrush, Coll. *Native Seattle: Histories from the Crossing-Over Place*. Seattle: University of Washington Press, 2007.

Townsend, Camilla. *Pocahontas and the Powhatan Dilemma*. New York: Hill and Wang, 2004.

Townsend, Kenneth William. *World War II and the American Indian*. Albuquerque: University of New Mexico Press, 2000.

Trachtenberg, Alan. *Shades of Hiawatha: Staging Indians, Making Americans, 1880–1930*. New York: Hill and Wang, 2004.

Trafzer, Clifford E. *As Long as the Grass Shall Grow and Rivers Flow: A History of Native Americans*. Fort Worth, TX: Harcourt College, 2000.

Trafzer, Clifford E., Jean A. Keller, and Lorene Sisquouc, eds. *Boarding School Blues: Revisiting American Indian Educational Experiences*. Lincoln: University of Nebraska Press, 2006.

Trahant, Mark N. *The Last Great Battle of the Indian Wars: Henry M. Jackson, Forrest J. Gerard and the Campaign for the Self-Determination of America's Indian Tribes*. Fort Hall, ID: Cedars Group, 2010.

Ulrich, Roberta. *American Indian Nations from Termination to Restoration, 1953–2006*. Lincoln: University of Nebraska Press, 2010.

Ulrich, Roberta. *Empty Nets: Indians, Dams, and the Columbia River*. 2nd ed. Corvallis: Oregon State University Press, 2007.

Usner, Daniel H. *Indians, Settlers & Slaves in a Frontier Exchange Economy: The Lower Mississippi Valley before 1783*. Chapel Hill: University of North Carolina Press, 1992.

Wallace, Anthony F. C. *The Long, Bitter Trail: Andrew Jackson and the Indians*. New York: Hill and Wang, 1993.

Wallace, Paul, and John Mohawk. *The White Roots of Peace: The Iroquois Book of Life*. Santa Fe, NM: Clear Light, 1994.

Watson, Blake A. *Buying America from the Indians: Johnson v. McIntosh and the History of Native Land Rights*. Norman: University of Oklahoma Press, 2012.

Weaver, Jace. *The Red Atlantic: American Indigenes and the Making of the Modern World, 1000–1927*. Chapel Hill: University of North Carolina Press, 2014.

Weber, David J. *The Spanish Frontier in North America*. New Haven, CT: Yale University Press, 1992.

Weisiger, Marsha. *Dreaming of Sheep in Navajo Country*. Seattle: University of Washington Press, 2009.

West, Elliott. *The Contested Plains: Indians, Goldseekers, and the Rush to Colorado*. Lawrence: University Press of Kansas, 1998.

West, Elliott. *The Last Indian War: The Nez Perce Story*. New York: Oxford University Press, 2009.

Westerman, Gwen, and Bruce M. White. *Mni Sota Makoce: The Land of the Dakota*. St. Paul: Minnesota Historical Society, 2012.

Whaley, Gray H. *Oregon and the Collapse of Illahee: U.S. Empire and the Transformation of an Indigenous World, 1792–1859*. Chapel Hill: University of North Carolina Press, 2010.

White, Richard. *The Middle Ground: Indians, Empires, and Republics in the Great Lakes Region, 1650–1815*. New York: Cambridge University Press, 1991.

White, Richard. *The Roots of Dependency: Subsistence, Environment, and Social Change among the Choctaws, Pawnees, and Navajos*. Lincoln: University of Nebraska Press, 1983.

Wilkins, David E., and K. Tsianina Lomawaima. *Uneven Ground: American Indian Sovereignty and Federal Law*. Norman: University of Oklahoma Press, 2002.

Wilkinson, Charles F. *Blood Struggle: The Rise of Modern Indian Nations*. New York: W. W. Norton, 2006.

Wilkinson, Charles F. *Messages from Franks Landing: A Story of Salmon, Treaties, and the Indian Way*. Seattle: University of Washington Press, 2006.

Wilson, James. *The Earth Shall Weep: A History of Native America*. New York: Grove Press, 2000.

Wishart, David J. *An Unspeakable Sadness: The Dispossession of the Nebraska Indians*. Lincoln: University of Nebraska Press, 1994.

Witgen, Michael. *An Infinity of Nations: How the Native New World Shaped Early North America*. Philadelphia: University of Pennsylvania Press, 2013.

Woodworth-Ney, Laura. *Mapping Identity: The Creation of the Coeur d'Alene Indian Reservation, 1805–1902*. Boulder: University Press of Colorado, 2004.

Zappia, Natale A. *Traders and Raiders: The Indigenous World of the Colorado Basin, 1540–1859*. Chapel Hill: University of North Carolina Press, 2014.

Index

About the Authors

Robert R. McCoy is an associate professor of history at Washington State University, Pullman, WA. He is the author of *Chief Joseph, Yellow Wolf, and the Creation of Nez Perce History in the Pacific Northwest* (Routledge Press) and coauthor of *Forgotten Voices: Death Records of the Yakama 1888–1964.*

Steven M. Fountain is a clinical assistant professor of history and coordinator of Native American Programs at Washington State University Vancouver. His first book *Horses of Their Own Making: An Equestrian History of Native America* is forthcoming from the University of Washington Press.